Dilapidations and Service Charge

Dilapidations and Service Charge

DENIS J GARRITY LLB (Hons), Dip LP
Advocate

LORNA RICHARDSON LLB (Hons), Dip LP
Lecturer in Commercial Law, University of Edinburgh
Solicitor (non-practising)

EDINBURGH
University Press

Edinburgh University Press is one of the leading university presses in the UK.
We publish academic books and journals in our selected subject areas across the
humanities and social sciences, combining cutting-edge scholarship with high editorial
and production values to produce academic works of lasting importance. For more
information visit our website: edinburghuniversitypress.com

© Denis J Garrity and Lorna Richardson, 2019

Edinburgh University Press Ltd
The Tun – Holyrood Road
12 (2f) Jackson's Entry
Edinburgh EH8 8PJ

Typeset in Adobe Caslon by
Waverley Typesetters, and
printed and bound in Great Britain

A CIP record for this book is available from the British Library

ISBN 978 1 4744 7390 3 (paperback)
ISBN 978 1 4744 7544 0 (webready PDF)
ISBN 978 1 4744 7545 7 (epub)

The right of Denis J Garrity and Lorna Richardson to be identified as authors of this
work has been asserted in accordance with the Copyright, Designs and Patents Act 1988
and the Copyright and Related Rights Regulations 2003 (SI 2003/2498).

Contents

Preface	vii
Table of Cases	ix
Table of Statutes	xv
Table of Orders, Rules and Regulations	xvi

1 Introduction — 1

  1.1 Commercial property, the common law and "urban leases" — 1
  1.2 Investment in commercial property — 2
  1.3 The repairing obligation in context — 3
  1.4 The commercial relevance of lease duration — 4
  1.5 Treatment of "repairs" towards expiry of the lease — 4
  1.6 Single-occupancy and multi-occupancy buildings — 5

2 Defining "the Premises" and "the Common Parts" — 6

  2.1 Introduction — 6
  2.2 Single-occupancy buildings — 6
  2.3 Multiple-occupancy buildings — 7
  2.4 "The premises" and "the common parts" — 7
  2.5 Fixtures – general — 11
  2.6 What is a fixture? — 11
  2.7 The role of intention in accession — 13
  2.8 Trade fixtures — 14
  2.9 Severance of items from the premises by agreement — 15

3 The Underlying Common Law — 16

  3.1 Introduction — 16
  3.2 The landlord's implied warranty at lease commencement – that the premises let are fit for purpose — 17
  3.3 The landlord's common law repairing obligation — 19
  3.4 Ordinary and extraordinary repairs — 21
  3.5 The tenant's duty to take reasonable care — 24
  3.6 The absent repairing obligation — 24

CONTENTS

4 The Tenant's Repairing Obligations: Reading the Lease and Other Documents — 28

    4.1 Introduction — 28
    4.2 Principles of interpretation — 28
    4.3 The FRI repairing clause — 35
    4.4 The repairing obligation in detail — 38
    4.5 Where the premises are not in good condition at lease commencement — 46
    4.6 Notice of wants of repair and schedules of dilapidations — 48
    4.7 Exclusions from the tenant's repairing obligations — 51
    4.8 "Hidden" repairing obligations — 53
    4.9 Sub-leases — 54

5 Remedies for Breach of the Repairing Obligation — 56

    5.1 Introduction — 56
    5.2 Serving a schedule of dilapidations — 56
    5.3 Remedies available at common law for breach of the lease — 56
    5.4 Remedies specifically provided for in the lease — 73
    5.5 Effect of tenant's breach of repairing obligation on rights the tenant has under the lease — 83
    5.6 Tenant's remedies for breach of the landlord's obligations in relation to the condition of the property — 83

6 Common Parts and Service Charge — 85

    6.1 Introduction — 85
    6.2 What is typically a common part and why? — 85
    6.3 Obligations in relation to common parts and services — 87
    6.4 Factors to take into account regarding works to common parts or services — 92
    6.5 The tenant's obligation to pay service charge — 96
    6.6 Reserve or sinking funds — 107
    6.7 Tenant's remedies for the landlord's breach of the lease — 110
    6.8 Landlord's remedies for the tenant's breach of the lease — 112

7 Dispute Resolution — 118

    7.1 Introduction — 118
    7.2 Nature of the dispute and remedy sought — 118
    7.3 When and how are dilapidations identified? — 119
    7.4 When to consider dispute resolution – specific implement and damages — 120
    7.5 Dispute resolution options — 122

Index — 131

Preface

This book was conceived in the context of teaching a course on the law of leases. There seemed to us a significant gap in the literature and a need for an in-depth analysis of the repairing obligation and service charge liability contained in a lease of commercial premises. These obligations are two key elements of the landlord/tenant relationship, with potentially significant financial and operational implications for both parties, and about which many disputes arise each year. This text aims to fill the gap by providing a detailed and comprehensive analysis of Scots law in respect of these important aspects of business life and professional practice.

The book is aimed at students of law, and of land economics, and also those who encounter dilapidations and service charge in daily practice, whether as a solicitor, surveyor, landlord or tenant. We are acutely aware that the law does not exist in a vacuum, perhaps especially so in this area of practice, and the book introduces the reader to the commercial objectives ever-present in the drafting, negotiation and operation of commercial leases. We have considered the common law of leases, as well as terms found in commercial leases, and how these have been interpreted by the courts. We have also set out relevant contract law rules and principles relevant to the landlord and tenant's rights, obligations and remedies. Uniquely, the book provides a detailed treatment of the law relating to service charge.

We have sought to draw on our experience in commercial leasing transactions, commercial litigation, and academia – with the aim of producing a text that is readable while comprehensively dealing with this area of law and practice. We hope it is of use to many.

We have aimed to state the law as at 7 July 2019.

DENIS J GARRITY and LORNA RICHARDSON
Edinburgh
July 2019

Table of Cases

Aberdeen City Council v Stewart Milne Group Ltd [2011] UKSC 56,
 2012 SC (UKSC) 240 33
Akorita v Marina Heights (St Leonards) Ltd [2011] UKUT 225 (LC) 102, 103
Allied Dunbar Assurance plc v Superglass Sections Ltd 2003 SLT 1420 83
Antaios Compania Naviero SA v Salen Rederiena (The Antaios) [1984] AC 191 33
Anderson v Pringle of Scotland Ltd 1998 SLT 754 60
Anstruther Gough Calthorpe v McOscar [1924] 1 KB 716 .... 38, 40, 41, 43
Arlington Business Parks GP Ltd v Scottish & Newcastle Ltd [2014] CSOH 77,
 2014 GWD 14-261 83
Arnold v Britton [2015] UKSC 36, [2015] 2 WLR 1593 .... 29-30, 31, 34, 76, 77, 100
Ashtead Plant Hire Co Ltd v Granton Central Developments Ltd
 [2018] CSOH 107 .... 125, 126–27
Assessor for Fife v Hodgson 1966 SC 30 13
Aubrey Investments Ltd v DSC (Realisations) Ltd (in receivership) 1999 SC 21 78–80
AWG Business Centres Ltd v Regus Caledonia Ltd and Cheshire West and Cheshire
 Council [2017] CSIH 22, 2017 GWD 9-131 .... 30, 90

Balfour Beatty Construction (Scotland) Ltd v Scottish Power plc 1994 SC (HL) 20 .. 64, 66
BAM Buchanan Ltd v Arcadia Group Ltd [2013] CSOH 107A 13, 128
Bank of East Asia Ltd v Scottish Enterprise 1997 SLT 1213 68
Bank of Scotland v Dunedin Property Investment Co Ltd 1998 SC 657 ...... 29, 31, 32-33
Batley (L) Products Ltd v North Lanarkshire Council [2014] UKSC 27,
 [2014] 3 All ER 64 .... 28, 46, 50, 54
Bayne v Walker (1815) 3 Dow 233, 3 ER 1049 .... 25, 51
Beatsons Building Supplies Ltd v Noble and Ors as Trustees of the Alex F Noble & Son
 Ltd Executive Benefits Scheme 2015 GWD 15-271 .... 6, 8, 36
Beech v Kennerley, 20 October 2010, unreported 92
Belcher v Mackintosh 2 Moo & R 186 39
Berrycroft Management Co Ltd v Sinclair Gardens Investments (Kensington) Ltd
 (1997) 29 HLR 444 92
Bishop v 3i Investments plc [2014] CSOH 152, 2014 GWD 33-634 34
Blackwell v Farmfoods Aberdeen Ltd 1991 GWD 4-219 19
Blythswood Investments (Scotland) Ltd v Clydesdale Electrical Stores Ltd
 (in receivership) 1995 SLT 150 .... 50, 78, 79, 80
BNP Paribas Securities Services Trust Co (Jersey) Ltd v Mothercare (UK) Ltd
 [2015] CSOH 47 .... 13, 128
Boldmark Ltd v Cohen (1987) 19 HLR 135 90
Boots UK Ltd v Trafford Centre Ltd 2008 EWHC 3372 (Ch) 89
Bradford & Bingley Building Society v Thorntons plc 1998 GWD 40-2071 99

TABLE OF CASES

Britannia Invest A/S v Scottish Ministers 2018 SLT (Sh Ct) 133, 2018 GWD 9-112 .. 100
Brown's Operating System Services Ltd v Southwark Roman Catholic Diocesan
  Corporation [2007] EWCA Civ 164, [2007] L &TR 25 109–10
Bunge SA v Nidera BV [2015] UKSC 43, [2015] 3 All ER 1082 62
Burgerking Ltd v Rachel's Charitable Trust Ltd 2006 SLT 224 79

Campbell v Edwards [1976] 1 WLR 403 .... 125, 127
Cantors Properties (Scotland) Ltd v Swears & Wells Ltd 1978 SC 310.............. 51
Capital Land Holdings Ltd v Secretary of State for the Environment
  1997 SC 109 50
Centre for Maritime and Industrial Safety Technology Ltd v Ineos Manufacturing
  Scotland Ltd [2014] CSOH 5, 2014 GWD 5-100..................................... 32
Chartbrook Ltd v Persimmon Homes Ltd [2009] 1 AC 1101 31
Charter Reinsurance Co Ltd v Fagan [1997] AC 313 .... 29, 33
Cine-UK Ltd v Union Square Developments Ltd [2019] CSOH 3.................. 127
Clarke (T) (Scotland) Ltd v MMAXX Underfloor Heating Ltd [2014] CSIH 83,
  2015 SC 233 61
Company, In re a [1984] 1 WLR 1090 113
Co-operative Insurance Society Ltd v Fife Council [2011] CSOH 76,
  2011 GWD 19-458... 23-24, 38, 43, 44, 60, 95
Coventry v British Gas Corporation, 15 August 1984, Outer House, unreported 59
Crieff Highland Gathering Ltd v Perth and Kinross Council [2011] CSOH 38,
  2011 SLT 992 70-72
Cummings v Singh [2019] SAC (Civ) 11, 2019 Hous LR 41 57
Czarnikow v Koufos (The Heron II) [1969] 1 AC 350 66

Dem-Master Demolition Ltd v Healthcare Environmental Services Ltd
  [2017] CSOH 14, 2017 GWD 5-72 48
Dickie v The Amicable Property Investment Building Society 1911 SC 1079.......... 20
Dolby Medical Home Respiratory Care Ltd v Mortara Dolby UK Ltd
  [2016] CSOH 74, 2016 GWD 19-344............................... 19, 86, 122
Dorchester Studios (Glasgow) Ltd v Stone 1975 SC (HL) 56..................... 81
Douglas Shelf Seven Ltd v Co-operative Wholesale Society Ltd [2007] CSOH 53,
  2007 GWD 9-167... 89
Douglas Shelf Seven Ltd v Co-operative Wholesale Society Ltd [2009] CSOH 3,
  2009 GWD 3-56.. 111

EDI Central Ltd v National Car Parks Ltd [2010] CSOH 141, 2011 SLT 75 69
EOP II Prop Co III SARL v Carpetright plc [2019] CSOH 40, 2019 GWD 19-305 ... 34
Euro Properties Scotland Ltd v Khurshied Alam and Randall Mitchell
  2000 GWD 23-896... 78, 79, 80-81, 82

Faill (A & J) v Wilson (1899) 7 SLT 148 59
Fehilly v General Accident Fire & Life Assurance Corporation Ltd 1982 SC 163 52
Ferguson v Paul (1885) 12 R 1222 15
Finchbourne Ltd v Rodriguez [1976] 3 All ER 581......................... 92, 103
Firstcross Ltd v Teasdale (1983) 8 HLR 112 92
Fluor Daniel Properties Ltd v Shortlands Investments Ltd [2001] 2 EGLR 103 ..91, 93-94
Fordell Estates Ltd v Deloitte LLP [2014] CSOH 55 123

TABLE OF CASES

Franborough Properties Ltd v Scottish Enterprise, 14 June 1996 (Lord Penrose) unreported 101, 127
Fry's Metals Ltd v Durastic Ltd 1991 SLT 689 24

Glebe Sugar Refining Co v Paterson (1900) 2 F 615 .... 18, 24
Golden Casket (Greenock) Ltd v BRS (Pickfords) Ltd 1972 SLT 146 .... 19, 20
Golden Strait Corporation v Nippon Yusen Kubishika Kaisha (The Golden Victory) [2007] UKHL 12, [2007] 2 AC 535 62
Grahame v Swan and Others (Magistrates and Police Commissioners of Kirkcaldy) (1882) 9 R (HL) 91 57
Grove Investments Ltd v Cape Building Products Ltd [2014] CSIH 43, 2014 Hous LR 35 .... 28, 33–34, 74–76
Gunn v National Coal Board 1982 SLT 526 20
Gyle Shopping Centre General Partners Ltd v Marks and Spencer plc [2016] CSIH 19, 2017 SCLR 221 30

Hadley v Baxendale (1854) 9 Ex 341 .... 62–64, 66, 67
Haveridge Ltd v Boston Dryers Ltd [1994] 49 EG 111 92
Highland and Universal Properties Ltd v Safeway Properties Ltd 2000 SC 297 .... 57, 58, 60
Hill v Stewart Milne Group Ltd and Gladedale (Northern) Ltd [2016] CSIH 35, 2017 SCLR 92 30
HMV Fields Properties Ltd v Skirt 'n' Slack Centre of London Ltd 1982 SLT 477 .. 81–82
Hoe International v Andersen [2017] CSIH 9, 2017 SC 313 .... 30, 34, 50
Hoult v Turpie 2004 SLT 308 68
House of Fraser plc v Prudential Assurance Co Ltd 1994 SLT 416 .... 22–23, 37

Inverclyde Council v John F McCloskey t/a Prince of Wales Bar 2015 SLT (Sh Ct) 57, 2015 GWD 6-126 116
Inveresk plc v Tullis Russell Papermakers Ltd [2010] UKSC 19, 2010 SC (UKSC) 106 .... 68, 69
Investors Compensation Scheme Ltd v West Bromwich Building Society [1998] 1 WLR 896 .... 31–32, 33

Jacey Property Ltd v De Sousa [2003] EWCA Civ 510 103
Johnstone v Hughan (1894) 21 R 777 38
Jones v Sherwood Computer Services plc [1992] 1 WLR 277 127
Joyner v Weeks [1891] 2 QB 31 62

Kilmacolm Hydropathic Co Ltd v Hall (1922) 38 Sh Ct Rep 233 72
Kirkham v Link Housing Group Ltd [2012] CSIH 58, 2012 Hous LR 87 20
Kodak Processing Companies Ltd v Shoredale Ltd [2009] CSIH 71, 2010 SC 113 115

Leonora Investment Co Ltd v Mott MacDonald Ltd [2008] EWCA Civ 857, [2008] 2 P&CR DG15 .... 102, 103
Lindley Catering Investments Ltd v Hibernian Football Club Ltd 1975 SLT (Notes) 56 72
Little Cumbrae Estate Ltd v Island of Little Cumbrae Ltd [2007] CSIH 35, 2007 SC 525 .... 24–27, 35, 37, 44, 51, 52

xi

TABLE OF CASES

Lloyds TSB Foundation for Scotland v Lloyds Banking Group plc [2011] CSIH 87,
   2012 SC 259; [2013] UKSC 3, [2013] 1 WLR 366 29
Lousada & Co Ltd v JE Lesser (Properties) Ltd 1990 SC 178..................... 69
Lowe v Quayle Munro Ltd 1997 SC 346 .... 37, 39, 42, 43, 46–47, 92
Lucas's Executor v Demarco 1968 SLT 89 81
Luminar Lava Ignite Ltd v Mama Group plc [2010] CSIH 1, 2010 SLT 147.......... 31
Lurcott v Wakely and Wheeler [1911] 1 KB 905 .... 38, 44

McCall's Entertainments (Ayr) Ltd v South Ayrshire Council (No 1)
   1998 SLT 1403 68
McCall's Entertainments (Ayr) Ltd v South Lanarkshire Council (No 2)
   1998 SLT 1421 .... 37, 47, 69, 83
MacDonald v Livingstone [2012] CSOH 31, 2012 GWD 11-218 102
McDougall v Easington District Council [1984] 1 EGLR 93 93
M'Gonigal v Pickard 1954 SLT 62.. 20
M'Laughlan v Craig 1948 SC 599 20
McNeill v Aberdeen City Council [2013] CSIH 102, 2014 SC 335 69
Macari v Celtic Football and Athletic Co Ltd 1999 SC 628....................... 68
Mackeson v Boyd 1942 SC 56 51
Makdessi v Cavendish Square Holdings BV [2015] UKSC 67,
   [2016] AC 1172 77
Mannai Investments Co Ltd v Eagle Star Assurance Co Ltd [1997] AC 749 ... 32, 33, 117
Mapeley Acquisitions Co (3) Ltd v City of Edinburgh Council [2015] CSOH 29,
   2015 GWD 13-284.. 34, 77
Marfield Properties v Secretary of State for the Environment 1996 SC 362........ 9–10, 86
Maris v Banchory Squash Racquets Club Ltd [2007] CSIH 30; 2007 SC 501 79
Marks and Spencer plc v BNP Paribas Securities Services Trust Co (Jersey) Ltd
   [2015] UKSC 72, [2016] AC 742 92
Mars Pension Trs Ltd v County Properties & Developments Ltd
   1999 SC 267 .... 16–17, 19, 100
Mechan v Watson 1907 SC 25 18
Mickel v McCoard 1913 SC 896 24
Middleton v Leslie (1892) 19 R 801.. 58
Moor Row Ltd v DWF LLP [2017] CSOH 63, 2017 GWD 14-213.............. 10, 62
Morgan v Hardy (1886) 17 QBD 770... 40
Morgan v Stainer (1993) 25 HLR 467 92
Mossman v Brocket 1810 Hume 850 .... 21, 22
Multi-Link Leisure Developments Ltd v North Lanarkshire Council
   [2010] UKSC 47, 2011 SC (UKSC) 53 29

Napier v Ferrier (1847) 9 D 1354 .... 21–22, 37, 44

Paton v MacDonald 1973 SLT (Sh Ct) 85....................................... 18
PDPF GP Ltd v Santander Ltd [2015] CSOH 40, 2015 Hous LR 45 .... 46, 54
Peace v City of Edinburgh Council 1999 SLT 712............................... 60
Penman v Mackay 1922 SC 385 68
PIK Facilities Ltd v Shell UK Ltd 2003 SLT 155...................... 57, 58, 59, 121
PIK Facilities Ltd v Shell UK Ltd 2005 SCLR 958............................. 121
Plough Investments Ltd v Manchester City Council [1984] 1 EGLR 244 93
Portland (Duke of) v Wood's Trs 1926 SC 640 62

Possfund Custodial Tr Ltd v Kwik-Fit Properties Ltd [2008] CSIH 65,
   2009 SLT 133 . . . . 49, 73, 112
Prenn v Simmonds [1971] 1 WLR 1381 31
Proudfoot v Hart (1890) 25 QBD 42 . . . . 37, 39–40, 41, 44
Prudential Assurance Co Ltd v James Grant & Co (West) Ltd 1982 SLT 423 62

Rafferty v Shofield [1897] 1 Ch 937. 68
Rainy Sky SA v Kookmin Bank [2011] UKSC 50, [2011] 1 WLR 2900 33
Ravenseft Properties Ltd v Davstone Holdings Ltd [1980] QB 12 94
Retail Parks Investments Ltd v The Royal Bank of Scotland Ltd (No 2)
   1996 SC 227 . . . . 57, 58, 60

Sanderson v Armour & Co 1922 SC (HL) 117 125
Scott v Muir 2012 SLT (Sh Ct) 179 . . . . 116, 117
Scottish Discount Co Ltd v Blin 1985 SC 216. 12–14
Scottish Mutual Assurance plc v Jardine Public Relations Ltd
   [1999] EG 43 (CS) 93, 94, 102
Scottish Power Generation Ltd v British Energy Generation (UK) Ltd 2002 SC 517. . . . 59
Scottish Tourist Board v Deanpark Ltd 1998 SLT 1121. 69
Secretary of State for the Environment v Possfund (North West) Ltd
   [1997] 2 EGLR 56 109
Sharp v Thomson 1930 SC 1092 . . . . 24, 38
Sinclair v Caithness Flagstone Co (1898) 25 R 703 . . . . 58, 121
@Sipp Pension Trs v Insight Travel Services Ltd [2015] CSIH 91,
   2016 SC 243 . . . . 28, 30, 34, 37, 47–48, 74–77
Sunlife Europe Properties Ltd v Tiger Aspect Holdings Ltd [2013] EWCA Civ 1656,
   [2014] 1 P & CR DG14. 63

Tay Salmon Fisheries Co Ltd v Speedie 1929 SC 593 51
Taylor v Secretary of State for Scotland 2000 SC (HL) 139. 29
Taylor Woodrow Property Co Ltd v Strathclyde Regional Council
   1996 GWD 7-397. . . . . 11, 13, 14, 38, 39, 42, 43–44
Todd v Clapperton [2009] CSOH 112, 2009 SLT 837 18
Tonsley 2 Trust Trs v Scottish Enterprise [2016] CSOH 138, 2016 GWD 31-554. 77
Transfield Shipping Inc v Mercator Shipping Inc (The Achilleas) [2008] UKHL 48,
   [2009] 1 AC 61. . . . . 64, 66
Turner's Trs v Steel (1900) 2 F 363 21

Universities Superannuation Scheme Ltd v Marks & Spencer plc [1999] L & TR 237 . . 103

Van Lynden v Gilchrist [2016] CSIH 72, 2017 SC 134. 15
Victor Harris (Gentswear) Ltd v The Wool Warehouse (Perth) Ltd 1995 SCLR 577. . . . 92
Victoria Laundry (Windsor) Ltd v Newman Industries Ltd [1949] 2 KB 528 . . . . . . 64, 66

Wade v Waldon 1909 SC 571. . . . . 69, 70, 111
West Castle Properties Ltd v Scottish Ministers 2004 SCLR 899 . . . . . 39, 40, 41–42, 42, 45
Westbury Estates Ltd v The Royal Bank of Scotland plc [2006] CSOH 177,
   2006 SLT 1143 . . . . 35, 38–39, 40, 41, 42, 44
Whyte and Mackay Ltd v Capstone International Incorporated [2010] CSIH 87,
   2011 SC 221 . . . . 59, 73

TABLE OF CASES

William Collins & Sons Ltd v CGU Insurance plc [2010] CSIH 37,
    2010 SLT 607 . . . . .59, 73, 74, 112
Wolfson v Forrester 1910 SC 675 . . . . 18, 19–20
Wood v Capita Insurance Services Ltd [2017] UKSC 24, [2017] AC 1173 . . . . . . 30, 32, 34
WW Promotions (Scotland) Ltd v De Marco 1988 SLT (Sh Ct) 43 . . . . 93, 99, 101

Table of Statutes

Arbitration (Scotland) Act 2010
    s 1 124
    Sch 1 (Scottish Arbitration Rules)
        rr 67, 68, 69, 70 125
Bankruptcy (Scotland) Act 2016
    s 2(1)(b)...................... 113
    s 7(1) 113
    s 16(1)(f) 114
        (i) 112, 113
        (3)(b)..................... 113
Bankruptcy and Diligence etc (Scotland)
    Act 2007
    s 183 114
    s 208 112
Buildings (Scotland) Act 2003 86
Court of Session Act 1988
    s 47(1) 60
        (2)...................... 59, 73
        (2A)....................... 59
Courts Reform (Scotland) Act 2014
    s 88 73
        (1)(b)...................... 59
Debt Arrangement and Attachment
    (Scotland) Act 2002
    s 19 114
Debtors (Scotland) Act 1987...........
    ss 73J, 73L.................... 114
Disability Discrimination Act 1995
    s 21(2)(a)-(c) 53
Equality Act 2010
    s 20 53

Factories Act 1961.................... 53
Fire (Scotland) Act 2005.............. 53
Health and Safety at Work Act 1974 ... 53
Insolvency Act 1986
    s 122 113
    s 123 114
        (1)...................... 113
        (a)..................... 112
Landlord and Tenant Act 1927
    s 18 .... 62, 63
Law Reform (Miscellaneous Provisions)
    (Scotland) Act 1940
    s 1 58
Law Reform (Miscellaneous Provisions)
    (Scotland) Act 1985 .... 71, 117
    ss 4-6......................... 72
    s 4(2)(a)...................... 115
        (3), (4).................... 115
    s 5 .... 72, 78, 84
        (3) 78–79
Legal Writings (Counterparts and
    Delivery) (Scotland) Act 2015....... 46
Occupiers' Liability (Scotland) Act
    1961.......................... 86
Office, Shops and Railway Premises Act
    1963.......................... 53
Requirements of Writing (Scotland) Act
    1995.......................... 46
Tenements (Scotland) Act 2004 87

Table of Orders, Rules and Regulations

Act of Sederunt (Rules of the Court of Session 1994) 1994 (SI 1994/1443)
    Chapter 34A. 129
    Chapter 47 127
    r 26.1(1)(b)(ii). 128
    rr 47.7, 47.12(2)(h), (i) 128
Act of Sederunt (Sheriff Court Ordinary Cause Rules) 1993 (SI 1993/1956)
    Chapter 20 128
    Chapter 27A. 129
Bankruptcy (Scotland) Regulations 2014 (SSI 2014/225)
    Sch 1 Form 2 112
Construction (Design and Management) Regulations 2007
    (SI 2007/320). 53
Construction (Design and Management) Regulations 2015
    (SI 2015/51). 53
Insolvency (Scotland) (Receivership and Winding up) Rules 2018
    (SSI 2018/347). 112
Non-Domestic Rating (Unoccupied Property) (Scotland) Regulations 2018
    (SSI 2018/77). 67

Chapter 1
Introduction

1.1 COMMERCIAL PROPERTY, THE COMMON LAW AND "URBAN LEASES"

This book deals with leasehold obligations concerning the maintenance, repair and renewal of commercial property – the repairing obligation and service charge liabilities. What is meant by "commercial property" in this context? Depending on the audience, it could be property that is being put to use for retail, industrial, office, or leisure purposes, with a few other categories and sub-categories no doubt being available. For present purposes, however, it is heritable property that is being used other than for residential or agricultural uses (i.e. all types of heritable property excluding residential property and agricultural property). The reason for that distinction is relatively simple – residential and agricultural leases are subject to their own statutes and case law, and have their own textbooks.[1] This book also deals only with commercial property located in Scotland, and again the reason is simple – Scots law is different from the law of England and Wales. While the overriding commercial objectives in commercial leasing are the same across the UK, the underlying law that the parties are working with (or seeking to overcome through specific lease terms) mostly comes from different sources. As there is no formal classification of "commercial property" within Scots law, the general common law of leases applies, and sets the background or foundation to particular lease terms agreed between the parties. It is important to note, however, that Scots law does not prevent parties from altering contractually the common law repairing obligation.

While there is no classification of commercial property as such, there is found within the common law a distinction between "urban leases" and "rural leases". The distinction between the two has been described as follows:

> *Rural and Urban Leases.* An important distinction is drawn between rural tenements on the one hand and urban tenements on the other. The distinction does not depend so much on the situation of the subject in the country or the town as on its nature. Where the main subject let is the use of the *solum*, its produce and what is naturally on it or below it, the lease is a Rural Lease. Where the main subject let is the use of the *superficies*, or what has been placed on the surface by the art of man, such as buildings of all kinds, the lease is an Urban Lease. The addition of an accessory to the main subjects of the lease

---

[1] This also reflects, in general terms, the classification adopted by the Scottish Law Commission in its Discussion Paper, *Aspects of Leases: Termination* (Scot Law Com DP No 165, 2018) at para 1.1.

makes no difference. Thus the existence of a farmhouse does not make the farm less of a rural tenement; and the existence of an area or garden does not make a villa less urban than a factory.[2]

Accordingly, the vast majority of what are generally understood to be "commercial leases" will be categorised as "urban leases" under Scots law (although it is technically possible for the subject matter of a commercial lease to be rural subjects). The particular importance of this for the purposes of this book is that the common law repairing obligation discussed in Chapter 3 is imposed on the landlord under an "urban lease" at common law, but not under a "rural lease".

1.2   INVESTMENT IN COMMERCIAL PROPERTY

Property might be acquired for various reasons. It has been said that:

> Buyers are those who propose to tie up capital in land or in land and building; there are three main angles from which they could view the transaction:
> 1. For occupation having regard to the personal, social or commercial benefits to be derived from that occupation.
> 2. For long-term investment having regard to the income (annual rent) expressed as a yield (percentage return) on the capital invested.
> 3. For short-term gain or profit, buying and reselling after improvement or repackaging.
>
> These motives are not mutually exclusive; a transaction might be entered into with more than one motive in mind.[3]

Those new to the UK commercial property industry can be forgiven for thinking that "property investors" buy and sell land, bricks, cement, steelwork, cladding, glass and other building materials. To a certain extent, of course, they do just that, but most investors in commercial property do not buy land or buildings for owner-occupation, or so that it can sit vacant until sold on to someone else at a higher price. Almost invariably in the context of property investment, commercial land and buildings are bought with a lease/tenant already in place, or with reasonable prospects of a tenant being found within a relatively short period of time – i.e. we are concerned with a type-2 buyer as listed above. In essence, the property investor is (or intends to become) a landlord, with the right to enforce the lease terms against the tenant, including payment of rent and service charge, and implementation of the repairing obligation – the "investment" is the value to the investor of regular rent payments and enforcement of the lease terms throughout its duration. Commercial property investment operates on the same basis as other investments – the investor seeks a return (or "yield") on capital expended. In very basic terms, the landlord obtains a return on his investment through payment of rent by the tenant of the property (although capital uplift in valuation might also be an objective).

For example, if a landlord buys a property for £1,000,000, and obtains an annual rent of £50,000 from a tenant, then the annual return (or yield) to

---

[2] G Paton and J Cameron, *The Law of Landlord and Tenant in Scotland* (1967) p 70.
[3] E Shapiro, D Mackmin and G Sams, *Modern Methods of Valuation* (12th edn, 2019) p 4.

the landlord on its investment is 5% (being £50,000/£1,000,000).[4] The return to the landlord (and value of the investment) can be affected by many factors, such as:

(a) lease duration (being the length of time the lease is in place, and during which the tenant is obliged to pay the rent);
(b) the tenant's financial strength over time – often referred to as the "covenant strength" (i.e. ability to pay the rent and comply with its other obligations under the lease);
(c) rent reviews during the currency of the lease (in terms of which the rent might be adjusted up or down, although usually upwards only);
(d) rent obtainable on re-letting following lease expiry (or possible obsolescence of the building); and
(e) the requirement to spend money on the land/building during the existence of the lease, or in order to re-let it on lease expiry.[5]

1.3 THE REPAIRING OBLIGATION IN CONTEXT

The importance that the lease terms and the identity of the tenant bear to the "value" of the investment (and the ability to obtain third-party funding for acquisition and/or development) is readily apparent. The investor is purchasing the future performance of the obligations of the tenant under the lease, as much as it is buying the bricks and mortar of the building that is the subject of the lease.

These basic commercial principles led to the development of the "Full Repairing and Insuring" (or "FRI") lease as an investment that institutional investors (such as pension providers or insurance companies) were willing to purchase to provide long-term returns on monies invested. The original FRI leases were "25 × 5", overall meaning:

- a 25-year duration;
- 5-yearly upwards-only rent reviews;
- tight control on assignation of the tenant's interest;
- the tenant pays the cost of insuring the property;
- the tenant meets the costs of all repairs/renewals during the currency of the lease (whether or not the tenant carries out the work); and
- the tenant leaves the property at lease expiry in a condition such that it can be re-let by the landlord immediately.

The focus of this book is the repairing obligation, service charge provisions, and dilapidations claims. Any uncertainty as to possible expenditure required of the landlord in addition to the initial acquisition costs impacts on the marketability and/or value of the investment. The terms of the repairing obligation also impact on other

---

[4] This is obviously a grossly simplified explanation of investment and return in this context. Readers will hopefully appreciate that property valuation and investment is considerably more complicated (and interesting) than this suggests: see Shapiro et al, *Modern Methods of Valuation*.
[5] Factors external to the lease might also impact on values, such as borrowing costs, returns available in other markets (e.g. stocks and shares), and general interest in/appetite for property investment.

provisions of a commercial lease, such as the proper construction of the hypothetical lease for rent review purposes and insurance/reinstatement obligations, but it is not intended to consider those aspects in any detail as part of this book.

1.4 THE COMMERCIAL RELEVANCE OF LEASE DURATION

As stated above, the original FRI leases would normally be entered into for a duration of 25 years. Apart from the requirement for an "investment grade" lease, in terms of which the tenant meets ongoing costs liabilities, it was generally considered that the tenant had a commercial interest in ensuring that "its" premises would be properly maintained to a good standard over that period of time.

Over the last twenty or so years, however, there has been a clear shift away from standard FRI lease terms in most sectors of the commercial property market. The trend has been for leases of shorter duration, or with break clauses that permit the tenant to bring the lease to an end at certain points in time. This, in turn, impacts on other commercial matters, such as the tenant's willingness to accept liabilities for repairs, reinstatement and dilapidations at lease expiry. Adjustment of one part of a lease will generally impact elsewhere in the lease, and the repairing obligation is not immune in that respect.

Reaching a compromise position on the repairing obligation can often be tricky, despite the best efforts of clients, surveyors and lawyers to do just that. Recording the condition of a building at the point of entry of the tenant is one thing. However, the "easy" drafting of providing that the tenant is not obliged to put the property into any better condition than that evidenced by a photographic schedule of condition ignores the possibility of a number of future events, such as destruction and reinstatement of a building (or part thereof), or the need to replace certain items that are beyond economic repair.[6]

1.5 TREATMENT OF "REPAIRS" TOWARDS EXPIRY OF THE LEASE

As the lease draws to an end, the landlord's mind will invariably turn towards the future of its investment. This might involve re-letting the premises in their current condition, refurbishment, or even demolition and/or redevelopment for alternative uses. If there is no tenant lined up to take on a new lease of the premises, then the landlord will have to consider very carefully whether to effect works that might not meet the requirements of future tenants. This might be as basic as decorating the premises in a particular style or might involve major refurbishment/redevelopment in the hope of attracting new tenants.

Meanwhile, the tenant will be considering its obligations to return the premises to the landlord in a particular condition, and the potential cost implications of doing that, bearing in mind that (a) the tenant will derive no commercial benefit from carrying out any repairs or redecoration, and (b) carrying out works during the currency of the lease will impact on the tenant's ability to use/trade from the premises for which it is otherwise paying rent.

---

[6] The use of schedules of condition is considered further in **4.5**.

It will not come as a surprise, therefore, that very often the "terminal dilapidations" under a lease are dealt with by way of a negotiated cash settlement between the parties, whether or not that is provided for in the lease itself.[7]

1.6 SINGLE OCCUPANCY AND MULTI-OCCUPANCY BUILDINGS

Before considering the detail of the repairing obligations imposed by a clause in a lease, it is of obvious importance to understand the "premises" that are affected by that clause.

In the case of a single-occupancy building, such as a stand-alone warehouse or factory, this will usually be readily apparent – the repairing obligation will be in respect of the entire building and all its constituent parts. The position might not be so clear in the case of multi-occupancy buildings, such as a shopping centre, or an office development with different tenants in various parts of the building. This topic is covered in more detail in Chapter 2.

In relation to multi-occupancy buildings, it is likely that the individual tenants will be leased an internal shell only,[8] with the landlord retaining the all-important common parts of the building, including the foundations, walls, roof, and areas used in common by the tenants. Instead of imposing a repairing obligation on the tenants in respect of common parts, the landlord will retain the right (if not obligation) to carry out repairs and maintenance, etc to the common parts, but charge the tenants for doing so by way of annual service charge. Service charge regimes are considered in more detail in Chapter 6.

---

[7] See Chapter 7 dealing with dispute resolution.
[8] Sometimes referred to as a "developer's shell".

Chapter 2

Defining "the Premises" and "the Common Parts"

2.1   INTRODUCTION

A commercial lease has many interdependent clauses and schedules, including the user clause, insuring and repairing obligations, service charge, and the rent review clause. Of central importance to these clauses is an understanding of what has actually been let to the tenant by the lease – "the Premises" – and what (if anything) is to be retained by the landlord, including items intended to form the "Common Parts".

2.2   SINGLE-OCCUPANCY BUILDINGS

If the entirety of a building or area of ground is let to the tenant for its sole occupation and use, the landlord will ordinarily want to impose a full repairing obligation onto the tenant in respect of those subjects. Presumably to reflect this intention, the practice has developed of using the conveyancing description from the landlord's title deeds to define the premises let by the lease. Certainly, if any other form of definition/description is used, care should be taken to ensure that there is no gap or discrepancy between the landlord's title and the subjects let to the tenant.[1] Notwithstanding that general position, the draftsperson in each case must give consideration to the rules of interpretation of contracts.[2] As is discussed below, use of a conveyancing description to define the premises is perhaps not the complete answer in all situations.

Additional care should be taken in respect of "individual" premises that form part of larger subjects, such as a shop forming the ground floor of a tenement building. Ordinarily, the lease will be of those premises (defined using the conveyancing description contained within the title deeds), with an additional obligation to comply with title conditions and burdens in respect of other elements of the building of which they form part. The title deeds might include an obligation to effect works to common parts of the tenement or building, such as a roof, mutual walls, access road or similar (or to contribute towards the costs of works). Accordingly, the tenant should be advised of potential liabilities in respect of subjects "outwith" the premises

---

[1] The case of *Beatsons Building Supplies Ltd v Noble and Ors as Trustees of the Alex F Noble & Son Ltd Executive Benefits Scheme* 2015 GWD 15-271 illustrates the ability of a tenant to challenge the application of the repairing obligation where the lease does not define the premises let solely by reference to the conveyancing description of the subjects owned by the landlord. This is discussed in more detail below.

[2] See Chapter 4 for a full analysis.

let, condition surveys undertaken as appropriate,[3] and the lease drafted to match the parties' expectations as to liabilities.

2.3 MULTIPLE-OCCUPANCY BUILDINGS

The landlord may own a building that has more than one "lettable area". This may be, for example, a shopping centre or multi-floor office development, in which different tenants are expected to lease/occupy distinct units. When dealing with multi-occupancy buildings (of whatever nature), the landlord will ordinarily lease only the internal airspace or "shell" to the tenant, including perhaps plasterwork and other finishes. The landlord does not lease structural elements, the roof, foundations or the like to the various tenants. Instead, the landlord retains possession of those "common parts" of the building, and will undertake to decorate, repair, maintain or renew them as required, subject to the tenants paying an appropriate proportion of the costs of doing those works via a regular service charge or one-off payment.

Accordingly, it is important when drafting or revising the lease to understand:

(a) how the building was constructed;
(b) what individual "premises" are being let to the tenant(s);
(c) what "common parts" are being retained by the landlord; and
(d) what the parties' rights and obligations are in respect of those premises/common parts.

From a tenant's perspective, it is of real importance to understand that a restricted repairing obligation in respect of "the premises" offers no protection against potentially major costs in respect of "the common parts". The service charge provisions must also be considered and revised as appropriate. Chapter 6 covers the topic of common parts and service charge in more detail.

2.4 "THE PREMISES" AND "THE COMMON PARTS"

2.4.1 General

It should not be forgotten that a lease is a commercial contract between the parties, and falls to be interpreted in the same manner as other commercial contracts.[4] This is of relevance not only for determining the proper construction of particular clauses of the lease, but also when considering the defined terms within the lease. The question of construing the definitions of "the Premises" and "the Common Parts" normally arises in disputes as to responsibility for effecting repairs and/or meeting the costs of those repairs.

2.4.2 Single-occupancy leases

Commercial leasing practitioners generally work on the basis that use of a conveyancing description to define the premises let in a single-occupancy lease is sufficient to let to the tenant all that is encompassed within the landlord's title.

---

[3] I.e. the tenant should understand the physical state and condition of all elements of the building that it might have responsibility for.
[4] See Chapter 4 for a full discussion of the principles of interpretation.

That is to say, use of a conveyancing description in a lease is evidence of a common intention between the parties that everything within the landlord's title is to be let to the tenant.

Situations can arise, however, where that general position may be open to challenge, as happened in the case of *Beatsons Building Supplies*.[5] In that case, the parties had defined the premises let by reference to a postal address and a plan (not a conveyancing description). The premises comprised an industrial shed with a large yard for storage of building supplies. Of relevance in relation to the definition of the premises let (the tenant argued) was the fact that the lease made separate provision for services conduits running above and below the premises let – indicating that it had been the intention of the parties to restrict the extent of the premises.

Unknown to the tenant when the lease was entered into, there was a burn several metres below the surface of the yard.[6] The burn had been culverted with a pipe. During the tenant's occupation, the pipe collapsed, leading to subsidence of the ground above, including the surface of the yard, rendering a significant part of it unusable.

The point that the court was ultimately asked to determine was this: which party had responsibility for repairing the culvert and the surface? Had the collapsed culvert been let to the tenant as part of "the premises" (as defined), such that the repairing obligation applied to it?[7] The landlord argued that the premises (as defined) included everything within the landlord's title *a coelo usque ad centrum*,[8] and that the responsibility rested with the tenant by virtue of its repairing obligation.

The tenant argued that the proper construction of the definition of "the premises" remained a question of establishing the intention of the parties at the outset of the lease. By reference to the terms of the lease, read as a whole, the tenant argued that:

(a) The intention of the parties was that the premises let comprised that which the tenant intended to use, namely (i) the building (from foundations to roof height), and (ii) the surface of the yard and airspace above it necessary for use of the premises as a whole.

(b) The repairing obligation did not, therefore, apply to an unseen culvert several metres below the surface of "the premises".

The court ultimately found in favour of the landlord, bringing the culvert within the definition of the premises let by the lease.[9]

---

[5] *Beatsons Building Supplies Ltd v Noble and Ors as Trustees of the Alex F Noble & Son Ltd Executive Benefits Scheme* 2015 GWD 15-271.

[6] The sheriff in reaching his decision appears to take it for granted that the tenant's lawyers would have examined the landlord's title and discovered the existence of the burn, notwithstanding that that did not form part of the landlord's arguments in the case.

[7] There was also a separate argument as to whether the necessary repair works amounted to "extraordinary repairs", thus falling outwith the tenant's repairing obligation under the lease, but that point was ultimately not decided by the court.

[8] Meaning "from the Heavens to the centre of the Earth".

[9] *Beatsons Building Supplies Ltd v Noble and Ors as Trustees of the Alex F Noble & Son Ltd Executive Benefits Scheme* 2015 GWD 15-271. The tenant instigated but subsequently abandoned an appeal against the decision.

2.4.3 Multi-occupancy leases

In a multi-occupancy lease there is even greater need for careful drafting to define the boundaries or split between individual premises/lettable areas and the common parts (which, together, should encompass all of the landlord's title). As well as ensuring there is a sufficiently clear definition of "the premises" for the purposes of the tenant's repairing obligation, the lease requires to regulate responsibility for repairs, renewals, etc to the common parts, and recovery by the landlord of costs incurred in implementing its obligations.

Some of the issues involved (and the problems associated with drafting that is less than clear) are discussed in the case of *Marfield Properties v Secretary of State for the Environment*.[10] That case involved a dispute over a tenant's liability for service charge in respect of common parts of a building. The building had a supermarket at ground floor level, with five floors of office space above. There was also a car park. The "premises" let to the tenant were defined as:

> (First) All and Whole part of the first floor above the street or ground floor ... and the whole of the second and third floors of the building comprising shops, offices and a supermarket fronting Graham Street, Airdrie and which floors are shown within red boundary lines on the [plan annexed]
>
> ...
>
> Together with a right in common with the Landlords and the occupiers of the remainder of the said building development to the following subjects and services (hereinafter referred to as "the common parts"); (a) the car parks and common service yard situated within the said building development; (b) the internal access roads and the pedestrian access way leading from Graham Street, Airdrie; (c) the landscaped area and footpaths within the said building development; (d) the safety fences and boundary walls and others bounding the said building development; and (e) all other parts of, fixtures and fittings used in connection with and services in the said building development which are common to the premises and other parts of said building development.

The tenant's repairing obligation was restricted to the interior of the premises let, and the tenant undertook in terms of the lease to pay a proportionate share of the expense of cleaning and maintaining the common parts as defined (see above). Furthermore, the landlord was obliged to uphold the structures of the building:

> ... and shall maintain the roofs, walls, floors, second floor screeds, drains, rhones, downpipes, water pipes, waste pipes and soil pipes and be responsible for all wind and watertight repairs and all external painting.

The dispute concerned whether the "common parts" included or did not include the roof and external walls of the building, as those items were not specifically referred to in the definition of the common parts. The case was originally heard in the sheriff court, where the sheriff found that the roof and walls did not form part of the common parts. That decision was appealed to the Inner House. The Inner House found that the roof and walls did form part of the common parts, even though not expressly referred to. In doing so, they relied heavily on the catch-all provision contained in section (e) of the definition of the common parts (narrated above) and took into

---

[10] *Marfield Properties v Secretary of State for the Environment* 1996 SC 362.

account the provisions of the lease as a whole. The Lord President (Hope), delivering the opinion of the court, also opined that:

(1) it was inappropriate to use the common law of the tenement to assist in interpreting the definition of "common parts" in the lease – that exercise must be done by reference to the wording of the lease and the ordinary rules for the interpretation of contracts;
(2) the *"contra proferentem"* rule for construction of contracts does not apply to commercial leases; and
(3) the more onerous or unusual the contractual burden/obligation is, the greater is the requirement for clarity.

This case is an example of the court adopting a purposive construction of the lease, with the construction exercise being approached with reference to the purpose of the lease as a whole. The additional comments of Lord President Hope, summarised above, are also welcome guidance for those seeking to advise landlords and tenants of their rights and obligations in this area.

2.4.4 Sub-lettings and the premises sub-let

A sub-letting might be of part or the whole of the premises let under the lease. For example, the tenant of four floors of an office building might sub-let one or more of those floors to different sub-tenants, or a tenant of one floor might create different lettable units within that single floor. On the assumption that there is some repairing obligation imposed upon the tenant under the head-lease (or what is soon to become a head-lease), it is likely that the tenant will wish to re-impose those liabilities, either in whole or in part, onto the sub-tenant(s).

When the sub-letting is of the whole of the premises let under the head-lease, there is no real issue in terms of defining the premises to be let under the sub-lease. The parties to the sub-lease will most likely consider the issue of the repairing obligation to be imposed on the sub-tenant in respect of those premises in the same way as a landlord/tenant would upon a head-lease being granted. There might be a simple "pass-through" of the head-lease repairing obligation onto the sub-tenant, although it will often be necessary to take into account the fact that the sub-tenant might be in occupation for a much more limited period than the tenant under the head-lease.[11] There is also every likelihood that the sub-tenant will wish to restrict its repairing obligation by reference to the state and condition of the premises as at the date of entry under the sub-lease. Ensuing difficulties with matching repairing obligations to a schedule of condition are discussed in Chapter 4.

The issue of the extent of "the premises" sub-let requires more careful consideration when a sub-letting of part is contemplated, and sub-division works are to be undertaken. It might then be necessary to create a sub-lease structure that reflects a multi-occupancy situation, even if the head-lease is in respect of a single-occupancy building and is otherwise a single-occupancy lease.

---

[11] It should be noted that rarely does the straightforward intention of transferring the repairing obligation to a sub-tenant result in a straightforward claim in respect of dilapidations: see *Moor Row Ltd v DWF LLP* [2017] CSOH 63, 2017 GWD 14-213.

2.5 FIXTURES – GENERAL

In considering what is included in "the premises" for the purposes of the repairing obligation, parties should not overlook the importance and value of fixtures, which might form part of the premises from the outset of the lease or might be introduced during the currency of the lease (usually by the tenant as part of initial fitting-out works or later alterations).[12] Whilst it is true that either landlord or tenant can introduce fixtures onto a property, categorisation into "landlord's fixtures" and "tenant's fixtures" can lead to unwarranted confusion as to whether or not a fixture forms part of the premises let, and this confusion is often transferred into the terms of the lease itself.[13]

The first matter to be established is whether something brought onto the premises becomes a fixture. This is examined in **2.6** below. If it is a fixture then it becomes part of the premises as a matter of law (i.e. its legal character changes from "moveable" to "heritable" property) and is owned by the landlord. That occurs irrespective of which party attached it to the premises, and in most cases irrespective of any provisions of the lease (or licence for works).

It is then necessary to consider whether the fixture is a "trade" fixture. As is examined in **2.8** below, a tenant is entitled at common law to remove a trade fixture without the consent of the landlord, whereupon its character reverts to moveable rather than heritable. Again, this distinction can be important – not only for the purposes of the repairing obligation, but also for considering what "the premises" might comprise at lease expiry.

Before looking at the common law applicable to fixtures, it is worth pointing out that most advisers will attempt to draft the lease and/or licence for works in such a way as to define and regulate the rights and obligations of the parties. When the cost of fitting out large retail premises can easily run into a seven-figure sum of money, for example, it is in the interests of the parties to agree up-front what is to happen to those works during and at the expiry of the lease. A landlord might want the tenant to leave fixtures in place for the benefit of a future purchaser or tenant but might want the fixtures removed to create a blank canvas for future fitting-out. Equally, a tenant might argue for the right to leave alterations/fixtures and fittings in place at the end of the lease, to avoid (a) removal/reinstatement costs, and (b) associated interruption to trading during the final months of the lease.[14]

2.6 WHAT IS A FIXTURE?

A fixture is a moveable item that is affixed to the premises, and through that process becomes part of the premises. This is based on the common law of "accession". Accession operates as follows:

---

[12] It is, of course, important to understand this for other aspects of the lease, such as the obligation on the landlord to insure "the premises" and effect repairs in respect of insured risk damage to "the premises".

[13] An example of this is seen in *Taylor Woodrow Property Co Ltd v Strathclyde Regional Council* 1996 GWD 7-397.

[14] Tenants' improvements and alterations should also be considered in the context of any rent review provisions. Most tenants would not expect to incur the costs of fitting out the premises only to find that, at rent review, the landlord obtains a higher rent as a result of those works having been effected.

Accession (*accessio*) occurs whenever two pieces of property become joined together in such a way that one (known as the "accessory") is considered to have become subsumed in the other (known as the "principal").[15]

Accession involves three distinct elements – physical attachment, functional subordination, and permanency.[16] Accession arises as a matter of law, based on the facts and circumstances of each case – it is not determined by reference to the terms of the lease or licence for works. The extent to which the terms of the documentation might be relevant in assessing whether accession has occurred is considered below. Accordingly, it might be the case that certain items are, as a matter of contract between landlord and tenant, defined as part of the premises, but do not, in questions with third parties, form part of the building owned by the landlord.

The leading modern case on the law of accession in the context of fixtures is *Scottish Discount Co Ltd v Blin*.[17] In that case (heard by a bench of seven judges in the Inner House), the Lord President (Emslie) adopts the following proposition:[18]

> ... the broad approach which the court must take is sufficiently explained in one or two selected statements of the law which are in line with the authorities as a whole. In his article on "Fixtures" in Green's *Encyclopaedia of the Laws of Scotland*, Vol 7, Professor Gloag in section 2, entitled "What constitutes a fixture", said this in paras. 362 and 363:—
>
>> "362. The question whether a particular thing has become a fixture, that is, has become a part of the soil, or of some building attached to the soil, is not to be solved by the mere consideration whether it is, as matter of fact, affixed to the soil or building. That consideration, as well as the degree or extent of its attachment, is to be taken together with other elements. These elements are: whether it can be removed *integre, salve et commode, i.e.* without the destruction of itself as a separate thing, or of the soil or building to which it is attached; whether its annexation was of a permanent or quasi-permanent character; whether the building to which it is attached was specially adapted for its use; how far the use and enjoyment of the soil or building would be affected by its removal; the intention of the party attaching it. Intention, however, in this question means intention discoverable from the nature of the article and of the building, and the manner in which it is affixed, not intention proved by extrinsic evidence, or deducible from the consideration, in cases between landlord and tenant, that the tenant in attaching a fixture is not likely to have intended to make a present to his landlord.
>>
>> "363. From the number of these considerations it is plain that it is impossible to lay down any very exact rules as to what constitutes a fixture, and that each case must depend greatly upon its particular circumstances. The degree of attachment may be conclusive in extreme cases. Thus if an article is so firmly attached to the *solum* or to

---

[15] K G C Reid, "Property" in *The Laws of Scotland: Stair Memorial Encyclopaedia*, vol 18, para 570. See paras 578–587 for a full discussion of accession of fixtures under the heading "Moveables to Land: Fixtures". The historical development of the law in this area is covered in detail in K G C Reid, "The Lord Chancellor's fixtures" (1983) 28 JLSS 49.
[16] Reid, "Property" in *Stair Memorial Encyclopaedia*, vol 18, para 571.
[17] *Scottish Discount Co Ltd v Blin* 1985 SC 216.
[18] *Scottish Discount Co* at p 232. It appears that counsel in the case were agreed on the law, with the exception of the relevance of "intention", which the court goes on to discuss separately.

a building that it cannot be removed without solving it into its constituent elements, there would seem no doubt that it is a fixture, whatever was the intention in so attaching it, or its adaptability to the structure to which it is attached."

It will be apparent that there is no closed list of items that might become fixtures. The question turns on the facts and circumstances of each case. Questions of fact as to whether an item does or does not form a fixture might be remitted to a reporter who is best placed to analyse the relationship between the item in question and the building to which it is affixed.[19] One example of this being done is found in the case of *Taylor Woodrow Property Co Ltd v Strathclyde Regional Council*.[20] A question had arisen as to whether electric storage heaters were fixtures of the premises. The Lord Ordinary (Penrose) noted the following:[21]

> The dispute in relation to storage heaters covered a number of topics. For the landlords it was contended that the heaters were heritable. They were of the standard type of storage heater, permanently wired into the electrical circuitry of the premises ... For the tenants it was contended that the heaters were moveable or, alternatively, that that they were tenants' fittings ... There is information available in photographs that might suggest that the heaters are of the standard storage heater variety, permanently wired into the electrical ring mains of the premises. However, it is not strictly a matter of admission and it will be for the reporter to examine the installation and to advise on the circumstances before a view is taken as to the character of the heaters in this case.
>
> The test to be applied where the issue of fixture is or relates to heritable right is now authoritatively laid down in *Scottish Discount Co Ltd v Blin* 1985 SC 216 ... In my view the proper course for the reporter to adopt is to apply the criteria set out in Lord President Emslie's opinion at pages 232–3 of *Scottish Discount Co Ltd v Blin*. In the case of storage heaters it will clearly remain a relevant consideration if it is ascertained that they are integrated into a dedicated electrical circuit, itself undoubtedly part of the premises, without which they could not function, and which, without the attachment of the heaters, would not be useable. There may be such mutual adaptation of heaters and circuitry that the reporter would have little difficulty in arriving at a view similar to that which resulted in *Hodgson*.[22] But the issue is one of fact in the absence of agreement and will require to be investigated.

2.7 THE ROLE OF INTENTION IN ACCESSION

The case of *Scottish Discount Co Ltd v Blin* concerned valuable machinery, for use in the scrap trade, which had been bolted onto specially prepared foundations in the scrapyard by the scrapyard owner.[23] When the owner defaulted under a loan, a heritable creditor with a security over the yard claimed that the machinery was

---

[19] This form of judicial remit is intended to save time and expense compared to a contested proof on a factual issue and is discussed in more detail in Chapter 7. Subject to a reporter acting within and otherwise meeting the terms of his remit, the parties effectively exclude probation of the matters covered in the report; see *BAM Buchanan Ltd v Arcadia Group Ltd* [2013] CSOH 107A and *BNP Paribas Securities Services Trust Co (Jersey) Ltd v Mothercare (UK) Ltd* [2015] CSOH 47.
[20] *Taylor Woodrow Property Co Ltd v Strathclyde Regional Council* 1996 GWD 7-397.
[21] *Taylor Woodrow Property Co* at pp 29–32.
[22] *Assessor for Fife v Hodgson* 1966 SC 30.
[23] The scrapyard in question was owner-occupied, and the case is not directly concerned with the landlord/tenant relationship as regards fixtures.

heritable, and therefore formed part of the yard covered by its security. It transpired, however, that the scrapyard merchant had acquired the machinery under a hire-purchase agreement, under which the seller retained ownership in the goods until all the hire-purchase payments were made. It was argued that the scrapyard merchant could not have intended that the machinery become heritable, since he did not own the machinery in the first place.

The court rejected this argument, saying that intention was to be looked at objectively (see above). Extrinsic evidence is not always to be ignored completely, however. In *Scottish Discount Co Ltd v Blin*, for example, it was held that the terms of the hire-purchase agreement under which the scrap merchant acquired the machinery could, in limited circumstances, assist in determining intention, but was not of itself conclusive.

As Lord President Emslie states:[24]

> I am not persuaded, however, that in asking the question whether an article has become a fixture it will never be permissible to notice that it was acquired by the person who installed it on his land, under a hire-purchase agreement. That circumstance, it seems to me, may, when the matter is otherwise in fine balance, be of some relevance in deciding whether the installation was or was not intended to be a permanent or quasi permanent addition to the land.

It has been questioned whether "intention" is properly a factor to be considered, notwithstanding the decision in *Scottish Discount Co Ltd v Blin*.[25] However, the criteria set out in that case have been applied subsequently with approval.[26] Objective intention, therefore, should not be dismissed altogether as part of the exercise of determining whether an item is or is not a fixture.

2.8 TRADE FIXTURES

A "trade fixture" is a fixture that is attached to the premises by the tenant for the purposes of the tenant's trade or business at the premises. Trade fixtures accede to the premises in the same way as all other fixtures and become the property of the landlord accordingly. The important distinction between fixtures generally and trade fixtures is that, at common law, trade fixtures can be removed from the premises by the tenant without the consent of the landlord. As Rankine states:

> It would seem that all trade fixtures are removeable by the tenant who (or whose author) set them up: provided that there be no custom or stipulation to the contrary, and that the fixtures can be recognised and disannexed *in specie*, or in such a way as permit of their being reinstated *in specie*. It would appear, moreover, that fixtures may be removed even if not capable of being so disannexed, if they are merely accessories to things removeable. The ground of exception is said to be the public advantage, as giving encouragement to tenants to improve the apparatus of their trade with the certainty of getting the full benefit of their outlay. Otherwise put, the tenant in annexing trade fixtures does so with no intention to improve the shop or factory or to make the landlord a gift of the reversion, but solely for the purpose of being the better able to make use of the machine or fitting in prosecution

---

[24] *Scottish Discount Co Ltd v Blin* 1985 SC 216 at 235.
[25] Reid, "Property" in *Stair Memorial Encyclopaedia*, vol 18, para 583.
[26] *Taylor Woodrow Property Co Ltd v Strathclyde Regional Council* 1996 GWD 7-397 (as quoted above).

of his trade or manufacture ... By the infixture he surrenders the ownership, retaining at best only the right to dissever and remove ...[27]

As with fixtures generally, there is no closed list of what might constitute a trade fixture. The facts and circumstances of each case must be considered before a decision can be arrived at. There might also be a degree of overlap between fixtures being considered as trade fixtures and a right of severance contained with the lease documentation itself. In *Van Lynden v Gilchrist*[28] a head-lease obliged the tenant to build between 20 and 40 holiday chalets onto the subjects let, "sell" those chalets to third parties (by granting sub-leases), and then remove the chalets at lease expiry. The question arose whether a sub-tenant, at lease expiry, was entitled to remove/sever the chalet from the ground. The case was ultimately decided by reference to the express terms of the leasehold documentation, but the Inner House referred to the fact that the case might also be capable of analysis on the basis that the chalets were "trade fixtures".

2.9 SEVERANCE OF ITEMS FROM THE PREMISES BY AGREEMENT

It is open to the parties to provide for removal or severance of fixtures from the premises, irrespective of whether the fixtures in question are trade fixtures. This agreement can be express or implied from the terms of the lease.[29] Fixtures will remain part of the premises within the landlord's ownership, and subject to any repairing obligation, unless and until severance occurs.

---

[27] J Rankine, *The Law of Leases in Scotland* (3rd edn, 1916) p 299.
[28] *Van Lynden v Gilchrist* [2016] CSIH 72, 2017 SC 134.
[29] *Ferguson v Paul* (1885) 12 R 1222; *Van Lynden v Gilchrist* [2016] CSIH 72, 2017 SC 134.

Chapter 3
The Underlying Common Law

3.1 INTRODUCTION

When drafting or considering the terms of a lease of commercial property, it is necessary to understand (1) the commercial objectives of the parties, and (2) any statute, common law rule or implied term that ought to be contracted out of for those commercial objectives to be met.[1] In the case of commercial leases, particularly relevant for this book generally, there are a number of provisions of the common law as regards condition and repair of leased property that should be at the forefront of the drafter's mind. A failure to appreciate the impact of the underlying common law provisions, as they affect both landlord and tenant, will most likely result in a lease that fails to express clearly (or perhaps not at all) the commercial intention of the parties at the outset.

In modern commercial leases, the common law default position in relation to condition and repair of commercial properties is almost invariably contracted out of/altered by agreement between the parties. There are two main reasons for that: (1) the common law obligations lack the certainty required for parties who want property maintained to a particular standard, and (2) the common law obligations do not reflect the commercial objectives of an FRI lease, as discussed in Chapter 1.

Where an FRI lease is the agreed commercial position between the landlord and tenant, it is to be expected that the terms of the lease will completely overwrite the common law, such that there is no need to consider it. However, where it is agreed that something less onerous than an FRI lease is to be put in place, the parties require to appreciate that they risk the common law having an impact on the repairing obligation as contained within the lease.[2]

It is important, therefore, to understand how the courts address the interface or interaction between the common law and the wording of the lease. From a drafter's perspective, this entails consideration of what drafting measures must be taken in order to contract out of the common law. General principles of contractual interpretation are covered in Chapter 4, but the following statement from Lord Prosser in *Mars Pension Trs Ltd v County Properties & Developments Ltd*[3] provides a suitable starting point for drafters in the present context:

---

[1] This applies to commercial contracts generally, but is readily apparent in the case of leases, given the longstanding provisions of the common law relating to such contracts. Agricultural and residential tenancies are more heavily regulated by statute, with contracting-out often precluded.
[2] The same point applies in respect of drafting that fails to meet the commercial objectives of the parties.
[3] *Mars Pension Trs Ltd v County Properties & Developments Ltd* 1999 SC 267.

LANDLORD'S IMPLIED WARRANTY AT LEASE COMMENCEMENT

Before considering what the clause means if properly construed, and whether it says what has to be said in order to achieve effective exclusion of the implied common law warranty by the landlord, it is necessary to consider a prior, underlying issue: what are the principles governing construction of such a clause, and what sort of thing must be said, if one is to exclude the liability which would flow from the implied common law warranty?

...

But apart from these quite general propositions, there are many instances of courts saying, in relation to some type or category of provision, that special, more stringent rules of construction apply, or that a particular effect can only be achieved by a provision which meets special, more stringent requirements than are usual.

...

According to the authorities thus far noted, it does not appear to me that "strictness" in interpreting a provision of the type in question involves anything more startling than this—that where the general common law imposes an obligation or liability upon one party to a contract, the contract will not be read as excluding that obligation or liability unless it makes it clear, at least by necessary implication, that that was the intention of the parties. I do not myself think that the word "strict" is particularly useful. And if all that is required is that the contract shows this clear intention, that seems to me to be consistent with what is said in Gloag on *Contract*, to the effect that no implied term is admissible "directly contradictory" of the terms that are expressed. To say that there is no special rule of construction is to my mind going too far: the proposition that the common law rule will prevail unless the contract clearly negates this, or unless there is a direct contradiction, is rather more demanding than our basic rules of construction. And much may depend on the particular context. But while such a rule may be described as special, it does not appear to me in its essence to be a particularly strict one, far less to involve any positive requirement that exclusion or exemption clauses must take particular forms, or describe or list excluded rights individually rather than generically. What is needed is clarity of intention.

3.2 THE LANDLORD'S IMPLIED WARRANTY AT LEASE COMMENCEMENT – THAT THE PREMISES LET ARE FIT FOR PURPOSE

3.2.1 The premises let

Rankine summarises the common law position as follows:

> [A] lease implies a warrandice on the landlord's part that its subject is reasonably fit for the purpose for which it is let. The rule is only of value where the subject let, or part of it, consists of artificial structures, such as buildings, fences and the like ... [If] a house is let for a dwelling, or a mill, or a shop, it must be fit to live, work, or trade in. If the immediately preceding predecessor left them in a condition not corresponding to the implied warranty, they must be repaired by the landlord.
>
> The rule of the common law, as applied to urban tenements, is that they shall be put into habitable or tenantable condition by the landlord at entry. ... The question whether a house is tenantable or habitable is one of fact to be determined on a proof, or by remit

to a man of skill; and the determination will greatly depend on the class of house let and the degree to which it has the advantage of modern improvements.[4]

This is often referred to as the landlord's implied warranty that the premises that are the subject matter of the lease will be fit for the purpose for which they are let.[5] The exact obligation on the landlord will be interpreted on a case-by-case basis, with reference to the type of premises involved, the reasonable requirements of tenants of that type of premises, and the value of premises.[6] It will be appreciated that this provides little guidance for advisers in relation to modern, potentially complex, buildings. The classic statement of the obligation is found in the opinion of the Lord President (Dunedin) in *Wolfson v Forrester*:[7]

> By the law of Scotland the lease of every urban tenement is, in default of any specific stipulation, deemed to include an obligation on the part of the landlord to hand over the premises in a wind and water tight condition, and if he does not do so, there is a breach of contract and he may be liable in damages ... But wind and water tight means only wind and water tight against what may be called the ordinary attacks of the elements, not against exceptional encroachments of water due to other causes.[8]

However, that statement, restricted to the requirement for the premises to be wind- and watertight, does not reflect the full scope of the landlord's obligation as set out above. While there is little clear guidance on the extent of the obligation, it is generally taken to be the case that the landlord must ensure that the premises let are safe, structurally sound for reasonable uses,[9] and wind- and watertight.[10] The common law obligation at the outset of the lease is a "one-off" obligation on the landlord, and is a separate obligation from that of ongoing repair and renewal during the currency of the lease.

---

[4] J Rankine, *The Law of Leases in Scotland* (3rd edn, 1916) pp 240 and 241. Also see J Erskine, *An Institute of the Law of Scotland* (1st edn, 1773, reprinted by Edinburgh Legal Education Trust 2014) at II.VI.43. Erskine actually says that 'where a subject is let for a particular purpose, the nature of the contract implies, that it be fitted for that purpose". This is said in the context of a dwelling house being in habitable condition at entry. There is no suggestion by the authors that a landlord must fit out premises according to the needs of a particular tenant.

[5] Rankine, *The Law of Leases*, p 207.

[6] *Mechan v Watson* 1907 SC 25 per Lord M'Laren at 28. In *Glebe Sugar Refining Co v Paterson* (1900) 2 F 615 Lord M'Laren says: "the building must be reasonably fit for the purpose for which it was let, and must be reasonably used by the tenant; the general and recognised practice of the trade being, in my opinion, the criterion of reasonable use". Thus, the landlord is not obliged to ensure that the premises are fit for all possible uses that the tenant might put them to. Also see *Paton v MacDonald* 1973 SLT (Sh Ct) 85.

[7] *Wolfson v Forrester* 1910 SC 675 at 680.

[8] The latter section of this quote also covers, in the opinion of the Lord President, any ongoing obligation on the landlord to maintain the premises in a wind- and watertight condition. Habitability might be assessed independently of the question as to whether the premises are wind- and watertight, perhaps of more relevance in relation to residential properties.

[9] *Glebe Sugar Refining Co v Paterson* (1900) 2 F 615; *Todd v Clapperton* [2009] CSOH 112, 2009 SLT 837.

[10] For a wider discussion of the implied warranty and the common law repairing obligation, see A McAllister, "The landlord's common law repairing obligation" 2012 JR 263. Issues of dampness and vermin are also discussed in this context, although the case law generally deals with residential tenancies and housing legislation, and the issue of fitness for habitation.

To displace this obligation, most commercial leases will contain an express provision of "acceptance" by the tenant of the premises let, with confirmation that the tenant accepts the premises as being in good and tenantable condition and fit for the purpose for which they are let in terms of the lease. It is not necessarily the case that the landlord's implied warranty is being "excluded", but rather that the tenant accepts that the landlord has fulfilled any duty owed to the tenant.[11] For obvious reasons, if the tenant's acceptance is qualified in any way, or otherwise fails to displace fully the landlord's implied warranty, then the potential exists for a residual liability to rest with the landlord. Parties should also take care to avoid possible drafting conflicts between acceptance of the premises in a particular state and condition on the one hand, and liability for ongoing repairs on the other.[12]

3.2.2 Multi-occupancy buildings – common parts

As was explained in more detail in Chapter 2, where the tenant leases only part of a larger building owned by the landlord, the landlord will retain possession and control of the major parts of the building, including structural elements, foundations, roof, etc. In the cases that have come before the courts, parties have accepted (apparently without debate) that the landlord's implied warranty extended to the relevant common parts also.[13] There is no clear authority for this proposition, however. The case of *Golden Casket (Greenock) Ltd v BRS (Pickfords) Ltd*[14] appears to take the alternative approach, with the landlord's duties very clearly confined to the premises let, albeit in relation to adjoining properties owned by the same landlord (and not common parts of a larger building/complex of which the premises formed only part).

Prudent drafters will in any event seek to displace the landlord's implied warranty in relation to the retained common parts of the larger building(s). The landlord will seek to achieve this position through an equivalent acceptance of the common parts by the tenant – any failure to do so arguably results in the landlord having a residual liability in respect of common parts if there is breach of the implied warranty.

3.3 THE LANDLORD'S COMMON LAW REPAIRING OBLIGATION

Rankine, after summarising the landlord's implied warranty, goes on to set out the landlord's common law repairing obligation in relation to the premises let:

> The landlord of an urban tenement is further bound at common law, and unless it be otherwise stipulated, to uphold it in a tenantable or habitable condition during the course of the lease.[15]

Again, this obligation is found in the opinion of the Lord President (Dunedin) in *Wolfson v Forrester*[16] where he states:

---

[11] *Mars Pension Trs Ltd v County Properties & Developments Ltd* 1999 SC 267 at 272G.
[12] *Dolby Medical Home Respiratory Care Ltd v Mortata Dolby UK* [2016] CSOH 74, 2016 GWD 19-344. See Chapter 4 for further discussion of this point.
[13] *Mars Pension Trs Ltd v County Properties & Developments Ltd* 1999 SC 267 at 269A, dealing with the common parts of a shopping centre; also *Blackwell v Farmfoods Aberdeen Ltd* 1991 GWD 4-219.
[14] *Golden Casket (Greenock) Ltd v BRS (Pickfords) Ltd* 1972 SLT 146.
[15] Rankine, *The Law of Leases*, p 241.
[16] *Wolfson v Forrester* 1910 SC 675 at 680.

> [The landlord] is also bound to put [the premises] into a wind and water tight condition if by accident they become not so. But this is not a warranty, and accordingly he is in no breach as to this part of his bargain till the defect is brought to his notice and he fails to remedy it.

It is clear that there is no absolute obligation on the landlord to remedy defects within the premises let. It is generally taken to be the case that liability to effect repairs to the premises let does not arise unless and until the defect is brought to the attention of the landlord, although that does not appear to be an absolute position.[17] As Lord Skerrington puts it:[18]

> [The] mere fact that the premises which form the subject of the lease are in a state of disrepair, does not in the ordinary case give rise to a claim of damages, unless, in the language of Erskine,[19] "the insufficiency arises from the inconsiderate or culpable act of the landlord." In other words, the landlord's obligation to repair, as implied by law or as usually expressed, is not a warranty.

Beyond the basic requirements of the premises being maintained in a wind- and watertight condition, there is little certainty from the common law as to the landlord's obligations throughout the duration of the lease.[20] There are, in any event, three important exceptions to this common law liability. The landlord is not liable for deterioration or destruction that arises as a result of:

(a) the tenant's fault or negligence;
(b) *damnum fatale* or pure accident; and
(c) the act or omission of a third party for whom the landlord is not responsible.[21]

Damnum fatale is described as follows:

> A loss arising from inevitable accident, such as no human prudence can prevent; - such, for example, as the losses occasioned by storms or tempests, lightening, floods, overblowing with sand, or, in general, by any calamity falling within the legal description of an act of God.[22]

---

[17] *Dickie v The Amicable Property Investment Building Society* 1911 SC 1079; *M'Laughlan v Craig* 1948 SC 599; *Kirkham v Link Housing Group Ltd* [2012] CSIH 58, 2012 Hous LR 87 (although this case was decided upon the terms of the lease); *Golden Casket (Greenock) Ltd v BRS (Pickfords) Ltd* 1972 SLT 146 at 148. See also McAllister, *Scottish Law of Leases* (4th edn, 2013) para 3.42 under the heading "Constructive Notice".

[18] *Dickie v The Amicable Property Investment Building Society* at 1085.

[19] Erskine, *Institute* at II.VI.43.

[20] In *M'Gonigal v Pickard* 1954 SLT 62 it was held that dampness spreading from foundations would not be a breach by the landlord of the obligation to keep the premises in a wind- and watertight condition. The Lord Ordinary (Mackintosh) comments in the case: "So far as I am aware and so far as our books seem to reveal, Lord Dunedin [in *Wolfson v Forrester* 1910 SC 675] is the only judge who appears to have attempted something like a definition of the meaning and scope of the obligations lying upon the landlord to put and to keep premises wind and water tight." *Gunn v National Coal Board* 1982 SLT 526 is a separate case dealing with dampness but decided by reference to the obligation to keep the premises let in a habitable condition.

[21] Rankine, *The Law of Leases*, p 242.

[22] J Bell, *Dictionary and Digest of the Law of Scotland* (7th edn, Watson (ed), 1890).

3.4 ORDINARY AND EXTRAORDINARY REPAIRS

The repairing obligation is split into two different types of repairs – ordinary repairs and extraordinary repairs. At common law, the landlord's repairing obligation is unqualified, and thus includes ordinary and extraordinary repairs. It is important to understand, however, that a "basic" repairing obligation of a tenant (in terms of a lease) imposes responsibility for ordinary repairs only, with extraordinary repairs remaining the responsibility of the landlord. As Rankine puts it:

> The burden of keeping the houses wind and water tight may be thus thrown on the tenant or it may be retained by the landlord, who will, in either case, unless it be otherwise stipulated, be liable also for the extraordinary repairs necessitated by lapse of time, natural decay, extraordinary accident, or latent defect.[23]

In the early case of *Mossman v Brocket*[24] the tenant under a 19-year lease had accepted the "houses" of a farm in the condition they were in as at the date of entry and had bound himself "to uphold and leave them tenantable at his removal". The case records that the houses were very old and in bad condition at the time of the tenant's entry to the subjects. The parties were in dispute at lease expiry as to the extent of the tenant's repairing obligation.[25] Some of the walls were decayed and would require to be rebuilt to make the houses fit for the accommodation of a new tenant under a subsequent 19-year lease. The Inner House found that the tenant was not liable for the repairs in question, deciding that:

> ... under such a clause, and in such circumstances, [the tenant] was liable for ordinary and petty repairs only from year to year, and not to reconstruct what had gone to decay through the necessary waste of time,

with the Lord President (Avondale) adding the following:

> What the word tenantable in such a clause truly means, depends in a great measure on the custom of the country where the farm is, and the condition of the houses at the tenant's entry.

The classic statement of the differing treatment of ordinary and extraordinary repairs is found in the subsequent case of *Napier v Ferrier*.[26] The case concerned "the mansion-house of Clippens" and ancillary premises,[27] to which the pursuer, Napier, was about to take entry under a lease. The lease provided that the tenant was obliged at his own expense:

> [To] keep the new mansion-house, offices, and porter's lodge in good and sufficient repair and condition during the lease, and to leave them so at the termination thereof.

---

[23] Rankine, *The Law of Leases*, p 247; see also *Turner's Trs v Steel* (1900) 2 F 363.
[24] *Mossman v Brocket* 1810 Hume 850.
[25] Disputes concerning liability for dilapidations at lease expiry are clearly not confined to the era of the FRI lease.
[26] *Napier v Ferrier* (1847) 9 D 1354.
[27] A photograph of the mansion house (taken some decades after the case) is found at https://canmore.org.uk/collection/1574515. It is still in existence, albeit converted into flats and surrounded by new-build houses within the town of Linwood.

The tenant refused to take entry due to the condition of the premises, and sought payment of the costs of remedying the defects, which are recorded as follows:

> 1st. That the ends of the whole joists in wall of drawing-room are less or more destroyed, being in an advanced state of decomposition. 2d. That the ends of the whole joists in wall of small back-room off dining-room are in a like decomposed condition. 3d. That in south front-room in top flat the whole ends of joists in wall there, are in a similar state of decomposition. 4th. That the rain water penetrates the house from parts in the roof where slates are off and broken; and 5th. From a number of cracks in the lead gutters, the front and back gutters especially being in a deplorable condition, we are of opinion that before the house can be considered safe and sufficient for the pursuer's occupancy during the period of his lease, a portion of the floors should be taken up, and new joists bolted to the old ones, with a rest in the walls, and extending from eight to ten feet inwards in the whole of the apartments we have enumerated, the deafening, deafening-boards, flooring, and finishing afterwards replaced, the lead in front and back gutters removed and replaced with new, and the slates, where broken and out, repaired.

The tenant founded on the landlord's implied warranty, arguing that:

> A party who lets a mansion-house for habitation ... is himself under the implied condition and obligation that the subjects so let shall be a habitable mansion-house, and not a ruin, or so verging to ruin as to be uninhabitable, without a reconstruction of the building *in essentialibus*.

The Inner House found that the landlord was responsible for bearing the costs of the majority of the necessary repairs. The Lord President (Boyle) provides the following opinion in relation to the tenant's repairing obligation:

> I cannot read the words "to make repairs" as having any further meaning than to keep the subjects in repair ... I have no hesitation in holding that the repairs of the roof and gutters, the putting to rights of the whole lead apparatus, fall under the category of ordinary repairs, and to that extent I would confirm the interlocutor[28] ... [The] whole other portion of the account is connected with the repairs necessarily made in consequence of the state of decomposition reported upon.
>
> I make a complete separation, therefore, between ordinary repairs and this decay, or extraordinary repairs. We are enabled to extract from the decision quoted from Baron Hume,[29] this general principle, that where a party undertakes an obligation to put the premises in good and sufficient repair, it covers all things that can come under ordinary repairs. But when it so happens that the floors are going – that the ends or centre of the joists are in a state of decay, I take the case to be one not covered by that obligation.
>
> ...
>
> I hold the principle of the law to be as clear as the sun at noon-day, that the landlord is liable for extraordinary repairs.

Despite Lord President Boyle's emphatic distinction between ordinary and extraordinary repairs in *Napier v Ferrier*, the boundary between the two, in practical terms, remains wide and blurred. In *House of Fraser v Prudential Assurance Ltd*,[30] Lord McCluskey, delivering the opinion of the court, comments:

---

[28] An earlier decision finding the tenant liable for those costs.
[29] *Mossman v Brocket* 1810 Hume 850.
[30] *House of Fraser plc v Prudential Assurance Co Ltd* 1994 SLT 416 at 419J–420C.

We observe, and neither party submitted otherwise, that the common law, as set forth in Rankine [*Law of Leases*] and the cases referred to, does not give any very precise method of distinguishing between ordinary and extraordinary repairs. In the cases, various notions, such as foreseeability, extraordinary cause, latent defect, inevitable deterioration over time, the extent of the damage, the nature of the damage etc, are all deployed in different sets of circumstances in order to make the distinction between what, according to the circumstances of each case, fall to be treated as ordinary and what as extraordinary repairs. No clear, universally applicable principle or talisman for distinguishing between the two emerges. Lord Ormidale, in *Sharp v Thomson*, spoke (at 1930 SC, p 1100; 1930 SLT, p 789) of the tenants' duty of keeping the lade "free from such defects as would be likely to result in ordinary course from the normal occupation and use of the lade; for example, to keep its bed clean and free from obstructions which might be calculated to impede the flow of the water and so cause it to spill over the side; and to patch and repair such defects in the bank as might from time to time be occasioned by the action of the flowing water so as to obviate serious injury by their gradual erosion; in other words, to protect the banks from avoidable erosion".

That passage gives a general guide which goes beyond the duty in relation to maintaining a lade, but neither it nor any other passage to which we were referred would enable parties to a modern commercial lease to reach ready agreement as to the borderline cases; indeed the no man's land might be very broad.

In the subsequent case of *Co-operative Insurance Society Ltd v Fife Council*,[31] Lord Glennie reviewed the main authorities on ordinary and extraordinary repairs and sought to offer some guidance as to categorisation into one or the other:

> I respectfully agree with Lord McCluskey in *House of Fraser* that the decided cases do not give any very precise method of distinguishing between ordinary and extraordinary repairs. No universally acceptable principle or formula emerges for distinguishing between them. But the cases do identify the main considerations that are apt to be taken into account. As appears from the Opinion of Lord Anderson in *Sharp v Thomson* [1930 SC 1092], these can be grouped under three broad heads: (i) the origin of the damage, (ii) its extent and (iii) its nature. The first head refers to how the damage came about. If it was caused by a fortuitous event, something unanticipated and outwith the control of either party, that would be a pointer to the repair being an extraordinary repair for which the tenant was not liable. The contrast there is with the ordinary effects of bad weather. It seems to me that the question of decay though lapse of time falls into this category, though the qualification here is that the landlord may not be held liable to repair (or replace), say, some part of the structure (be it a wall or a roof) which has collapsed or is on the point of collapse through natural wastage (something which would *prima facie* be an extraordinary repair) if the structure was only allowed to get into that state through neglect on the part of the tenant: see e.g. *Johnstone v Hughan* [(1894) 21 R 777]. The scope for argument in this area is likely to be very great — for example, the passages in the authorities to which I have referred reveal some uncertainty about how ordinary wear and tear is to be treated. The second head relates to the extent or seriousness of the damage, and the likely cost of repairs — thus, if a wall or roof collapses, it may point to the necessary repair being an extraordinary repair for which the landlord is liable, but subject to the qualification already made about the condition which caused it to collapse having come about through the tenant's own neglect. The third head relates to the nature of the damage and the

---

[31] *Co-operative Insurance Society Ltd v Fife Council* [2011] CSOH 76 at para 19, 2011 GWD 19-458.

necessary repair. Does it amount to total reconstruction? There is an obvious overlap with the second head, but it was under this head that Lord Anderson[32] drew the distinction between repair and renewal.

Despite the best efforts of Lord Glennie in *Co-operative Insurance Society*, it remains the case that categorisation is not straightforward, and that detailed investigation into the facts and circumstances may well be required before any advice can be offered or a decision taken.

3.5 THE TENANT'S DUTY TO TAKE REASONABLE CARE

The tenant under an urban lease has no repairing obligation at common law, in contrast to the obligations on the landlord. It remains the case, however, that the tenant is liable in respect of any damage or destruction caused through negligence or inappropriate use of the premises let. This is often referred to as a duty on the tenant to take reasonable care of the premises.[33] The tenant is in breach of contract and liable to the landlord in damages if this duty is breached. That is not the same as the tenant having a repairing obligation, although in practice it is likely to be treated as such.[34]

3.6 THE ABSENT REPAIRING OBLIGATION

It will be apparent from a consideration of the paragraphs above that the common law does not provide a seamless dovetail between the respective obligations placed on the landlord and tenant. Whilst unusual, circumstances can arise whereby damage occurs to premises let for which neither landlord nor tenant has liability to effect repairs, either at common law or in terms of the lease. Whether or not the repairs are carried out in those circumstances, and which party undertakes responsibility to pay for them, will no doubt depend on the point at which the need for the repairs arises. If towards the end of the lease then the tenant might decide simply to leave the premises, with the disrepair left for the landlord to remedy prior to re-letting the premises. If, however, the disrepair occurs early in the period of the lease then the tenant might well take the view that it must undertake the repairs in order to derive the greatest use and benefit of the premises during the period of the lease.[35]

This situation arose in the case of *Little Cumbrae Estate Ltd v Island of Little Cumbrae Ltd*.[36] The pursuer was the owner and landlord of the Island of Little Cumbrae. The entire island had been let to the defender for a period of five years. The subjects of lease included approximately 793 acres of land, a mansion house, five cottages, and a harbour and jetty.[37] The tenant had an obligation to repair, maintain

---

[32] In *Sharp v Thomson* 1930 SC 1092.
[33] McAllister, *Scottish Law of Leases*, para 3.7; R Rennie et al, *Leases* (2015) para 14-24.
[34] See, e.g. *Glebe Sugar Refining Co v Paterson* (1900) 2 F 615; *Mickel v McCoard* 1913 SC 896; *Fry's Metals Ltd v Durastic Ltd* 1991 SLT 689.
[35] See Rankine, *The Law of Leases*, p 225. Other issues might arise, such as insurance, whether the tenant is entitled to a rent abatement in respect of damaged premises, or whether *rei interitus* operates to bring the lease to an end altogether.
[36] *Little Cumbrae Estate Ltd v Island of Little Cumbrae Ltd* 2007 SC 525.
[37] It was therefore considered to be a "rural" lease.

and renew the premises let in terms of the lease, but insured risk damage was excepted from the repairing obligation. There was no express obligation on the landlord to effect repairs in respect of insured risk damage, although there was an obligation that any insurance proceeds were to be "forthwith laid out in reinstating the Premises".

Three years into the five-year lease, a storm caused damage to roofs of the buildings, the jetty, a sewer outfall pipe, a storm wave break, a harbour marker post and mooring points. The tenant had effected certain repairs and counterclaimed against the landlord for the expense incurred in doing so (insofar as the expenditure had not been met by insurance proceeds – i.e. the insurance shortfall). The tenant argued that the lease contained an implied term to the effect that the repairing obligation fell upon the landlord in the particular circumstances of the case:

> [10] The action came before the sheriff for debate. Put very shortly, the first contention of counsel then appearing for the defenders was that cl 3 of Pt II of the schedule to the lease was to be construed as expressly imposing an obligation on the landlord to repair damage caused by an insured risk. The sheriff rejected that contention and it was not further advanced either before the sheriff principal or before us. The alternative submission for the defenders advanced to the sheriff was that there was to be implied into the lease a provision that repairs to damage arising from the occurrence of one of the insured risks required to be carried out by the landlord. That contention was advanced on the basis, again put shortly, that such repairs were excepted from the tenant's repairing obligations in cl 3 of Pt II of the schedule; someone would need to carry out the repairs, ergo the landlord must be that someone; that view was consistent with the requirement that the landlord was to lay out the insurance money on repairs; and such an implication was required by "business efficacy". That contention found favour with the sheriff.

The tenant succeeded at first instance in the sheriff court, and also at appeal before the sheriff principal.[38] The Inner House took a different view, however:

> [16] In our opinion the position adopted by the defenders is misconceived. As already mentioned, it is accepted that the repairs with which this action is concerned are repairs resulting from storm damage and hence are *damnum fatale*. The decision of the House of Lords in *Bayne v Walker*[39] settled that in the case of accidental destruction or damage for which no-one was at fault neither landlord nor tenant was under any obligation to rebuild or repair, though each might have an interest to do so. The civilian law rule expressed in the maxim *res suo perit domino* meant that the subject perished to each of the parties according to his interest in it. The speeches of Lord Redesdale and the Lord Chancellor (Lord Eldon) discuss the practical and commercial considerations justifying a rule (in a modern parlance, a default rule) that the loss should rest where it fell, each according to his own interests in the case of property subject to a tenancy. Thus, to take the example of the destruction of a farmhouse occurring shortly before the ish, it would be unreasonable to impose on the tenant the obligation to rebuild or repair when his occupation was about to cease; and equally the landlord might prefer to have a different farmhouse in a different location with a view to the future letting of the holding. The later authorities to which we were referred by counsel for the pursuers make clear that, at least since *Bayne v Walker*, the common law position in both urban and rural tenancies has been that in the event of damage or destruction constituting *damnum fatale* neither party is under any obligation,

---

[38] *Little Cumbrae Estate* at paras 10 and 11.
[39] *Bayne v Walker* (1815) 3 Dow 233.

owed to the other, to repair or rebuild. Each may have an interest to do so; the tenant to resume enjoyment; the landlord to recover his rental income, since otherwise the rent is subject to whole or partial abatement.

[17] As was recognised by the Lord Chancellor in his speech, it is, of course, open to the parties to a lease to modify, or depart from, the common law rule by clear express provision. Since the rule applies in respect of loss or damage which is now more readily capable of being covered by insurance, its consequences in modern practice are usually addressed through that means. That is indeed what has been done in the present case, there being agreement on insurance; the ultimate responsibility for the meeting of the *premia*; and an obligation on the landlord to lay out the insurance monies on repairs. But in so far as the insurance arranged against *damnum fatale* should prove lacking, the common law rule will apply to the uninsured *damnum fatale*. In that respect we note in particular the passage in the practitioners' handbook by Ross and McKiechan [sic], *Drafting and Negotiating Commercial Leases in Scotland*[40] (para 10.6) where, having discussed insurance by the landlord, the authors then address the type of question arising in the present case in these terms:

> "The question then arises as to the position if the insurance monies proved insufficient to meet the cost of rebuilding or reinstatement. Where the obligation is to 'lay out all monies received in respect of such insurance' in reinstatement (as opposed simply to 'reinstate') it would seem that the landlord would not have to complete the work at his own expense — he would have complied with his obligation by laying out all the insurance monies received. Thus the tenant should call for a specific obligation from the landlord to make up any shortfall. Clearly the tenant needs this protection to prevent a situation in which the landlord refused to complete the work of rebuilding. This would be of particular concern if the underlying common-law rule in Scotland (providing for termination of the lease in the event of total destruction and abatement of rent in the event of partial destruction) had been displaced and if the abatement of rent proviso which had been substituted was expressed to operate for a limited period, because on the expiry of such period the tenant would become liable for rent. The tenant should argue most strongly for the inclusion of an obligation compelling the landlord to re-instate."

We would add that, in our view, the lease appears to have been drafted against a proper understanding of the common law on *damnum fatale* in leases. Thus the provisions in cl 5 of Pt II of the schedule exhibit awareness of the common law rule on termination and abatement of rent in the event of *damnum fatale* and seek to restrict it to a limited extent. But the further provision in favour of the tenant suggested by the authors of this handbook is not to be found.

...

[19] In so far as the express terms of a lease do not cover, or replace, the provisions implied at common law in such contracts, those provisions will apply. Contracts of lease must be drafted against the existence of common law default rules. In our view it is clear that the common law default rule relating to liability — or perhaps more accurately the absence of liability — for *damnum fatale*, while partially displaced in cl 5(2) of the lease, as respects abatement of rent and *rei interitus* is not displaced by any express obligation on the landlord to carry out storm damage repairs. Where an hiatus in the express terms of a nominate contact is filled by a term implied *ex lege*, one never really enters the territory of implying terms justified on the basis of a need to give basic "business efficacy", since

---

[40] M Ross, D McKichan, A Primrose and M Fleming, *Drafting and Negotiating Commercial Leases in Scotland* (2nd edn, 1993).

that need has indeed been addressed by the term implied at common law. To suggest that the common law solution might be improved is not to the point.

[20] In these circumstances we consider that the pursuers are correct in their submission that the decisions of the sheriff and the sheriff principal are unsound. In our view the defenders are mistaken in contending that the pursuers as landlords were under any legal obligation to execute the storm damage repairs beyond their obligation to apply the insurance monies thereto (which it is not disputed has been done).

In different circumstances, it might still be possible to argue for a construction of the lease in question to the effect that it was not the intention of the parties to the lease to leave such a lacuna in the repairing obligation (or in respect of the liability for the costs of effecting repairs).[41] Express drafting regulating the position between the parties, taking into account any obligations as regards insurance, is undoubtedly the more straightforward approach to adopt.

---

[41] Given the terms of the judgment in *Little Cumbrae Estate Ltd v Island of Little Cumbrae Ltd* 2007 SC 525 (as set out above), it would seem wise to advance any such argument based on a "proper construction" of the terms of the lease, rather than argue for implication of a separate or new term.

Chapter 4

The Tenant's Repairing Obligations: Reading the Lease and Other Documents

4.1 INTRODUCTION

Having considered the common law rights and obligations of landlord and tenant in the previous chapter, this chapter considers the agreement reached between the parties, namely the lease along with other documents, which impact on the condition of the premises. In commercial leases it is almost inevitable that parties will enter into a lease contracting out of the position at common law. Most commercial leases are full repairing and insuring leases (FRI leases).[1] In an FRI lease the landlord seeks to exclude as far as possible any liability for repair of the premises that would attach to him at common law. The landlord aims to receive a certain financial return from letting the property and wants the property to be handed back to him at lease expiry in a condition which will allow him to re-let it to another tenant at a market rent. As such, the landlord will seek to ensure the tenant is under a number of obligations in relation to repairs, and the condition of the property more generally, throughout and at the end of the lease. Tenants generally accept that they will be under repairing obligations. The extent of the obligations may differ depending on the negotiating strength of the parties and the market in which the lease is being negotiated. Obligations in terms of the lease and other letting documents are the focus of this chapter.

4.2 PRINCIPLES OF INTERPRETATION

Before going on to consider the types of clause commonly found in a commercial FRI lease it is important to remember that leases are contracts, to which some special rules apply.[2] As such, the normal rules of contractual interpretation apply to them. Indeed, many cases in which important rules of commercial contract interpretation have been stated and developed have involved commercial leases.[3]

---

[1] The FRI lease is discussed in Chapter 1. This form of lease has been the most common since the 1970s and was a significant change from leases encountered before that period: see R Rennie et al, *Leases* (2015) para 26-32.

[2] Such as the ability for the tenant to obtain a real right by virtue of the Leases Act 1449.

[3] Recent examples include *L Batley Products Ltd v North Lanarkshire Council* [2014] UKSC 27, [2014] 3 All ER 64; *Grove Investments Ltd v Cape Building Products Ltd* [2014] CSIH 43, 2014 Hous LR 35; and *@SIPP Pension Trs v Insight Travel Services Ltd* [2015] CSIH 91, 2016 SC 243.

There are a number of methods of interpretation that can be used in the interpretative exercise.[4] Discussions on this subject generally consider the differences between the literal approach to interpretation, on the one hand, and the contextual or purposive approach on the other. Commercial common sense has also featured prominently in recent years.

4.2.1 Literal approach

The focus of a literal approach to interpretation is to discern the parties' intention from the words used in the clause in question, with the words being given their natural and ordinary meaning. Lord Mustill's statement in *Charter Reinsurance Co Ltd v Fagan* encapsulates this approach:[5]

> I believe that most expressions do have a natural meaning, in the sense of their meaning in ordinary speech ... the inquiry will start, and usually finish, by asking what is the ordinary meaning of the words used.

Account is taken of other clauses in the document in which the disputed clause appears, such that the disputed words are taken in the context of the document as a whole.[6] Scottish courts traditionally used a literal approach to interpretation and this approach continued to be evident in contemporary Scottish cases.[7] The extent to which a more literal approach should prevail has been the subject of significant debate before the Inner House and the Supreme Court in recent years. In *Arnold v Britton*[8] the Supreme Court reiterated the importance of the words used by the parties in their contract. The dispute in that case revolved around the correct interpretation of a service charge provision in the leases of holiday chalets. The landlord advocated a literal approach, which would see the service charge sum begin at £90 at the beginning of the leases and increase by 10% each year on a compound basis, such that when the 99-year leases ended in 2072 the service charge payment for each chalet would amount to £550,000. The tenants argued that the disputed clause had two possible meanings and, as such, the court could choose the more commercially sensible construction. The majority found in favour of the landlord.[9] Lord Neuberger was at pains to stress the importance to be attached to the words in the contract, noting:[10]

---

[4] On contract interpretation generally see W W McBryde, *The Law of Contract in Scotland* (3rd edn, 2007), ch 8; Scottish Law Commission Discussion Paper on *Interpretation of Contract* (Scot Law Com DP No 147, 2011).

[5] *Charter Reinsurance Co Ltd v Fagan* [1997] AC 313 at 384, quoted with approval by Lord President Rodger in *Bank of Scotland v Dunedin Property Investment Co Ltd* 1998 SC 657 at 661.

[6] *Taylor v Secretary of State for Scotland* 2000 SC (HL) 139 per Lord Hope at 144; *Multi-Link Leisure Developments Ltd v North Lanarkshire Council* [2010] UKSC 47, 2011 SC (UKSC) 53 per Lord Hope at para 11.

[7] See, e.g., Lord Hope in *Multi-Link Leisure Developments* at para 11; Lord President Rodger in *Bank of Scotland v Dunedin Property Investment Co Ltd* 1998 SC 657; the Inner House decision in *Lloyds TSB Foundation for Scotland v Lloyds Banking Group plc* [2011] CSIH 87, 2012 SC 259, such an approach being criticised by the Supreme Court: [2013] UKSC 3, [2013] 1 WLR 366.

[8] *Arnold v Britton* [2015] UKSC 36, [2015] 2 WLR 1593. For discussion of the case see C Connal, "Has the Rainy Sky dried up? *Arnold v Britton* and commercial interpretation" (2016) 20 Edin LR 71.

[9] The majority decision was delivered by Lord Neuberger with whom Lords Sumption and Hughes agreed. Lord Hodge gave a separate opinion. Lord Carnwath dissented.

[10] *Arnold v Britton* at para 17.

the reliance placed in some cases on commercial common sense and surrounding circumstances ... should not be invoked to undervalue the importance of the language of the provision which is to be construed.

The court found that while commercial common sense is an important factor to take into account, a court should be very slow to reject the natural meaning of a provision as correct because it appears to be a very imprudent term for one of the parties to have agreed. In interpreting the contract the court must identify what the parties have agreed and not what the court thinks they should have agreed.[11] The Scottish courts generally followed the approach set out in *Arnold v Britton*,[12] with some exceptions.[13] The Inner House, in *@SIPP Pension Trs v Insight Travel Services Ltd*,[14] expressly followed *Arnold*. The Inner House noted the emphasis placed by Lord Neuberger on the fact that commercial common sense should not be invoked to undervalue the importance of the language used in the contractual provision, and that the court should be slow to reject the natural meaning of a provision simply because it seemed to be a very imprudent term for one of the parties to have agreed: the purpose of interpretation was not to identify what the court thought the parties ought to have agreed but what they, in fact, agreed.[15]

However, the Supreme Court in *Wood v Capita Insurance Services Ltd*[16] noted that the court's approach to interpretation was not solely literal. The court had to ascertain the objective meaning of the language used. This also involved taking into account the context in which those words were used.[17] There was also a role for commercial common sense where there were rival interpretations.[18] The process of interpreting a contract was an iterative process and the court had to balance the indications given by the words used, the context and the commercial consequences of the possible interpretations available.[19] However, the court indicated that the extent to which each interpretative tool will assist varies according to the circumstances, with the court noting that where a document was sophisticated, complex and drafted by professionals a textual analysis may be most useful.[20] Most FRI leases will be professionally drafted, complex documents.

As such, it seems that while there is an important role for the words used in the parties' contract, there may also be a role for other interpretative tools. These are discussed below.

---

[11] *Arnold v Britton* at para 20.
[12] See *Gyle Shopping Centre General Partners Ltd v Marks and Spencer plc* [2016] CSIH 19, 2017 SCLR 221; *Hill v Stewart Milne Group Ltd and Gladedale (Northern) Ltd* [2016] CSIH 35, 2017 SCLR 92; *AWG Business Centres Ltd v Regus Caledonia Ltd and Cheshire West and Cheshire Council* [2017] CSIH 22, 2017 GWD 9-131.
[13] Principally *Hoe International v Andersen* [2017] CSIH 9, 2017 SC 313, discussed in **4.2.3**.
[14] *@SIPP Pension Trs v Insight Travel Services Ltd* [2015] CSIH 91, 2016 SC 243. This case is discussed below in **4.2.3** and **5.4.2**. See L Richardson, "Commercial common sense revisited: further developments in contract interpretation and commercial leasing" (2016) 20 Edin LR 342.
[15] *@SIPP Pension Trs* per Lady Smith at para 17.
[16] *Wood v Capita Insurance Services Ltd* [2017] UKSC 24, [2017] AC 1173.
[17] *Wood v Capita* per Lord Hodge at para 10.
[18] *Wood v Capita* per Lord Hodge at para 11.
[19] *Wood v Capita* per Lord Hodge at para 12.
[20] *Wood v Capita* per Lord Hodge at para 13.

PRINCIPLES OF INTERPRETATION

4.2.2 Contextual approach

A contextual approach to interpretation is based on the premise that words do not exist in a vacuum. Parties choose words to express their contractual intention based on the facts and circumstances that exist at the time the contract is entered into. As such, on this approach, a court interpreting the contract cannot determine the meaning of the words used without understanding the background circumstances or "matrix of fact". Lord Hoffmann's opinion in *Investors Compensation Scheme Ltd v West Bromwich Building Society*[21] was, for some,[22] a significant development in using a contextual approach to interpretation and is a significant point of reference in many interpretation cases. Lord Hoffmann set down five principles (the comments in the bullet points have been added to provide additional analysis on the principles):[23]

(1) Interpretation is the ascertainment of the meaning which the document would convey to a reasonable person having all the background knowledge which would reasonably have been available to the parties in the situation in which they were at the time of the contract.

- Interpretation is not a purely objective exercise. There is the subjective element of what the particular parties knew at the time the contract was entered into.

(2) Subject to point (3), the background circumstances which can be considered include absolutely anything which would have affected the way in which the language of the document would have been understood by a reasonable man.

- It should, however, be noted that the parties' subjective intentions or matters known to only one of the parties will not form part of the relevant background circumstances. Only facts or information available to both parties at contract formation are relevant[24] such as the state of the market or industry in which the parties operated and in which the contract was to be performed.

(3) The parties' pre-contractual negotiations and their declarations of subjective intent are not relevant in the interpretive exercise.[25]

- However, pre-contractual negotiations will be relevant where they evidence circumstances existing at contract formation, such as that a particular fact was known to both parties.[26] They will also be relevant

---

[21] *Investors Compensation Scheme Ltd v West Bromwich Building Society* [1998] 1 WLR 896.
[22] See the contrary view expressed by Lord Bingham, writing extra-judicially, in T Bingham, "New thing under the sun: interpretation of contract and the ICS decision" (2008) 12 Edin LR 374.
[23] *Investors Compensation Scheme* at 912–913.
[24] *Arnold v Britton* [2015] UKSC 36, [2015] 2 WLR 1593 per Lord Neuberger at para 21.
[25] See the discussion of this rule in *Chartbrook Ltd v Persimmon Homes Ltd* [2009] 1 AC 1101, in particular paras 28–41; see also *Prenn v Simmonds* [1971] 1 WLR 1381 especially Lord Wilberforce at 1384 and *Luminar Lava Ignite Ltd v Mama Group plc* [2010] CSIH 1, 2010 SLT 147.
[26] See Lord President Rodger in *Bank of Scotland v Dunedin Property Investment Co Ltd* 1998 SC 657 at 665.

where they demonstrate any objectively apparent consensus on meaning between the parties.[27]

(4) The meaning which a document (or any other utterance) would convey to a reasonable man is not the same thing as the meaning of its words. The meaning of words is a matter of dictionaries and grammar; the meaning of the document is what the parties using those words against the relevant background would reasonably have been understood to mean. The background may not merely enable the reasonable man to choose between the possible meanings of words which are ambiguous but even (as occasionally happens in ordinary life) to conclude that the parties must, for whatever reason, have used the wrong words or syntax.[28]

(5) The "rule" that words should be given their "natural and ordinary meaning" reflects the common-sense proposition that we do not easily accept that people have made linguistic mistakes, particularly in formal documents. On the other hand, if one would nevertheless conclude from the background that something must have gone wrong with the language, the law does not require judges to attribute to the parties an intention which they plainly could not have had.

- Principles 4 and 5 make clear that as part of the interpretative exercise the court can find that the contract contains a mistake in language or syntax. However, Lord Hoffmann sets a high bar to overcome if seeking to show that a mistake has been made when he says we do not easily accept such mistakes in formal documents.

The background against which the words are used is an important factor in interpreting the words in the contract. Indeed, in *Wood v Capita* Lord Hodge noted that:[29]

[I]t has long been accepted that [interpretation] is not a literalist exercise focused solely on a parsing of the wording of the particular clause but that the court must consider the contract as a whole and, depending on the nature, formality and quality of drafting of the contract, give more or less weight to elements of the wider context in reaching its view as to that objective meaning.

4.2.3 The commercially sensible approach

The commercially sensible approach has proved most controversial in recent years. This approach allows the court to consider the commercial purpose of the contract, and the parties' objectives in entering the contract, in interpreting its meaning. This approach to interpretation was highlighted in *Bank of Scotland v*

---

[27] See the discussion of this issue in *The Centre for Maritime and Industrial Safety Technology Ltd v Ineos Manufacturing Scotland Ltd* [2014] CSOH 5, 2014 GWD 5-100.
[28] Lord Hoffmann cites *Mannai Investments Co Ltd v Eagle Star Assurance Co Ltd* [1997] AC 749 as an example of this rule.
[29] *Wood v Capita Insurance Services Ltd* [2017] UKSC 24, [2017] AC 1173 at para 10.

Dunedin Property Investment Co Ltd[30] where Lord President Rodger preferred a commercially sensible construction to the contextual approach advocated by Lord Hoffmann in *Investors Compensation Scheme*.[31] The commercially sensible approach to interpretation has tended to be used along with either the literal or contextual approach as a "check"[32] or makeweight[33] on the interpretation reached using either of these other methods. In many cases the commercially sensible approach to interpretation is raised where there is more than one possible interpretation of a provision. In such a situation the court should prefer the construction most consistent with business common sense.[34]

In *Grove Investments Ltd v Cape Building Products Ltd*[35] the Inner House determined the interpretation of a dilapidations provision in a commercial lease on the basis of commercial common sense. The court essentially equated the common law with a commercially sensible construction. The court characterised a commercial contract as a co-operative enterprise which parties entered into for their mutual benefit.[36] As such it should be construed in such a way that the benefits reasonably expected from the contract accrued to both parties and without an excessive or disproportionate burden falling on one party.[37] For the court excessive or disproportionate results were those which were objectively excessive or disproportionate according to the expectations of reasonable parties in the position of the parties to the contract. The common law was integral to a decision on the most commercially sensible construction:

> [I]ts rules represent the considered attempts of judges, over many years, to strike a fair balance between the interests of contractual parties. Usually, therefore, the common law will achieve a result in accordance with common sense. For this reason, when a contract is interpreted, the common law can often serve as a benchmark against which considerations of fairness can be measured. If a particular construction of a contractual term achieves a result that is radically different from the rules of the common law, that is a factor that may in some circumstances indicate that that construction is commercially unreasonable.[38]

The court went on to qualify this statement. Being radically different from the common law is unlikely to be of great importance in construing the main terms of the contract (terms dealing with the parties' substantive rights and obligations) as such terms will generally have been the subject of negotiation. A divergence from

---

[30] *Bank of Scotland v Dunedin Property Investment Co Ltd* 1998 SC 657.
[31] See Lord Rodger's comments in *Bank of Scotland v Dunedin* at 661 where he approves Lord Steyn's comments in *Mannai Investments Co Ltd v Eagle Star Assurance Co Ltd*. Lord Rodger also found Lord Mustill's comments in *Charter Reinsurance Co Ltd v Fagan* [1997] AC 313 at 384 helpful. Lord Mustill's comments are set out at **4.2.1**. See also the comments of Lord Caplan in *Bank of Scotland v Dunedin Property Investment Co Ltd* at 666.
[32] See Lord Diplock's comments on the effect of the commercially sensible approach on a literal approach in *Antaios Compania Naviera SA v Salen Rederiena AB (The Antaios)* [1985] AC 191 at 201.
[33] *Aberdeen City Council v Stewart Milne Group Ltd* [2011] UKSC 56, 2012 SC (UKSC) 240 per Lord Hope at para 22.
[34] *Rainy Sky SA v Kookmin Bank* [2011] UKSC 50, [2011] 1 WLR 2900.
[35] *Grove Investments Ltd v Cape Building Products Ltd* [2014] CSIH 43, 2014 Hous LR 35. For further discussion of this case see **5.4.2**.
[36] *Grove Investments* at para 11.
[37] *Grove Investments* at para 11.
[38] *Grove Investments* at para 12.

the common law will be an important factor in relation to subsidiary terms, as the consequences of the wording of such terms may not have been well thought through. In dealing with subsidiary terms the common law may provide considerable assistance in deciding what is commercially sensible.[39]

Grove Investments was initially followed in a number of cases[40] but was criticised in *@SIPP Pension Trs v Insight Travel Services Ltd* with the Inner House noting:

> Commercial contracts may, equally, be hard fought with each party intent on securing their own particular objective.... Care must be taken to avoid reading anything said in *Grove* as being to the effect that the court can correct a bad bargain or even an unfair one; there is no general rule that a commercial contract requires to be fair ... It is not legitimate to re-write parties' agreement,[41]

and that:

> the observations in *Grove* predated the guidance provided by the Supreme Court in *Arnold* and must, accordingly, be regarded with an appropriate degree of caution.[42]

Yet despite the criticisms of *Grove* the Inner House has subsequently noted the central importance of commercial common sense in interpretation. In *Hoe International Ltd v Andersen*[43] the court noted that *Arnold v Britton* did not set out general principles of contract interpretation but was a discussion of matters relevant to that case, which had been an "unusual case".[44] For the court in *Hoe* use of commercial common sense in interpretation was of central importance and would, said the court, lead to shorter contracts with reduced transaction costs, as well as greater predictability.[45]

There is therefore a conflict within the Scottish authorities as to the extent of the role for commercial common sense in interpretation. The decision in *Hoe* was handed down a few days before the Supreme Court's decision in *Wood v Capita*,[46] discussed above. It is therefore suggested that the Scottish courts will give some weight to commercial common sense where there is clearly more than one possible meaning for a contractual provision, but that, mindful of the decision in *Arnold v Britton* and *@SIPP Pension Trs*, the courts will not use commercial common sense to innovate on the contractual wording where that is unambiguous.[47]

---

[39] *Grove Investments* at para 12. For further discussion see L Macgregor, "Crossing the line between business common sense and perceived fairness in contractual interpretation" (2015) 19 Edin LR 378.

[40] *@SIPP Pension Trs v Insight Travel Services Ltd* [2014] CSOH 137, 2014 Hous LR 54; *Mapeley Acquisitions Co (3) Ltd v City of Edinburgh Council* [2015] CSOH 29, 2015 GWD 13-284; in a non-commercial leasing context, see *Bishop v 3i Investments plc* [2014] CSOH 152, 2014 GWD 33-634.

[41] *@SIPP Pension Trs v Insight Travel Services Ltd* [2015] CSIH 91, 2016 SC 243 at para 44.

[42] *@SIPP Pension Trs* per Lady Smith at para 44.

[43] *Hoe International Ltd v Andersen* [2017] CSIH 9, 2017 SC 313. For discussion of this case see L Richardson, "Commercial common sense in contractual interpretation: further views from the Inner House" (2017) 21 Edin LR 423.

[44] *Hoe International* per Lord Drummond Young at para 20.

[45] *Hoe International* per Lord Drummond Young at para 25.

[46] *Wood v Capita Insurance Services Ltd* [2017] UKSC 24, [2017] AC 1173.

[47] See, e.g., *EOP II Prop Co III S.A.R.L. v Carpetright plc* [2019] CSOH 40, 2019 GWD 19-305.

4.3 THE FRI REPAIRING CLAUSE

Having considered the approaches to contract interpretation more generally, this section considers the meaning given to repairing obligations likely to be found in commercial leases. As noted above, in a commercial FRI lease the landlord seeks to contract out of his obligations in relation to the condition of the property at common law, both at commencement and throughout the lease, and to impose obligations on the tenant in relation to the condition of the premises. The landlord must ensure that all matters he wishes to address in relation to repair are made by clear express provision in the lease.[48] Where the express terms do not deal with an issue the common law rules will apply to fill the gap:

> In so far as the express terms of a lease do not cover, or replace, the provisions implied at common law in such contracts, those provisions will apply. Contracts of lease must be drafted against the existence of the common law default rules.[49]

4.3.1 Tenant's acceptance of the premises

Typically before the tenant's repairing obligations are set out in detail there is a clause in terms of which the tenant accepts the premises as being in good and/or tenantable repair and fit for the purpose for which they are let.[50] In some leases, generally those where the condition of the property is evidenced by a schedule of condition,[51] the tenant will accept the premises in their present condition and fit for the purpose for which they are let. Such clauses displace the landlord's warranty at common law that the premises let are fit for purpose.[52]

4.3.2 Repairing obligations

The tenant is likely to be under separate but related obligations in relation to the condition of the leased premises during and at the end of the lease. The tenant's exact obligations depend on the provision in the lease in question. Different leases will, of course, contain different repairing obligations. As the courts have noted, the use of reported cases is of limited assistance given the obligations will depend on the specific wording used in the lease. However, reported cases can be referred to where they lay down a principle of interpretation[53] or where the words under construction are a phrase found in many leases.[54] A relatively modern example of an ongoing repairing obligation is as follows:

> The tenant shall at all times throughout the duration of the lease at its own expense well and substantially maintain, repair, renew, rebuild, reinstate, decorate and clean, and

---

[48] *Little Cumbrae Estate Ltd v Island of Little Cumbrae Ltd* [2007] CSIH 35, 2007 SC 525 in particular the discussion at paras 17–19.
[49] *Little Cumbrae Estate* per Lord Eassie (giving the opinion of the court) at para 19.
[50] A clause to this effect is found in the style multi-occupancy lease in *Greens Practice Styles: Commercial Leases*, pp 113–211, clause 2.2.
[51] On which see **4.5**.
[52] On which see **3.2** above. On contracting out of the implied warranty see McAllister, *Scottish Law of Leases* (4th edn, 2012) para 11.12; Rennie et al, *Leases*, para 26.31.
[53] On interpretation generally see **4.2**.
[54] *Westbury Estates Ltd v The Royal Bank of Scotland plc* [2006] CSOH 177, 2006 SLT 1143 per Lord Reed at para 16.

THE TENANT'S REPAIRING OBLIGATIONS

generally in all respects put and keep in good and substantial repair and condition the Premises ... provided that the obligations specified in this [clause] shall apply irrespective of the age or state of dilapidations of the Premises or the cause or extent of the damage, deterioration or destruction whether by a defect latent, inherent or patent, which may exist in the Premises at the date of entry or which may subsequently develop, or from any other cause or source whatever.[55]

An example of the obligation[56] imposed on the tenant at lease end in relation to the condition of the premises is:

At date of expiry of the lease the tenant shall quietly surrender the Premises to the landlord, with vacant possession, in good and substantial repair and condition, and in all respects in accordance with the tenant's obligations under the lease.[57]

Having set out the obligations that might be found in an FRI lease the following section considers matters that must be borne in mind when interpreting FRI lease repairing obligations.

4.3.3 Obligation in relation to the premises

When an issue regarding repair or condition arises the first thing to consider is the definition of the premises.[58] Where the landlord owns the premises and lets his entire interest in them to the tenant, this will include the landlord's rights above and below the premises, unless the lease provides otherwise. This reflects the property law rule that land is owned *a coelo usque ad centrum*,[59] and where what is owned by the landlord is let to the tenant, with the tenant having repairing obligations in relation to the premises let, the tenant will be responsible for repairs to any parts above or beneath the premises unless the lease states otherwise.[60]

Considering the definition of the premises is particularly important in a multi-occupancy building where the premises let will form only part of the property owned by the landlord. If the part of the building requiring work does not fall within the definition of the premises, such as where it is a common part,[61] the tenant will have no obligation to carry out repairs. The tenant's repairing obligations in the clause noted above relate to the premises only. The tenant may also come under repairing obligations in relation to items of plant or service media which exclusively serve the premises. Where that is the case it will be important to consider the definition of plant and service media,[62] as appropriate, and to be clear on whether the items on

---

[55] See clauses 1.1 and 1.2 of Schedule Part 12 of the style commercial multi-occupancy lease in *Greens Practice Styles: Commercial Leases*, pp 113–211.
[56] For further obligations that might be imposed on the tenant see **4.8.3**.
[57] Clause 8.1 of Schedule Part 12 of the style multi-occupancy lease in *Greens Practice Styles: Commercial Leases*, pp 113–211.
[58] On what constitutes the premises see the discussion at **2.4**.
[59] From the heavens to the centre of the earth.
[60] This was the case in *Beatsons Building Supplies Ltd v Noble and Ors as trustees of the Alex F Noble & Son Ltd Executive Benefits Scheme* 2015 GWD 15-271 where Sheriff Ross found the tenant liable for the repair of a culvert underneath the yard, which formed part of the premises let.
[61] As to which see Chapter 6.
[62] Plant might include items such as lifts, heating and air-conditioning equipment. Service media might include pipes, wires and cables.

which work is required exclusively serve the premises or also serve areas outwith the leased premises.

4.3.4 Does an obligation to keep in repair include an obligation to put and keep in repair?

Until recently it was thought that there was a difference on this issue between Scots and English law. In Scotland where a tenant was under an obligation to "keep the premises in good and substantial repair and condition" the tenant was not under an obligation to put the premises into that condition and then keep them in said condition.[63] Whereas, in English law, an obligation to keep property in "good tenantable repair" requires the tenant not only to keep the premises in such repair but to put them into such condition and keep them in that condition.[64] However, following the decision of the Inner House in *@SIPP Pension Trs v Insight Travel Services Ltd*[65] there is now no difference between Scots and English law, with the court holding that in a Scottish lease an obligation to "keep premises in good and substantial repair" included an obligation to put the premises into and thereafter keep them in that condition.[66]

Given the previous understanding of the position in Scotland, it is not uncommon to see leases oblige the tenant to "put and keep the premises in good and substantial repair".[67] Where such provision is made in the lease it is clear that the tenant is obliged to put and thereafter keep the premises in the stipulated condition.

4.3.5 Extraordinary repairs

As noted in Chapter 3, at common law the tenant is liable for ordinary repairs only. The landlord is liable for extraordinary repairs. Where express provision is made in the lease in relation to repairs, the question arises whether the tenant is liable for ordinary repairs only or whether he will be liable for extraordinary repairs also. This will depend on the terms of the lease.

Express provision is needed to impose an obligation on a tenant to carry out extraordinary repairs.[68] That this is the intention of the parties should be set out clearly and unambiguously.[69] It is common in commercial leases for the tenant's repairing obligations to expressly apply irrespective of the age or state of dilapidations of the premises or the cause or extent of the damage, deterioration or destruction whether by a defect latent, inherent or patent.[70] A further formulation is seen in the

---

[63] *Napier v Ferrier* (1847) 9 D 1354 per Lord Fullarton at 1360.
[64] *Proudfoot v Hart* (1890) 25 QBD 42.
[65] *@SIPP Pension Trs v Insight Travel Services Ltd* [2015] CSIH 91, 2016 SC 243.
[66] For criticism of this aspect of the decision see L Richardson, "Commercial common sense revisited: further developments in contract interpretation and commercial leasing" (2016) 20 Edin LR 342.
[67] As is provided in the repairing obligation set out at **4.3.2**.
[68] *McCall's Entertainments (Ayr) Ltd v South Lanarkshire Council (No 2)* 1998 SLT 1421 per Lord Hamilton at 1427–1428. It is less difficult for a landlord to be liable for extraordinary repairs where he is subject to express repairing obligations under the lease given the common law background – see *House of Fraser plc v Prudential Assurance Co Ltd* 1994 SLT 416.
[69] *Little Cumbrae Estate Ltd v Island of Little Cumbrae Ltd* [2007] CSIH 35, 2007 SC 525; see **4.3**.
[70] See the provision cited at **4.3.2** and *Lowe v Quayle Munro Ltd* 1997 SC 346 at 350–351.

THE TENANT'S REPAIRING OBLIGATIONS

lease considered in *Westbury Estates Ltd v The Royal Bank of Scotland*[71] in terms of which the tenant's obligations extended to

> all work necessary ... whether structural or otherwise and whether of the nature of maintenance, repair, renewal or rebuilding and whether normally the obligation of a landlord or of a tenant.

This or similar wording[72] will make the tenant liable for all repairs whether ordinary or extraordinary. An obligation on the tenant to renew, rebuild or replace may not, of itself, make the tenant liable for extraordinary repairs as such obligations may be aspects of the tenant's repairing obligation, limited to ordinary repairs.[73]

Where a tenant is not liable for extraordinary repairs under the lease he will not avoid liability where he fails to comply with his ordinary repairing obligations with the result that there arises a defect in the premises that requires extraordinary repair.[74] For example, if a tenant fails to comply with his ordinary repairing obligations in relation to the roof of the leased premises such that the roof is at the point of collapse due to the passing of time (such decay over time tending to indicate an extraordinary repair) the landlord will not have to carry out an extraordinary repair (by substantially repairing or replacing the roof) if the roof got into the decayed condition due only to the tenant's failure to comply with his ordinary repairing obligations.

4.4 THE REPAIRING OBLIGATION IN DETAIL

The tenant's obligations regarding the condition of the property depend on the terms of the lease itself. As such, when a question on repair or condition arises the first thing to do is carefully consider the lease. However, some general principles have been developed in the case law. Furthermore, commercial leases tend to be drafted using the same or very similar wording, such that assistance can be derived from cases where the courts have considered the meaning of phrases found in many commercial leases. These cases are considered in this section. Having an understanding of this body of case law as well as the general principles of contractual interpretation discussed above[75] will help in determining what the repairing obligations set out in the lease require the tenant to do.

In considering the language of the repairing obligation the court should in principle give full effect to each word used.[76] However, the way in which commercial leases are drafted, with the use of, in effect, "standard" or "tried and tested" wording

---

[71] *Westbury Estates Ltd v The Royal Bank of Scotland* 2006 SLT 1143.
[72] The wording should make clear that the parties intend to subvert the position at common law. It is suggested that this is most clearly done by referring to all three factors discussed in *Co-operative Insurance Society Ltd v Fife Council* [2011] CSOH 76, 2011 GWD 19-458 – the origin of the damage; the extent of the damage and the nature of the damage.
[73] *Co-operative Insurance Society Ltd v Fife Council*, in particular the discussion of Lord Anderson's opinion in *Sharp v Thomson* 1930 SC 1092. See also the discussion at **4.4.3**.
[74] *Johnstone v Hughan* (1894) 21 R 777. See the discussion of this case in *Co-operative Insurance Society Ltd v Fife Council* [2011] CSOH 76, 2011 GWD 19-458.
[75] See **4.2**.
[76] *Taylor Woodrow Property Co Ltd v Strathclyde Regional Council* GWD 7-397 (otherwise unreported), 15 Dec 1995 at p 6, referring to *Anstruther Gough Calthorpe v McOscar* [1924] 1 KB 716; *Westbury Estates Ltd v The Royal Bank of Scotland plc* [2006] CSOH 177, 2006 SLT 1143 at para 32 referring to *Lurcott v Wakely and Wheeler* [1911] 1 KB 905 and *Anstruther Gough Calthorpe*.

may leave the court with little scope for finding a precise meaning for every word used.[77] It has been held that there is no difference between the terms "habitable repair" and "tenantable repair".[78]

4.4.1 When is the repairing obligation triggered?

When considering when the repairing obligation is triggered a distinction must be made between a continuing repairing obligation and an obligation to leave the premises in good repair at lease end.[79] Clearly the tenant's obligation in relation to the latter is triggered when the lease comes to an end, whether at the ish or prematurely. It is more difficult to say when the tenant's continuing obligation to repair is triggered given this obligation arises at the commencement of the lease and subsists throughout the period of the lease.

It has been suggested that where the tenant is under an obligation to keep the premises in good and substantial repair the obligation will be triggered when there is disrepair. Where, however, the tenant is obliged to keep the premises in good and substantial repair and condition all that is needed to trigger the repairing obligation is that the premises are not in that condition.[80] In *Lowe v Quayle Munro Ltd* Lord Penrose commented that "the tenant's obligations ... were triggered by identification of a state of fact within the scope of the obligation".[81] Lord Reed has, however, opined that, regardless of the way in which the obligation is worded, the obligation will require the physical condition of the premises to be maintained to a given standard. The tenant's obligation will be triggered when the physical condition of the premises falls below that standard.[82] The tenant may be under an obligation to carry out certain works, such as replacing, renewing or rebuilding the premises or plant serving the premises where necessary. This obligation will be triggered when it is necessary that the works specified be carried out[83] to keep the premises in the condition required by the lease.[84]

4.4.2 Determining whether the premises are in the condition required by the lease

The next issue then is what condition does the lease require the subjects to be in and what does that entail? In *Proudfoot v Hart* it was held that "good tenantable repair" is:

---

[77] *Westbury Estates Ltd* at para 32.
[78] *Belcher v Mackintosh* 2 Moo & R 186, cited with approval by the Court of Appeal in *Proudfoot v Hart* (1890) 25 QBD 42.
[79] Examples of both are given in **4.3.2**.
[80] *Taylor Woodrow Property Co Ltd v Strathclyde Regional Council* GWD 7-397; *Lowe v Quayle Munro* 1997 SC 346. *Taylor Woodrow* was cited with approval in *West Castle Properties Ltd v Scottish Ministers* 2004 SCLR 899. Note, however, the reliance by Lord Penrose on English authority in *Taylor Woodrow* and the then difference between Scots and English law on an obligation to keep premises in good repair discussed at **4.3.4**. See also the doubts expressed about the difference between "good and substantial repair and condition" and "good and substantial repair" by Lord Reed in *Westbury Estates Ltd v The Royal Bank of Scotland plc* [2006] CSOH 177, 2006 SLT 1143 at para 34.
[81] *Lowe v Quayle Munro* 1997 SC 346 at 350.
[82] *Westbury Estates* at para 34.
[83] *Taylor Woodrow Property Co Ltd v Strathclyde Regional Council* GWD 7-397.
[84] *Westbury Estates* at para 33.

such repair as having regard to the age, character, and locality of the house, which would make it reasonably fit for the occupation of a reasonably minded tenant of the class who would be likely take it.[85]

Taking each of the factors identified in turn it was explained that "nobody could reasonably expect that a house 200 years old should be in the same condition of repair as a house lately built".[86] In relation to the character of the property, "the same class of repairs as would be necessary to a palace would be wholly unnecessary to a cottage".[87] Finally, the locality is important because:

> the state of repair necessary for a house in Grosvenor Square would be wholly different from the state of repair necessary for a house in Spitalfields.[88]

The tenant will not be required to keep the premises in perfect repair[89] or as new a condition as they were at lease commencement.[90] The premises need only be in such condition as a hypothetical reasonably minded tenant of the class who would be likely to take a lease of them would require.

One must look at the class of tenant who would have taken a lease of the premises at the *commencement* of the lease, not at any later stage, and not at lease end.[91] Initially this may seem counter-intuitive given a landlord wants to have the premises returned to him at lease expiry in a condition which will allow him to re-let them to another tenant at a market rent. This, coupled with the fact that the majority of disputes regarding wants of repair arise at lease end, suggest that the focus should be on the condition of the premises and who would be willing to lease the premises at that stage. Yet, consider the fact that the parties enter into their respective obligations under the lease when the lease is entered into. Parties' rights and obligations do not fluctuate over the period of the lease due to changes during the life of the lease. Changes to the area in which the premises are located do not alter the tenant's repairing obligation. If, when the lease was entered into, the locality was good and property there was in demand, such that a high class of tenant would have taken a lease, the tenant's repairing obligation does not diminish if during the lease the area deteriorates such that only a lower class of tenant would take a lease of the premises at lease end. Similarly the tenant's obligation under the repairing covenant does not increase if the locale improves such that leases in the area are being taken by a better class of tenant than when the parties' lease was entered into.[92] The tenant's obligation applies and has the same meaning on the first day of the lease as on the last.[93]

---

[85] *Proudfoot v Hart* (1890) 25 QBD 42 per Lopes LJ at 55, with which Lord Esher MR entirely agreed.
[86] *Proudfoot v Hart* per Lord Esher MR at 52.
[87] *Proudfoot v Hart* per Lord Esher MR at 52.
[88] *Proudfoot v Hart* per Lord Esher MR at 52.
[89] *Proudfoot v Hart* per Lord Esher MR at 52.
[90] *West Castle Properties Ltd v Scottish Ministers* 2004 SCLR 899 at para 55. While it is perfectly possible that a lease could specify that the tenant is to keep the subjects in "as new" condition, which would require them to be kept in such condition, a tenant should not agree to such a term.
[91] *Anstruther Gough Calthorpe v McOscar* [1924] 1 KB 716; *West Castle Properties Ltd v Scottish Ministers* 2004 SCLR 899 at para 52.
[92] See the discussion in *Anstruther Gough* on this issue by Bankes LJ at 726, Scrutton LJ at 731 and Atkin LJ at 732 under reference to the decision of the Court of Appeal in *Morgan v Hardy* (1886) 17 QBD 770.
[93] *Westbury Estates Ltd v Royal Bank of Scotland plc* [2006] CSOH 177, 2006 SLT 1143 at para 33.

Account is taken of the increasing age of the premises in determining the standard of repair. As Lord Mackay explains:

> Whilst the premises became older, as the lease ran its course, the passage of time did not alter the nature of the obligations on the tenants. Nevertheless, in fulfilling those obligations the tenants were entitled to take into account the increasing age of the building.... Accordingly in assessing whether or not the defendants had complied with their obligations ... allowance can be made for the age of the premises and the age of their various component parts.[94]

An alternative to the "hypothetical tenant" formulation used in *Proudfoot v Hart* can be found in *Anstruther Gough*.[95] In this case the repairing obligation required the tenant to "well and sufficiently repair support uphold maintain ... amend and keep [the premises]". The court held that the tenant was under an obligation to keep the premises in the condition they would be in if they were managed by a reasonably minded owner, having regard to the age of the premises, their character and ordinary uses. The court's view on what was required of the tenant did not turn on the differently worded repairing obligation to that under consideration in *Proudfoot v Hart*.[96] The Court of Appeal's concern in *Anstruther Gough* was to set out a working rule of general application to be used in determining the extent of the tenant's repairing obligations under a lease.[97] However, simply because a prudent owner would have carried out certain works, the tenant will not be under an obligation to do so where the works do not fall within the ambit of the repairing obligation in the lease. For instance a prudent owner might replace items of plant that were nearing the end of their economic life with modern apparatus. A tenant will not be obliged to do so where the condition of the plant does not result in the subjects falling below the condition required by the lease.[98]

That the "hypothetical tenant" test and the "reasonably prudent owner" test are tests of general application is evident in *West Castle Properties Ltd v Scottish Ministers*[99] where Lord Mackay noted that consideration must be given to any works which a prudent owner of the premises would have carried out in order to maintain the premises so that they could be expected to last for their normal life as well as considering the requirements of the tenants of the class that would be likely to occupy

---

[94] *West Castle Properties Ltd v Scottish Ministers* 2004 SCLR 899 per Lord Mackay at para 55.
[95] *Anstruther Gough Calthorpe v McOscar* [1924] 1 KB 716.
[96] Indeed Bankes LJ noted that he attached no importance to the particular form of words used in the covenant stating "[t]he effect is the same in my opinion whatever words the parties use, provided they plainly express the intention that the premises are to be repaired, kept in repair, and yielded up in repair". Scrutton LJ similarly did "not think there is any substantial difference in construction between 'repair,' which must mean 'repair reasonably and properly' and 'keep in good repair,' or 'sufficient repair' or 'tenantable repair,' or most of the various phrases cited to us". However, cf the comments of Atkin LJ that it is not useful to take a number of terms which may be found in different leases, treat them all as synonymous and impute to all of them a special meaning attached by authority to one of them. Note also modern authority that the precise terms of the lease must be considered, for instance, *Westbury Estates Ltd v Royal Bank of Scotland plc* [2006] CSOH 177, 2006 SLT 1143.
[97] *Anstruther Gough Calthorpe v McOscar* [1924] 1 KB 716, in particular Bankes LJ at 728.
[98] *Westbury Estates Ltd v Royal Bank of Scotland plc* [2006] CSOH 177, 2006 SLT 1143 at para 37. See the discussion of this case below. See also Lord Penrose's comments in *West Castle Properties Ltd* at para 56.
[99] *West Castle Properties Ltd v Scottish Ministers* 2004 SCLR 899.

the premises.¹⁰⁰ In that case the tenant was required "well and substantially to repair, maintain, renew, restore, cleanse and keep in the like good tenantable condition and repair the whole premises".

A repairing obligation requiring the tenant to "repair and maintain the subjects … all to the satisfaction of the landlord" means the reasonable satisfaction of the landlord. Where the word "reasonable" does not appear in the repairing covenant the court will imply it to give practical business sense to the operation of the provision, which without such qualifying language is of indefinite content.¹⁰¹ In determining whether a landlord has acted reasonably, the landlord is entitled to have regard to his own interest as owner but must also take into account the position of the tenant.¹⁰²

Plant and equipment

When considering whether items of plant or service media are in good repair the degree of reliability of the equipment is taken into account.¹⁰³ This will include the number and frequency of breakdowns as well as how long the item is out of order while repairs are carried out. Simply because items of plant are at the end of their economic life does not mean that they are in disrepair or result in the subjects being other than in good condition. This issue arose in *Westbury Estates Ltd*.¹⁰⁴ In this case the tenant was obliged to "uphold, maintain, repair and renew the Let Subjects … so as to keep the Let Subjects in good and substantial repair and condition". The landlord wanted the tenant to replace items of plant on account of the items having reached the end of their economic life according to guidelines issued by the Chartered Institute of Building Services Engineers (CIBSE).¹⁰⁵ The landlord argued that it was necessary for the items to be replaced because the plant no longer represented the least expensive method of performing its proper function. For Lord Reed the question of whether an item of plant was the least expensive method of performing its function was an entirely different question from whether its replacement was necessary to keep the premises in good and substantial repair and condition as required by the lease. The fact that an item was less efficient than a more modern equivalent told one nothing about whether the item was in good and substantial repair and condition.¹⁰⁶ The fact that an item is at, or approaching, the end of its economic life does not mean that the premises are below the condition required in the lease. That is especially so where the items of plant are capable of being operated and where the landlord cannot point to problems with reliability or significant servicing costs of the plant.¹⁰⁷ Furthermore, simply because component parts of the premises do not,

---

¹⁰⁰ *West Castle Properties* at paras 52 and 61.
¹⁰¹ *Taylor Woodrow Property Co Ltd v Strathclyde Regional Council* GWD 7-397; *Lowe v Quayle Munro* 1997 SC 346.
¹⁰² *Taylor Woodrow Property*, p 4.
¹⁰³ *Westbury Estates Ltd v The Royal Bank of Scotland plc* [2006] CSOH 177, 2006 SLT 1143 at para 34.
¹⁰⁴ *Westbury Estates v The Royal Bank of Scotland plc* [2006] CSOH 177, 2006 SLT 1143.
¹⁰⁵ The CIBSE Guidelines set out the expected number of years items of plant are expected to last before needing to be replaced.
¹⁰⁶ *Westbury Estates* at para 35.
¹⁰⁷ *Westbury Estates* at para 36.

at lease end, have exactly the same lifespans that they had at lease commencement does not automatically mean that the tenant had failed to keep the premises in good tenantable condition and repair.[108]

4.4.3 What work will the tenant have to carry out?

How much work the tenant will have to carry out depends on the wording of the repairing clause. Some clauses may require a tenant to repair the premises let. Others will go beyond repair and require any or all of the following: renewal, rebuilding, reinstatement and/or replacement of the premises. If clear words are used the tenant could be required to rebuild or reinstate the entire subjects let.[109] The words used and the way that they have been used is of vital importance. The common law background against which the parties are contracting must also be borne in mind.[110]

In *Co-operative Insurance Society Ltd v Fife Council*[111] it was held that an obligation on the tenant to "repair and keep in good and substantial repair and maintained, renewed and cleansed in every respect all to the satisfaction of the Landlords the leased subjects" did not make the tenant responsible for anything beyond ordinary repairs. The landlord argued that the use of the word "renewed" imposed extraordinary repairs on the tenant. For Lord Glennie the description "maintained, renewed and cleansed" was subordinate to the general purpose of the clause and was descriptive of the good and substantial repair in which the leased subjects were to be kept.[112]

Where the tenant is required to repair and also renew or replace the premises the test for repair may not be the same as the test for replacement. This occurred in *Taylor Woodrow Property Co Ltd v Strathclyde Regional Council*.[113] The lease required the tenant:

> To accept the Premises ... and at their own cost and expense to repair and keep in good and substantial condition and repair and maintained, decorated, paved and cleansed in every respect all to the satisfaction of the Landlords ... and to replace, renew or rebuilt [sic] whenever necessary the Premises.

Lord Penrose found that, given the wording of the clause, replacement, renewal and rebuilding were subject to a test of necessity, while repair was subject to the test of the landlord's satisfaction.[114]

It has been noted that "repair connotes the idea of making good damage so as to leave the subjects so far as possible as though it had not been damaged".[115] It is clear that an obligation to repair the premises includes renewal or replacement of

---

[108] *West Castle Properties Ltd v Scottish Ministers* 2004 SCLR 899 at para 68.
[109] Generally work required to the premises caused by an insured risk is excepted from the tenant's repairing obligation, as to which see **4.7.1**.
[110] On a tenant's liability for extraordinary repairs see **4.3.5**.
[111] *Co-operative Insurance Society Ltd v Fife Council* [2011] CSOH 76, 2011 GWD 19-458.
[112] *Co-operative Insurance Society* at para 21. See also *West Castle Properties Ltd v Scottish Ministers* 2004 SCLR 899 at para 74.
[113] *Taylor Woodrow Property Co Ltd v Strathclyde Regional Council* GWD 7-397.
[114] *Taylor Woodrow Property* at p 7; see also *Lowe v Quayle Munro Ltd* 1997 SC 346 which is to the same effect.
[115] *Anstruther Gough Calthorpe v McOscar* [1924] 1 KB 716 per Atkin LJ at 734.

parts of the premises in order that the subjects as a whole are in the condition of repair required by the lease.[116] For instance, in keeping the premises in the condition required by the lease it may be necessary to carry out repairs to the roof. In carrying out roof repairs individual roof tiles might need to be replaced. Replacement of the individual tiles is required to keep the roof in repair.

In English law renewal of significant component parts of leased subjects has been held to fall within a tenant's obligation to repair, for instance demolishing and rebuilding the front external wall of a house[117] or replacing a rotten floor, that could not be repaired, with a new one.[118] The test in English law is whether the work to be done is in substance renewal or replacement of defective parts or the renewal or replacement of substantially the whole of the premises.[119] English case law must be used with caution on this issue. As already mentioned, in Scots common law a tenant is not liable for extraordinary repairs (although the lease may expressly make the tenant so liable).[120] In English law there is no direct parallel between ordinary and extraordinary repairs.[121] Scottish judges have questioned whether some of the English authorities on this issue would have been decided the same way in Scotland.[122] It is suggested that they would not have been decided in the same way. In Scots law it is necessary to consider what caused the damage; the extent or seriousness of the damage; and what must be done to repair the damage. These issues must be taken into account to determine whether or not a repair is an extraordinary repair.[123] If it is an extraordinary repair it will not fall on the tenant as part of a general obligation to repair. Further clear and unambiguous language to that effect is required[124] such as a clear obligation to repair, replace, renew or rebuild the premises irrespective of the age or state of dilapidations of the premises or the cause or extent of the damage, deterioration or destruction whether by a defect latent, inherent or patent.[125]

When the tenant is carrying out repair works there is likely to be an element of betterment. For example, if sections of waterproof sheeting on the roof require to be replaced in order to repair the roof new waterproof sheeting may be of better quality or a higher specification than the material being removed. When the tenant carries out repairs there may, therefore, be inevitable upgrading or incidental betterment of the premises. This comes within a tenant's obligation to repair.

---

[116] *Taylor Woodrow Property* at p 7 where Lord Penrose referred to *Lurcott v Wakeley and Wheeler* [1911] 1 KB 905; *Co-operative Insurance Society Ltd v Fife Council* [2011] CSOH 76 at para 21, 2011 GWD 19-458.
[117] *Lurcott v Wakeley and Wheeler* [1911] 1 KB 905.
[118] Discussed *obiter* by Lord Esher MR in *Proudfoot v Hart* (1890) 25 QBD 42 and commented on in *Lurcott v Wakeley and Wheeler*.
[119] *Lurcott v Wakeley and Wheeler* per Buckley LJ at 924.
[120] See the discussion at **4.3.5**.
[121] *Westbury Estates Ltd v The Royal Bank of Scotland plc* [2006] CSOH 177, 2006 SLT 1143 per Lord Reed at para 17.
[122] See Lord Reed in *Westbury Estates* who suggests that the decisions in *Proudfoot v Hart* and *Lurcott v Wakeley and Wheeler* can be contrasted with the opinions in *Napier v Ferrier* (1847) 9 D 1354.
[123] *Co-operative Insurance Society Ltd v Fife Council* [2011] CSOH 76, 2011 GWD 19-458 per Lord Glennie at para 19.
[124] *Little Cumbrae Estate Ltd v Island of Little Cumbrae Ltd* [2007] CSIH 35, 2007 SC 525.
[125] See the clause set out in **4.3.2**.

Determining whether a defective part of the premises should be repaired or renewed is a question of fact and degree, determined by taking into account the nature and extent of the defect and the costs involved.[126] One must consider what the defect is and what options exist for repair or renewal, together with the costs and effect of both courses of action. If for instance repairs to a boiler that is prone to breakdowns would cost £400 but would solve the problem for only a year before further work would be needed, whereas renewal of the boiler would cost £2,000 but would last for a further 10 years, it might be that renewal of the boiler should be carried out by the tenant. The tenant will not be required to replace parts of the premises where there is another reasonable way for him to have complied with his repairing obligations under the lease.[127]

Unless there is express provision in the lease to that effect, the tenant will not be obliged to strip out parts of the premises which are serviceable and have periods of useful life left simply to ensure that the component parts once replaced will have, at the expiry of the lease, the same life expectancy as the predecessor parts had at lease commencement.[128]

Many commercial leases will specify that the tenant is to repair, renew, rebuild and reinstate the premises. A commercial lease will also generally provide that this obligation exists regardless of the age or state of dilapidations of the premises or the cause or extent of the damage, deterioration or destruction.[129] Such a clause will make the tenant responsible for almost any want of repair or destruction of the subjects.[130]

4.4.4 The repairing obligation at lease expiry

While the tenant will be under an obligation to keep the premises in repair throughout the lease, it is at lease end that most dilapidations disputes arise. In many cases a landlord will not be too concerned with the condition of the premises during the currency of the lease. During this time the tenant will be in occupation of the property and paying rent. However, as the lease draws to its end the landlord will turn his mind to what will happen to the premises following the end of the lease. It is at this time that the landlord will start to think about re-letting the property and the condition it will have to be in to attract a new tenant.

As noted above, as well as the tenant of a commercial lease being under an ongoing repairing obligation he will also be obliged to leave the premises in good repair and condition and in accordance with the tenant's obligations under the lease.[131] In determining whether the tenant has complied with his obligations the discussion in the preceding paragraphs on what the lease requires the tenant to do are equally relevant to the position at lease end. Of course, the trigger for liability under this obligation is failing to return the premises back to the landlord in the condition

---

[126] *West Castle Properties Ltd v Scottish Ministers* 2004 SCLR 899 at para 58.
[127] *West Castle Properties* at para 58.
[128] *West Castle Properties* at para 56.
[129] See the clause set out at **4.3.2**.
[130] Although damage or destruction caused by insured risks will normally be excluded from the tenant's obligation: see the discussion at **4.7.1**.
[131] See the clause set out at **4.3.2**.

THE TENANT'S REPAIRING OBLIGATIONS

required by the lease. A notice from the landlord to the tenant specifying breaches of the repairing obligations by the tenant is not required.[132]

4.5 WHERE THE PREMISES ARE NOT IN GOOD CONDITION AT LEASE COMMENCEMENT

A schedule of condition is often used to record and evidence the condition of premises at lease commencement where the premises are not in good condition. Rather than the tenant accepting the premises as being in good condition and repair, the tenant accepts the premises in their present condition by reference to the schedule of condition. The purpose of a schedule of condition is to limit the tenant's repairing obligations. A schedule of condition will often be used where a sub-tenant takes a sub-lease part of the way through the tenant's lease. The sub-tenant wants to restrict his repairing obligation to wants of repair or deterioration due to his occupation and use of the premises, and to exclude any wants of repair caused by the tenant.

A schedule of condition typically includes a description of the problems with the condition of the premises at the start of the lease. In many leases photographs are included. Problems, however, arise when leases are copied in black and white and copies are taken of copies – often the photographs in a schedule of condition look nothing more than a series of indiscernible blobs. Given recent advances in technology, in particular the prevalence of digital photography, it is hoped that schedules of condition might serve their function more usefully now and in future than they have done hitherto.[133]

It is important that the tenant's repairing obligation takes account of the fact that at lease commencement the property is not in good condition. When the tenant simply accepts the premises in their present condition without reference to a schedule of condition, or where there are discrepancies between the condition at lease commencement and the tenant's ongoing and/or terminal repairing obligation problems can arise.

In *Lowe v Quayle Munro*[134] the tenant agreed to:

> accept the premises in their present condition and at [the tenant's] own cost and expense to repair and keep in good and substantial repair and maintained ... and to replace or renew or rebuild whenever necessary the leased subjects ... and that regardless of the age or state of dilapidation of the buildings ... comprised in the leased subjects and irrespective of any latent or inherent defects therein.

The tenant argued that there needed to be an identifiable condition at the commencement of the lease which he would have a responsibility to maintain. Here

---

[132] *L Batley Pet Products Ltd v North Lanarkshire Council* [2014] UKSC 27, [2014] 3 All ER 64; *PDPF GP Ltd v Santander Ltd* [2015] CSOH 40, 2015 Hous LR 45. See the discussion on a notice of wants of repair and schedule of dilapidations at **4.6**.

[133] That said, it is important that the schedule of condition forms part of the lease and so it seems likely that schedules of condition will continue to form a hard copy annex or schedule to the lease. Changes to the Requirements of Writing (Scotland) Act 1995 and the enactment of the Legal Writings (Counterparts and Delivery) (Scotland) Act 2015 may result in some changes to practice but the fact that many leases are registered, whether in the Land Register or Books of Council and Session, suggests that a hard copy lease will continue to be produced.

[134] *Lowe v Quayle Munro* 1997 SC 346.

there was no benchmark, the tenant having simply accepted the premises in their present condition. There was no schedule of condition to evidence the condition at lease commencement. However, Lord Penrose was of the opinion that while the clause was "anything but free from difficulty" the better view was that the words "and that regardless of the age or state of dilapidation of the buildings ... comprised in the leased subjects and irrespective of any latent or inherent defects therein" should be read into the opening expression. The same words of disregard then qualified each of the obligations of repair or renewal from a clear benchmark at the beginning of the lease.[135] As such the tenant was responsible for repairs beyond those required to keep the premises in the condition at lease commencement. Lord Penrose came to this conclusion notwithstanding that the lease was for five years,[136] noting that the result was "perhaps surprising" but that it was open to parties to a commercial lease to make whatever arrangements they wished in relation to their obligations.

In *McCall's Entertainments (Ayr) Ltd v South Ayrshire Council (No 2)*[137] the tenants accepted the premises in their present condition as evidenced by a schedule of condition. They bound themselves to keep the premises at all times during the lease in good repair, condition and decoration and to leave the premises in a condition no less good and substantial than their present condition. There therefore appeared to be an inconsistency between the tenants' ongoing repairing obligation (to keep in good repair and condition) with their obligation at lease end (to return the premises in a condition no less good than the condition at the outset). While a schedule of condition had clearly been anticipated it appeared that no such schedule had been produced. That was not critical to the interpretation of the tenants' repairing obligation. For Lord Hamilton the tenants' obligation at the end of the lease would be discharged by the tenants handing the premises back to the landlord in the same general state as they were in at the start of the lease. That was inconsistent with the tenants being under an obligation to leave the premises in a state of overall improvement. The ongoing repairing obligation was to be measured by comparison with the "present condition" of the premises.[138] Lord Hamilton was influenced by the factual matrix when the lease was entered into: at that time the premises were in an advanced state of dilapidation and substantial works were needed if the subjects were to have a long-term future. Such works would have constituted or, at least, included extraordinary repairs. If the tenant was to be responsible for such works Lord Hamilton would have expected to see clear words to that effect, such as an obligation to replace or renew or rebuild as necessary regardless of the age or state of dilapidations of the buildings, as seen in *Lowe v Quayle Munro*.

In *@SIPP Pension Trs*[139] the tenants had accepted premises in their present condition; had agreed at their own cost and expense to repair and keep the premises in good and substantial repair; and to replace, renew or rebuild the premises whenever necessary to at least as good condition as they were in when accepted by the tenants, and that regardless of the age or state of dilapidation of the buildings for the time

---

[135] *Lowe v Quayle Munro Ltd* at 349.
[136] Although the tenant had been in occupation of most of the leased subjects for nine years prior to the execution of a new lease extending the premises let.
[137] *McCall's Entertainments (Ayr) Ltd v South Ayrshire Council (No 2)* 1998 SLT 1421.
[138] *McCall's Entertainments* at 1427.
[139] *@SIPP Pension Trs v Insight Travel Services Ltd* [2015] CSIH 91, 2016 SC 243.

being comprised in the premises. The Inner House considered the fact that a schedule of condition was not appended to the lease as weighing significantly against a construction which limited the tenants' responsibilities.[140] For the court the natural meaning of the obligation demonstrated the parties' intention that the overriding, and minimum repairing standard, was good and substantial repair. If the condition of the premises was below that standard at lease commencement the tenants must, when performing their obligation to repair and keep in good and substantial repair, do so in such a way as to achieve that standard.[141]

As noted above,[142] the court in this case determined that an obligation to keep premises in a certain condition obliged the tenant to put, and thereafter keep, the premises in such condition. This will result in the tenant having to improve the condition of the premises due to an ongoing repairing obligation of a higher standard than the premises at lease commencement. This case therefore highlights the importance of having an ongoing repairing standard at the same level as the condition of the premises at the beginning of the lease and using a schedule of condition to set out what that standard actually is.

In *Dem-Master Demolition Ltd v Healthcare Environmental Services Ltd*[143] the tenant had accepted the premises as being in the condition shown by a schedule of condition purported to be attached to the lease, and obliged itself to repair, maintain and renew (and, if necessary for the purposes of maintenance and repair, to replace and rebuild) in like condition during the lease. The tenant was obliged to leave the premises at lease end in such state and condition as was in accordance with the repairing obligations undertaken during the lease. No schedule of condition was attached to the lease. The tenant's position was that the premises were in a poor state of repair at lease commencement. The landlord's position was that the premises were in a much better condition than contended by the tenant. The problem for the tenant, without a schedule of condition, was the need for a proof[144] which required them to lead evidence to establish the condition of the premises at the outset of the lease.

As noted above, a schedule of condition is likely to be most beneficial to the tenant, qualifying and limiting the extent of his repairing obligations. Without a schedule as a point of reference as to the standard of repair the tenant faces a real difficulty in finding witnesses and proving what the condition of the property was, on the balance of probabilities, at lease commencement. This is a significant risk to the tenant.

4.6 NOTICE OF WANTS OF REPAIR AND SCHEDULES OF DILAPIDATIONS

As noted above, as a lease approaches expiry a landlord is likely to take a more significant interest in the condition of the premises. He will likely instruct a surveyor to carry out an inspection of the premises to determine their condition and note

---

[140] *@SIPP Pension Trs* per Lady Smith at para 19.
[141] *@SIPP Pension Trs* at para 20.
[142] At **4.3.4**.
[143] *Dem-Master Demolition Ltd v Healthcare Environmental Services Ltd* [2017] CSOH 14, 2017 GWD 5-72.
[144] A court hearing at which evidence is heard.

any wants of repair.[145] The landlord in a commercial lease will generally reserve to himself the right to take access to the leased premises during the term of the lease for the purpose of inspection.[146] It should be noted that this right can be exercised by the landlord at any time during the term of the lease but it is likely to be utilised as lease expiry approaches. The right to inspect should be reserved to the landlord in the lease given that it will not be implied[147] and without it an inspection may be an interference with the tenant's right to possession of the premises.[148]

During an inspection the landlord's surveyor will look at the condition of the premises and note where there are wants of repair or other breaches of the lease by the tenant. The extent of the landlord's right to inspect will depend upon the terms of the lease. In *Possfund Custodial Tr Ltd v Kwik-Fit Properties Ltd*[149] the landlord was prevented from drilling five boreholes to a depth of approximately 6 metres below ground level to assess potential contamination from the premises' prior use.[150] The Inner House held that the provisions in the lease, including the fact that there was no obligation on the landlord to carry out the inspection causing the least practicable disturbance to the tenant or to make good any damage caused,[151] showed that the parties had not intended the landlord to have such extensive rights by virtue of a clause allowing the landlord and his workmen to enter the premises and inspect them to view their condition.

Following inspection by a surveyor a schedule of dilapidations (also referred to as a notice of wants of repair) will generally be produced.[152] Where this is served on the tenant during the term of the lease it is referred to as an interim schedule of dilapidations. When this schedule is served close to lease end it is referred to as a terminal schedule of dilapidations. The schedule of dilapidations need not be in any particular form but is often in the form of a table or spreadsheet setting out line by line the items which are not in the condition required by the lease (or any other documents such as a licence for works)[153] and what works need to be done to bring the premises into the required condition. The schedule of dilapidations may also specify the clause in the lease said to have been breached by the tenant in failing to keep the property in the standard required by the lease.[154] As such the landlord or his surveyor may seek legal advice in the production of the schedule of dilapidations,

---

[145] Guidance on the approach surveyors should take to inspecting premises and dealing with dilapidations disputes can be found in RICS Professional Guidance, *Dilapidations in Scotland* (2nd edn, 2015), available at https://www.rics.org/globalassets/rics-website/media/upholding-professional-standards/sector-standards/building-surveying/dilapidations-in-scotland-2nd-edition-rics.pdf.
[146] See, e.g., clause 4.1 of Schedule Part 6 of the style multi-occupancy lease in *Greens Practice Styles: Commercial Leases*, pp 113–211.
[147] K Gerber et al, "Landlord and Tenant" (Re-issue) in *The Laws of Scotland: Stair Memorial Encyclopaedia* vol 10 (2001) para 500.
[148] *Possfund Custodial Tr Ltd v Kwik-Fit Properties Ltd* [2008] CSIH 65, 2009 SLT 133.
[149] *Possfund Custodial Tr Ltd v Kwik-Fit Properties Ltd* [2008] CSIH 65, 2009 SLT 133.
[150] Use of the underground storage tanks had come to an end before the lease between the parties' predecessors had been entered into, *Possfund Custodial Tr* at para 2.
[151] *Possfund Custodial Tr* at para 14.
[152] A worked example can be found in Appendix B of RICS Professional Guidance, *Dilapidations in Scotland*.
[153] See **4.8.3**.
[154] This is the approach advocated by the RICS: see *Dilapidations in Scotland*, para 9.1.10.

to ensure that the wants of repair are matters the tenant is liable for in terms of the lease or other leasehold documents. A schedule of dilapidations may be costed or uncosted. A costed schedule sets out the sum the landlord considers the works said to be required will cost. An uncosted schedule does not contain estimated costs. An interim schedule of dilapidations is less likely to be costed than a terminal schedule of dilapidations.

The schedule of dilapidations will then be sent with a notice to the tenant, requiring the tenant to take steps to rectify the wants of repair, specified in the schedule of dilapidations, perhaps within a set period of time. Commercial leases may provide that on receipt of a notice of wants of repair the tenant must commence works and thereafter complete works within a particular period.[155] The lease might provide that notices must be sent in a particular manner and where that is the case the notice and schedule of dilapidations should be sent in accordance with those requirements.[156] However, the lease may simply state that if notices are sent in a particular manner they will be deemed to be sufficiently served after a certain period of time.[157] Where that is the case the notice can be sent in another manner but will not benefit from the deemed service provisions.[158] However, failure to serve a valid notice on the tenant is unlikely to be fatal given the tenant's general obligation to keep the premises in good repair and to leave the premises in such condition at lease end.[159]

While it is very common for landlords to serve a schedule of dilapidations, particularly in the run-up to lease expiry, there is no need to do so, unless the lease specifically so provides, to trigger the tenant's repairing obligation.[160] The lease may contain an obligation on the tenant to comply with any schedule of dilapidations served on him by the landlord.[161] Such an obligation will likely be in addition to the tenant's ongoing repairing obligations and his obligation to leave the premises in a particular condition at lease end. To engage the tenant's obligation to comply with a schedule of dilapidations a schedule has to be served. However, there is no need for a notice or schedule of dilapidations to be served for the tenant to be under obligations to keep the premises in good condition throughout the lease or to leave them in good condition at lease end.[162] The landlord will use a schedule of dilapidations to set out his position regarding the condition of the premises and the tenant's breach of repairing obligations and, as noted below, use it as a precursor to pursuing a remedy or settlement with the tenant.

---

[155] See clauses 4.2 and 4.3 of Schedule Part 6 of the style multi-occupancy lease in *Greens Practice Styles: Commercial Leases*, pp 113–211.

[156] *Capital Land Holdings Ltd v Secretary of State for the Environment* 1997 SC 109. Although note the more relaxed approach taken to the service of notices in *Hoe International v Andersen* [2017] CSIH 9, 2017 SC 313.

[157] See clause 10 of the style multi-occupancy lease in *Greens Practice Styles: Commercial Leases*, pp 113–211.

[158] *Blythswood Investments (Scotland) Ltd v Clydesdale Electrical Stores Ltd (in receivership)* 1995 SLT 150.

[159] Although it may be an issue where the landlord wants to enter the premises and carry out the repairs himself during the period of the lease – as to which see **5.4.1**.

[160] As to which see **4.4.1**.

[161] See clause 4.2 of Schedule Part 6 of the style multi-occupancy lease in *Greens Practice Styles: Commercial Leases*, pp 113–211.

[162] *L Batley Pet Products Ltd v North Lanarkshire Council* [2014] UKSC 27, [2014] 3 All ER 64.

EXCLUSIONS FROM THE TENANT'S REPAIRING OBLIGATIONS

Notice may be required where the landlord wants the tenant to remove any alterations the tenant has carried out and for the property to be reinstated to the condition it was in pre-alteration.[163]

The landlord may wish the tenant to carry out the works prior to lease end or may serve the notice and schedule as a precursor to exercising a remedy[164] or to start discussions on a possible monetary payment to be made to the landlord by the tenant as compensation due for the tenant's failure to comply with his repairing obligations in terms of the lease.[165]

4.7 EXCLUSIONS FROM THE TENANT'S REPAIRING OBLIGATIONS

4.7.1 Insurance

It is common for repairs required as a result of damage caused to the premises by an insured risk to be excluded from the tenant's repairing obligation.[166] This exclusion is often subject to the tenant having paid the landlord the insurance premiums and any irrecoverable insurance monies due to acts or omissions of the tenant. How then are repairs or reinstatement works required as a result of an insured risk dealt with?

At common law neither landlord nor tenant is obliged to repair or reinstate the premises where they are damaged or destroyed by *damnum fatale*.[167] If the premises are destroyed or damaged so that they are no longer fit for the purpose for which they are let the lease comes to an end by *rei interitus*.[168] If the damage is not so significant as to destroy the premises or render them entirely unfit for purpose the tenant will be entitled to an abatement of rent in proportion to the extent of the damage to the premises let.[169] Parties almost invariably contract out of the common law position, with specific provision to deal with damage or destruction of the premises.

It is common, particularly in a multi-occupancy building, for the landlord to insure the building with the tenants paying him a proportion of the insurance premium. There are a number of reasons for this. The landlord will want to be sure that the premises and the building in which they are situated are insured rather than leaving this to the tenant to do as an obligation under the lease. While failure by a tenant to insure the premises when required to do so will be a breach of the lease, the landlord will not want to take the risk that the premises are not insured with only a right of action against the tenant for breach of the lease. Furthermore, the landlord clearly has an insurable interest in the property. The tenant is likely to have an insurable interest

---

[163] This issue is considered at **4.8.3** below.
[164] Discussed in Chapter 5.
[165] Discussed in Chapter 7.
[166] See for instance clause 1.3 of Schedule Part 12 of the style multi-occupancy lease in *Greens Practice Styles: Commercial Leases*, pp 113–211.
[167] *Bayne v Walker* (1815) 3 Dow 233, 3 ER 1049; *Little Cumbrae Estate Ltd v Island of Little Cumbrae Ltd* [2007] CSIH 35, 2007 SC 525 at para 16.
[168] The lease has become impossible to perform due to the damage or destruction of the subjects. On frustration generally see McBryde, *The Law of Contract in Scotland*, paras 21.19–21.36; on the effect of a supervening event on a lease see in particular *Cantors Properties (Scotland) Ltd v Swears & Wells Ltd* 1978 SC 310; *Tay Salmon Fisheries Co v Speedie* 1929 SC 593; and *Mackeson v Boyd* 1942 SC 56.
[169] McAllister, *Scottish Law of Leases*, paras 4.47–4.49.

also but that interest will not extend to the reinstatement value of the property if the tenant is not obliged to reinstate the property on damage or destruction by an insured risk.[170] In such circumstances the tenant's insurable interest is limited to the market value of the remainder of his lease.[171]

In a commercial lease the landlord is likely to be obliged to lay out the insurance proceeds to reinstate the property following damage or destruction. The lease will set a period within which the reinstatement must be completed, failing which either the landlord or the tenant can bring the lease to an end. The lease will provide that it is to continue during the period of reinstatement. During this period the rent or a fair proportion of it will be suspended.[172] Provision must also be made for any shortfall between what is received in insurance monies and the cost of reinstating the premises.[173] Any irrecoverable money due to acts or omissions of the tenant or those for whom he is responsible will generally be payable by the tenant. Any other shortfall is likely to be picked up by the landlord.[174]

4.7.2 Construction documents or collateral warranties

Where the premises or the building in which the premises are situated are relatively new or have recently been refurbished the tenant may agree with the landlord that there will be excepted from the tenant's repairing obligation any works required due to any latent and/or inherent defects in the design and construction of the building or as a result of the refurbishment works. It might be that the landlord is only prepared to except any defects that appear during a specified period of time following completion of the building or the works, as appropriate, or a set period from the start of the lease and, if that is the case, the exception might be time limited. In such a situation the landlord will have rights against the construction/design team either under the construction contract or a collateral warranty. It has been suggested that it is in order for a tenant to accept full repairing obligations in new build or refurbished premises provided that the tenant has an appropriate warranty package from the design team/contractors and appropriate indemnity insurance.[175] However, the better option from the tenant's point of view is to exclude liability for repairs as a result of the construction/works and leave this to be taken up by the landlord against the design team or contractors, with an obligation on the landlord to carry out repairs to the premises required as a result of such a defect.[176]

---

[170] *Fehilly v General Accident Fire & Life Assurance Corporation Ltd* 1982 SC 163.
[171] On insurable interest more generally see F Davidson et al, *Commercial Law in Scotland* (5th edn, 2018) paras 6.4–6.4.3.
[172] To protect his position in these circumstances the landlord will likely have loss of rent insurance, which is paid for by the tenant.
[173] If no such provision is made, notwithstanding provision for insuring the premises and laying out insurance monies, the common law will apply: *Little Cumbrae Estate Ltd v Island of Little Cumbrae Ltd* [2007] CSIH 35, 2007 SC 525.
[174] See, e.g., clause 2.3 of Schedule Part 14 of the style multi-occupancy lease in *Greens Practice Styles: Commercial Leases*, pp 113–211.
[175] Rennie et al, *Leases*, para 26-40.
[176] This would make it clear that this was the landlord's responsibility rather than relying on the common law (discussed in **3.4**) to operate in relation to this exclusion from the tenant's repairing obligation.

4.8 "HIDDEN" REPAIRING OBLIGATIONS

So far this chapter has focused on the tenant's obligations under clauses that require the tenant to keep the premises in a certain standard of repair. There will, however, be other obligations which, while not requiring repair of the premises let, impose obligations on the tenant in relation to the condition of the premises and which, as such, have a bearing on the tenant's repairing obligations.

4.8.1 Decoration

In a commercial lease it is common for a tenant to be under obligations in relation to both external and internal decoration of the subjects let in addition to a general repairing obligation. Such clauses usually require the tenant to treat and paint external parts of the premises and internal surfaces.[177] A tenant is likely to be obliged to decorate the exterior of the subjects once every three years, and the interior once every five years, as well as towards the end of the lease. Such an obligation does not require consideration of whether it is needed to keep the premises in a particular standard of repair. This work needs to be carried out as the tenant is obliged to do it at set times throughout the term of the lease.

4.8.2 Compliance with statute and title conditions

The tenant is likely to be under obligations to comply with statute and title conditions affecting the premises.

Compliance with statute creates a potentially wide-ranging liability. Many disputes arose between landlords and tenants when work was thought necessary for premises to comply with disability discrimination legislation.[178] A tenant will often be under a comprehensive duty to comply at his own expense and to carry out any work required by any statute, statutory instrument, order or regulation emanating from statute and any requirement of a public, local or other authority in relation to the premises; use of the premises; works carried out to the premises; and any fittings, fixtures, plant and machinery on the premises. Commercial leases often specifically mention the requirements of the Factories Act 1961, the Office, Shops and Railway Premises Act 1963, the Health and Safety at Work Act 1974, the Fire (Scotland) Act 2005 and the Construction (Design and Management) Regulations.[179] A tenant will, as a result of such an obligation, have to ensure, for instance, that the fire alarm sounders are of the required decibel level in various parts of the premises let and that adequate firefighting equipment is on site.

---

[177] See, e.g., the obligations found in clauses 4 and 5 of Schedule Part 12 of the style multi-occupancy lease in *Greens Practice Styles: Commercial Leases,* pp 113–211.
[178] Disability Discrimination Act 1995, s 21(2)(a)–(c) came into force on 1 October 2004. These provisions placed a duty on a provider of services to the public to (a) remove a feature; (b) alter a feature; or (c) provide a means of avoiding the feature where a physical feature (such as one arising from the design or construction of a building or the approach or access to premises) made it impossible or unreasonably difficult for a disabled person to make use of a service. For a discussion of the limits of such a duty see M Marsh and Z Bhaloo, "The Disability Discrimination Act 2005 (and Part III of the Disability Discrimination Act 1995 revisited): Part 1" (2005) 9(5) L & T Review 123–126. See now the Equality Act 2010, s 20.
[179] Previously SI 2007/320, now SI 2015/51.

4.8.3 Alterations

There is normally provision in a commercial lease that the tenant will not make any structural or external alterations to the premises or make any internal alterations without the landlord's consent being obtained. Where works have been carried out in breach of this prohibition the landlord may set out in a schedule of dilapidations work that needs to be done to reinstate the premises to their pre-altered state.

Where the tenant has sought and obtained the landlord's consent to alterations the lease and any licence for works, in terms of which consent was granted, need to be checked to determine whether the tenant must remove alterations and reinstate the property at lease end or not. It might be that the tenant is to reinstate the property to its pre-alteration state if required to do so by the landlord. If that is the case the issue is then whether the landlord has required the tenant to do so by notifying the tenant that the alterations must be removed and the premises made good. Depending on the provisions in the lease and licence for works, written notice to remove alterations and reinstate the premises may or may not be needed.[180] Where the lease provides that immediately prior to expiry of the lease the tenant will, if so requested by the landlord, remove and make good all alterations and reinstate the premises, a term will not be implied that reasonable notice of the need to remove alterations and reinstate has to be given.[181] Where neither the lease nor the licence provide a time limit within which reinstatement must be notified to the tenant it would be prudent for the tenant to enquire whether the landlord requires removal of alterations in the run-up to anticipated lease end, and at the very latest, following service of a notice to quit.

4.9 SUB-LEASES

Where a tenant has sub-let the premises the sub-tenant will have repairing obligations, as well as obligations to comply with statute, not to alter the premises and possibly also to decorate. As noted above[182] a sub-tenant is likely to agree to return the premises in the same condition as he accepted them rather than in good condition, as the tenant will generally have been in occupation of the premises for a period of time prior to the sub-lease. In those circumstances the sub-tenant does not want to be liable for improving the premises by returning them in good condition if he did not receive them from the tenant in such a condition. Thus, when a lease and sub-lease are coming to an end it is likely that the sub-tenant will have work to do to the property to put it into the condition required by the sub-lease and the tenant will have further work to do to bring the premises into the condition required by the lease.

Throughout and at the end of the lease the landlord will look to the tenant to comply with the repairing obligations. It is for the tenant to seek compliance from the sub-tenant and do any further work taking account of differences in standards of repair under the lease and sub-lease. The landlord is not in a contract with

---

[180] *L Batley Pet Products Ltd v North Lanarkshire Council* [2014] UKSC 27, [2014] 3 All ER 64.
[181] *PDPF GP Ltd v Santander Ltd* [2015] CSOH 40, 2015 Hous LR 45.
[182] See **4.5**.

the sub-tenant and as such has no direct right of action against the sub-tenant. The existence of a sub-lease can complicate any discussions on dilapidations at lease end given the involvement of another party. Dispute resolution is considered in Chapter 7.

Chapter 5
Remedies for Breach of the Repairing Obligation

5.1 INTRODUCTION

Having considered, in Chapter 4, the repairing obligations incumbent on the parties to a commercial lease this chapter looks at the rights of the parties where the repairing obligation has been breached. The main focus of discussion will be on the landlord's remedies against the tenant given that the tenant is the party with significant obligations in relation to the condition of the premises, while the landlord has few, if any, obligations in relation to the condition of the premises in an FRI commercial lease.

5.2 SERVING A SCHEDULE OF DILAPIDATIONS

It will be remembered[1] that the landlord in a commercial lease will generally have reserved to himself the right to inspect the premises and that he may have served a schedule of dilapidations on the tenant highlighting breaches of the tenant's repairing obligations. In many cases this will be a preliminary step to the landlord exercising a legal remedy. However, this is not a necessary precursor to the landlord seeking a remedy for the tenant's breach of the lease.

First, the various remedies available to the landlord at common law for breach of the tenant's repairing obligations will be explored. The remedies discussed in **5.3** are generally available on breach of contract. In **5.4** consideration is given to provisions commonly found in a commercial lease making express provision for landlords' rights when the tenant is in breach of his repairing obligations.

5.3 REMEDIES AVAILABLE AT COMMON LAW FOR BREACH OF THE LEASE

5.3.1 Specific implement

The landlord can seek an order of specific implement (an order *ad factum praestandum*) against the tenant to compel the tenant to carry out works required in terms of the lease.

Specific implement is sometimes referred to as the primary remedy available to a party faced with a breach of contract.[2] The court has a discretion on whether to

---

[1] See **4.6**.
[2] See the discussion in L Macgregor and H L MacQueen, "Specific Implement, interdict and contractual performance" (1999) 3 Edin LR 239 at 239. However, as the authors note, in practice implement is rarely sought and even more rarely granted. See also W W McBryde, *The Law of Contract in Scotland* (3rd edn, 2007) para 23.08.

grant implement. However, the pursuer is entitled to implement unless the court in the exercise of its discretion decides to refuse the order. The court may refuse implement only in "exceptional cases" where there is some "very cogent reason for depriving litigants of the ordinary means of enforcing their legal rights".[3] The court will consider whether the grant of the order would be inconvenient and unjust or cause exceptional hardship for the defender.[4] There are certain categories of case where the court will not grant specific implement. It has been suggested that the categories are not categories as such but are instances in which the court will always exercise its discretion to refuse implement.[5] The court will not grant specific implement in the following situations:

- where it would require the defender to do the impossible;
- where performance is readily available from another source (as where goods are not delivered and the disappointed purchaser can go into the market and acquire the goods); or
- contracts involving a personal relationship (such as employment contracts and partnership contracts).[6]

It is unlikely that any of these categories will prevent a landlord obtaining specific implement. Considering the inconvenience and injustice of an order may be a more pertinent factor. Lack of proportionality between the harm to the defender against the benefit to the pursuer if the order is granted has featured in cases where the court has refused implement.[7] However, it seems that in actions regarding breach of repairing obligations, the cost and inconvenience to the tenant will be proportionate to the benefit to the landlord – the work carried out by the tenant is likely to benefit the landlord commensurately. Furthermore, the Scottish courts have shown themselves willing to hold a tenant to his obligations under a commercial lease even where there will be a burden to the tenant as a result.[8]

It must be possible for the court to issue an order which is sufficiently precise. The tenant must be left in no doubt as to what he is required to do to comply with the court's order.[9] If this cannot be done the court will refuse to order specific implement.[10]

---

[3] *Grahame v Swan and Others (Magistrates and Police Commissioners of Kirkcaldy)* (1882) 9 R (HL) 91 per Lord Watson at 91; and more recently *Highland and Universal Properties Ltd v Safeway Properties Ltd* 2000 SC 297 per Lord President (Rodger) at 300 and Lord Kingarth at 311.

[4] *Highland and Universal Properties Ltd* per Lord President Rodger at 300 and Lord Kingarth at 311.

[5] L Macgregor, "Specific performance in Scots law" in J Smits, D Haas, and G Hesen (eds), *Specific Performance in Contract Law: National and Other Perspectives* (2008) p 76.

[6] See McBryde, *Contract*, paras 23.15–23.22 and Macgregor, "Specific performance in Scots law", p 76.

[7] See the discussion in Macgregor, "Specific performance in Scots law", p 75.

[8] See, e.g., Lord President Rodger's comment in *Highland and Universal Properties Ltd v Safeway Properties Ltd* 2000 SC 297 at 302 that "the decree simply requires the party in question to perform the obligation which it deliberately undertook in a formal contract", and Lord McCluskey's view in *Retail Parks Investments Ltd v The Royal Bank of Scotland Ltd (No 2)* 1996 SC 227 at 243 that "the court order sought by the pursuers would merely require them to continue to honour their obligation for the remaining six or so years of the lease". Both these cases concerned the tenants' obligation to keep open and trade from the leased premises.

[9] See the discussion on this issue in *Retail Parks Investments*, in particular Lord McCluskey at 238–244. See also *Cummings v Singh* [2019] SAC (Civ) 11, 2019 Hous LR 41.

[10] *PIK Facilities Ltd v Shell UK Ltd* 2003 SLT 155 at paras 39–41.

The penal sanctions for failure to comply with an order for specific implement have shaped the remedy. Lord President Robertson noted that:[11]

> failure to implement such a decree exposes a defender to the penalty of imprisonment ... I therefore think that in the case of decrees which may be thus enforced, or which expose a defender to penal consequences, it is right that the Court should so express the decree that the defender shall be in no doubt regarding the obligation he has to discharge.

At the time the Lord President made his comments the pursuer could seek the defender's imprisonment for failure to obtemper the decree without having to return to court. Despite procedure having changed[12] the penal consequences of failing to comply with the court's order continue to influence the availability of the remedy. In 1996 Lord McCluskey commented:[13]

> the general rule that the citizen should not be exposed to the risk of imprisonment or "other penal consequence" unless for a clear breach of an obligation which has been previously expressed, and made known to him, in terms that leave him in no doubt as to what it is that has to be done or avoided.

However, there might be said to be some relaxation on the requirement for precision. It has been held that it is not necessary that the court set out exactly how the defender should comply with the decree. The order may specify the end to be achieved but leave open the precise means by which the defender achieves that end.[14] In a dilapidations dispute a schedule of dilapidations is likely to have been produced. Requiring the tenant to carry out works to remedy the wants of repair set out in the schedule of dilapidations would seem to set out the end the tenant must achieve provided the schedule itself is sufficiently clear and specific.[15]

Specific implement will not be granted to require the tenant to do works once the lease has ended.[16] If a landlord wants the tenant to carry out works to the premises he will have to think about this well in advance of lease expiry. A tenant will not be ordered to do work once the lease has come to an end notwithstanding that the action for implement was raised prior to lease end.[17] It might take a year or more for the case to be heard and a decision issued. There is also, of course, the prospect of the decision being appealed. However, where the tenant is under a specific obligation to

---

[11] *Middleton v Leslie* (1892) 19 R 801 at 802.

[12] See Law Reform (Miscellaneous Provisions) (Scotland) Act 1940, s 1 and Lord McCluskey's comments on the effect of the changes in *Retail Parks Investments*, particularly at 241, quoted with approval in *Highland and Universal Properties Ltd v Safeway Properties Ltd* 2000 SC 297.

[13] *Retail Parks Investments* at 239.

[14] *Retail Parks Investments* per Lord McCluskey at 241, in which the court granted a decree ordering the defender to keep open and use the premises as bank offices during all normal business hours. See also *Highland and Universal Properties* where the tenant was ordered to keep the premises open for retail trade in any such goods as were from time to time sold in a high class retail store throughout the normal hours of business in the retail trade.

[15] Lack of precision of the order, with the pursuer landlord relying on two (presumably expert) reports in his pleadings, was a problem in *PIK Facilities Ltd v Shell UK Ltd* 2003 SLT 155: see paras 39–41.

[16] *Sinclair v Caithness Flagstone Co* (1898) 25 R 703; *PIK Facilities Ltd v Shell UK Ltd* 2003 SLT 155.

[17] In *PIK Facilities Ltd* the action was raised in 1998 and the lease ended on 31 December 2000. The decision is dated 3 May 2002.

carry out works to the premises at lease end an order for specific implement might be granted despite the lease having come to an end. This occurred in *Coventry v British Gas Corporation*.[18] In this case the tenant was under a specific obligation to do works at lease expiry to restore the ground to its original condition. That obligation could not arise before lease end. The tenant was entitled to work the land up to and including the end of the lease and was then required to carry out restoration works. As noted in Chapter 4 the tenant of a commercial lease is likely to be under an ongoing repairing obligation during the currency of the lease, as well as an obligation to leave the premises at lease end in the condition required by the lease. The obligation to leave the premises in the required condition is not a specific obligation at lease expiry that will allow the landlord to obtain specific implement that works be carried out post lease end.[19] Lord President Robertson noted that:[20]

> where at the expiry of a lease which contains what is sometimes called a redding-up clause, the landlord founds not on it but on violation of the course of works prescribed to the tenant during the whole course of his occupancy, the natural claim is for damages, and not for the execution of remedial works.

It is possible to seek interim specific implement.[21] While there was previously some doubt as to whether specific implement could be sought in the Court of Session on an interim basis[22] the introduction of subsection (2A) to section 47 of the Court of Session Act 1988 puts the matter beyond doubt. In determining whether to grant interim specific implement the court must consider (a) whether the pursuer has a *prima facie* case against the defender that there is a continuing breach of an obligation which is incumbent on the defender, which the order sought will address; and (b) the balance of convenience, bearing in mind the harm to either party if the order is granted or refused, and the relative strength of the parties' cases.[23] It is suggested that a landlord seeking interim implement of a tenant's repairing obligation under the lease will have a clear *prima facie* case. While each case will depend on its own facts it seems unlikely in most cases that the balance of convenience will favour the landlord. There are likely to be significant implications on a tenant's business operations while works, other than relatively minor works, are carried out to the premises. The premises may have to be closed and staff moved out for a period for works to be done and staff relocated elsewhere. The landlord will have other remedies available. He will, at least, have a damages action at common law provided

---

[18] *Coventry v British Gas Corporation* 15 August 1984, Outer House (Lord Allanbridge), unreported.
[19] There was such an obligation in *PIK Facilities Ltd v Shell UK Ltd* 2003 SLT 155 where specific implement was refused.
[20] *A & J Faill v Wilson* (1899) 7 SLT 148 at 150.
[21] In the Court of Session this is based on the Court of Session Act 1988, s 47(2) and (2A); in the sheriff court this is based on the Courts Reform (Scotland) Act 2014, s 88(1)(b).
[22] Given the terms of the Court of Session Act 1988, s 47(2); see the discussion of this issue in *William Collins & Sons Ltd v CGU Insurance plc* [2010] CSIH 37, 2010 SLT 607 at para 27; as to the order in the sheriff court see T Welsh, *Macphail's Sheriff Court Practice* (3rd edn, 2006) para 21.79 and the Courts Reform (Scotland) Act 2014, s 88(1)(b).
[23] *Scottish Power Generation Ltd v British Energy Generation (UK) Ltd* 2002 SC 517. For discussion of the criteria considered in making a decision on the grant of interim decrees see *Macphail's Sheriff Court Practice*, paras 21.89–21.92 and Rt Hon Lord Carloway et al (eds), *Court of Session Practice* (2015) paras H424–465; as to interim specific implement see the discussion in *Whyte and Mackay Ltd v Capstone International Incorporated* [2010] CSIH 87, 2011 SC 221.

the tenant's breach has caused a loss.[24] He may have other remedies such as payment of a sum of money if the premises are not left in the condition required by the lease.[25] Unless the landlord can point to a reason why the works need to be carried out by the tenant during the period of the lease it seems likely, in most cases, that the balance of convenience will favour the tenant notwithstanding the strength of the landlord's claim.

The position in Scots law on the availability of specific implement must be contrasted with the approach in English law to specific performance. In English law specific performance will not be granted unless damages are considered an inadequate remedy.[26] The difference in approach can be seen clearly in the differing outcomes of "keep open" cases in Scotland and England.[27] Given the availability of damages, it is unlikely that an English court will order specific performance requiring a tenant to carry out works in terms of the repairing obligations in the lease.

5.3.2 Interdict

The landlord may seek interdict against the tenant. Unlike specific implement, which requires positive action on the part of the tenant, an interdict can only be sought to prevent the tenant from doing something, rather than requiring the tenant to do something. In this way it might be said that specific implement is a positive order whereas interdict is a negative order.[28] How can interdict be useful when considering breach of repairing obligations?

While the focus of Chapter 4 was on the tenant's obligation to repair there was also discussion of "hidden" repairing obligations.[29] One such obligation related to the prohibition on a tenant carrying out alterations without the landlord's consent.[30] Where the landlord finds out that the tenant is planning on carrying out works without his consent he might seek to prevent the tenant from doing so by seeking interdict. The landlord must act before the prohibited alterations have been completed. An interdict will only prevent the prohibited activity from beginning or continuing and will be of no use once the alterations have been carried out. Interdict is also available on an interim basis.[31] Again the court must consider whether the pursuer has a *prima facie* case and where the balance of convenience

---

[24] On which see **5.3.3**.

[25] On which see **5.4.2**.

[26] *Co-operative Insurance Society Ltd v Argyll Stores (Holdings) Ltd* [1998] AC 1 per Lord Hoffmann at 11.

[27] See, e.g., the Scottish Inner House cases of *Retail Parks Investments Ltd v The Royal Bank of Scotland Ltd (No 2)* 1996 SC 227 and *Highland and Universal Properties Ltd v Safeway Properties Ltd* 2000 SC 297 and the English House of Lords case *Co-operative Insurance Society Ltd v Argyll Stores (Holdings) Ltd* [1997] 2 WLR 898. See in particular the comments made in *Highland and Universal* on the concerns raised by the House of Lords in *Co-operative Insurance*.

[28] Although see the use of interdict to effectively enforce an employment contract in *Anderson v Pringle of Scotland Ltd* 1998 SLT 754 and *Peace v City of Edinburgh Council* 1999 SLT 712. The cases are discussed in L Macgregor "Specific performance in Scots law" (n 5) pp 80–82.

[29] See **4.8**.

[30] See **4.8.3**.

[31] For the Court of Session see Court of Session Act 1988, s 47(1); for the sheriff court see *Macphail's Sheriff Court Practice*, paras 11.04 and 21.85 *et seq*.

lies.[32] The landlord is likely to have a *prima facie* case based on the tenant's obligations regarding alterations in the lease. Whether the landlord is successful on the balance of convenience will depend on the facts of the case, including the extent of the alterations the tenant intends to carry out and the impact of those obligations on the premises and surrounding property.

5.3.3 Damages

The landlord may seek damages from the tenant for breach of the repairing obligation. The landlord must establish that the tenant has breached the lease, in particular, that the tenant was required by the lease to do the works the landlord claims he should have done.[33] Given a damages action by a landlord is simply an action for breach of contract, issues such as causation, remoteness and mitigation of loss must be considered.[34]

Damages are most likely to be sought when the tenant fails to return the property to the landlord in the condition required by the lease rather than for breach of the tenant's ongoing repairing obligation. In many cases there will be no, or only nominal, loss to the landlord as a result of the tenant's failure to keep the premises in the condition required during the period of the lease. The tenant will be paying the rent under the lease and, in most cases, no other party will have any interest in the condition of the leased premises. The landlord suffers a loss when he cannot let the subjects when the tenant leaves at lease end; can only rent the premises following work he has to carry out to the premises; or can only lease the premises at a lower than market rent given their condition.

The landlord may, however, suffer a loss due to the tenant's failure to comply with his repairing obligations during the lease where the landlord seeks to sell the property and the condition of the leased premises results in a diminution in value of the property. While any purchaser will become the tenant's landlord and will be able to enforce the repairing obligation against the tenant the purchaser may take account of the potential difficulties in doing so and reflect that in the price he is willing to pay for the property. In a multi-occupancy property a potential tenant of another unit may decide not to take a lease of the unit due to the condition of the tenant's unit, or the condition of the tenant's unit might be bringing down the character of the property overall. If the landlord can show that he has suffered a loss as a result he can seek damages. In such a situation the landlord may wish to utilise another remedy such as implement[35] or carry out the works at the tenant's cost[36] instead of, or along with, damages so that the issue is resolved.

This part focuses on the more common claim of a landlord seeking damages for a tenant's failure to comply with his terminal repairing obligation. This loss will be assessed at the date of the breach. This will be lease expiry, when the tenant fails

---

[32] See, e.g., the discussion in *T Clarke (Scotland) Ltd v MMAXX Underfloor Heating Ltd* [2014] CSIH 83, 2015 SC 233.
[33] On what is required of a tenant in terms of an FRI lease see the discussion in Chapter 4.
[34] For discussion of damages generally see McBryde, *Contract*, ch 22. For a detailed examination of the law of damages see J Edelman, S Colton and J Varuhas, *McGregor on Damages* (20th edn, 2017).
[35] See **5.3.1**.
[36] See **5.4.1**.

REMEDIES FOR BREACH OF THE REPAIRING OBLIGATION

to leave the property in the condition required by the lease.[37] The damages claim may include a number of different heads. Typically these will be claims in relation to (a) the physical condition of the premises; (b) loss of rent and similar sums; and (c) landlord's costs. Each of these heads is considered in detail below, but before detailed consideration of these elements of the landlord's damages claim, it is useful to consider how the court goes about assessing damages more generally.

Assessing damages is more of an art than a science. There is no one way to assess damages. Instead the court looks at the various methods by which damages can be assessed and uses all of them to come to a view of the sum that should be awarded. In a claim for breach of a lease by a tenant Lord President Clyde stated:[38]

> The measures employed to estimate the money value of anything (including the damage flowing from a breach of contract) are not to be confounded with the value which it is sought to estimate; and the true value may only be found after employing more measures than one – in themselves all legitimate, but none of them necessarily conclusive by itself – and checking one result with the other.

It is not for the pursuer landlord to set out all methods of assessing his loss and to come to a figure sought by way of damages having evaluated the differing ways of assessing his loss. The landlord is entitled to seek damages on whatever basis of assessment of loss he wishes. Generally a landlord will assess his claim based on the cost of the works required to put the premises into the condition they should have been in at lease end. It is for the defender tenant to aver and prove that the landlord's loss is less than that assessed by considering the cost of the works.[39] The tenant might do this by considering the diminution in value of the reversionary interest. It is for the court to then consider the various ways of assessing the landlord's loss and cross-check each of these against the other to work out a sum which the court considers compensates the landlord for the tenant's breach of contract.

The position in England is different. In *Joyner v Weeks*[40] the Court of Appeal held that the landlord was entitled to the cost of the works even where a new tenant leased the premises on termination of the old lease, was paying a market rent and was under an obligation to demolish and alter part of the subjects let. The measure of loss was the cost of the works and that measure was not affected by the fact that, by reason of the terms of the new lease, the landlord was no worse off than he would have been if the tenant had complied with his obligations under the lease. The Scottish courts are clear that *Joyner v Weeks* is not part of Scots law.[41] The effect of *Joyner v Weeks* was ameliorated by the coming into force of the Landlord and Tenant Act 1927.[42] Section 18 of the Act provides that damages for breach of a repairing obligation shall not exceed the amount, if any, by which the value of the reversion is diminished owing to the breach, thus limiting the damages available to a

---

[37] Although events after the date of breach and before the date of assessment of damages by the court can be taken into account: see *Golden Strait Corporation v Nippon Yusen Kubishika Kaisha (The Golden Victory)* [2007] UKHL 12, [2007] 2 AC 535; and *Bunge SA v Nidera BV* [2015] UKSC 43, [2015] 3 All ER 1082.
[38] *Duke of Portland v Wood's Trs* 1926 SC 640 at 651.
[39] *Prudential Assurance Co Ltd v James Grant & Co (West) Ltd* 1982 SLT 423.
[40] *Joyner v Weeks* [1891] 2 QB 31.
[41] *Duke of Portland v Wood's Trs* per Lord President Clyde at 651.
[42] Section 18 of the 1927 Act came into force on 25 March 1928. The Act does not apply to Scotland.

landlord. The conventional way of calculating the diminution in value is by valuing the reversion in the condition it is in at the end of the lease and comparing that to the value based on the condition the leased premises should have been in had the tenant complied with the lease.[43]

5.3.3.1 *The condition of the property*

The landlord will likely use the schedule of dilapidations to base an action for damages on the cost of the works, but other ways of assessing the landlord's loss must be considered. What difference is there, if any, in the reversionary interest in the property between (i) the premises at lease end in the condition in which they are in, as measured against (ii) the condition the premises should have been in? Is there a difference in the market value of the property? Is that difference a lower figure than the cost of the works? Could the landlord let the premises albeit at a reduced rental? Is the capitalised value of that reduced rent a lower figure than the cost of the works?[44] These are all questions that must be asked by a tenant when seeking to defend a claim for breach of the terminal repairing obligation.

The parties must also consider causation. It is for the landlord to show that the breach by the tenant has caused him loss.[45] In defending an action for damages the tenant will want to consider causation also. The landlord will not suffer a loss due to the tenant's breach if the landlord intends to demolish the lease premises following lease expiry.[46] As such a tenant should check what the landlord plans to do with the property, of which the premises form part, following lease end. The tenant or his advisers can look at notifications made public by local authorities in terms of planning and building consents sought to try to establish this. In a similar vein, what is the landlord's loss if he plans to carry out extensive renovation works to the premises or the building, such that any works the tenant should have carried out to comply with his obligations under the lease, would have been rendered redundant?[47] There is no point painting walls if the walls are to be torn down. If an incoming tenant plans to carry out fitting-out works for his use of the premises what works that the outgoing tenant should have carried out would be rendered useless?

In terms of remoteness of loss it will often be the case that the landlord's loss will fall within the first limb of the test in *Hadley v Baxendale*[48] as a loss that may fairly and reasonably be considered as arising naturally, i.e., according to the usual course of things, from the tenant's breach. It is likely that a failure on the part of the tenant to comply with his repairing obligations will result in the landlord suffering a loss due to the condition of the premises, be that the cost of doing work to the property

---

[43] *Sunlife Europe Properties Ltd v Tiger Aspect Holdings Ltd* [2013] EWCA Civ 1656, [2014] 1 P & CR DG14 per Lewison LJ at 39.
[44] Although if the new tenant is not obliged to put the premises into the same condition as the outgoing tenant was required to, the landlord will suffer a loss regarding the condition of the property as a result of the outgoing tenant's breach.
[45] *Moor Row Ltd v DWF LLP* [2017] CSOH 63 per Lady Wolffe at paras 82–83, 2017 GWD 14-213.
[46] See Landlord and Tenant Act 1927, s 18 which makes express provision on this in English law.
[47] Landlord and Tenant Act 1927, s 18 provides that no damage shall be recovered for breach of a repairing covenant if it is shown that structural alterations were made to the premises that render valueless the repairs covered by the covenant.
[48] *Hadley v Baxendale* (1854) 9 Ex 341.

or diminution in value of the reversionary interest. As such it is suggested that it will only be in extraordinary cases where the second limb of the test in *Hadley v Baxendale* may come into play. This element of the test provides that damages will be recoverable if the landlord's loss is such as may reasonably be supposed to have been in the contemplation of both parties, at the time they entered the lease, as the probable result of its breach. Using this limb the landlord has to show that the loss, while not arising as a usual consequence of the breach, was nonetheless in the parties' contemplation due to facts known to both parties at the time the lease was entered into.[49] This limb of the test might allow recovery where the loss suffered by the landlord is significantly higher than one would normally expect, such as where extensive works are required to the premises to remedy the tenant's breach[50] but which the parties had in their contemplation as a consequence of a breach, perhaps due to an idiosyncrasy in the premises or the market known to both parties. In *Transfield Shipping Inc v Mercator Shipping Inc (The Achilleas)*[51] certain members of the House of Lords held that the presumed intention of the parties as to liability for loss was important and, as such, may have to be taken into account.[52]

It is sometimes said that a pursuer has a duty to mitigate his loss. Mitigation is not a duty – the defender has no right to force the pursuer to mitigate.[53] A failure to mitigate does not preclude the pursuer's claim. However, the pursuer will not be able to recover any sum as damages which he would not have suffered as a loss had he mitigated his loss.[54] The pursuer landlord is not required to go to the ends of the earth to minimise the impact of the tenant's breach but need only take reasonable steps to mitigate his loss.[55] It is for the pursuer to set out his loss, and for the defender to show that the loss is unreasonably high due to a failure to mitigate.[56]

5.3.3.2 *Loss of rent, etc*

The landlord faced with a breach of the terminal repairing obligation by the tenant may also seek loss of rent, as well as loss of service charge and insurance premiums.[57]

---

[49] Not the time of the breach.
[50] See *Balfour Beatty Construction (Scotland) Ltd v Scottish Power plc* 1994 SC (HL) 20 in which damages were held to be too remote; see also *Victoria Laundry (Windsor) Ltd v Newman Industries Ltd* [1949] 2 KB 528 where the Court of Appeal allowed recovery of general loss of profits under the first limb of *Hadley v Baxendale* but not the profits of the lucrative dyeing contracts with the Ministry of Supply of which the defender had not been advised and as such did not fall within the second limb of *Hadley v Baxendale*.
[51] *Transfield Shipping Inc v Mercator Shipping Inc (The Achilleas)* [2008] UKHL 48, [2009] 1 AC 61; see also Lord Hoffmann, "The Achilleas: custom and practice or foreseeability?" (2010) 14 Edin LR 47.
[52] See the discussion of this case at **5.3.3.2**.
[53] McBryde, *Contract*, para 22.37.
[54] McBryde, *Contract*, para 22.37.
[55] McBryde, *Contract*, para 22.38 and the authorities cited there.
[56] McBryde, *Contract*, para 22.45 and the authorities cited there. Mitigation is important for the loss of rent claim and is discussed in **5.3.3.2**.
[57] The landlord in a multi-occupancy property will still have to perform the services as set out in his lease with other tenants and many commercial leases provide that any proportion of the service charge which relates to a void unit are paid for by the landlord rather than split among the tenants in occupation. Similar provision is often made in relation to insurance arranged by the landlord for the entire property, the cost of which is repaid by the tenants.

Where the landlord is unable to re-let the premises at a market rent following lease end, due to the subjects not being in the condition required by the lease, the landlord can seek loss of rent from the tenant. The loss of rent claim is likely to cover any period in which the landlord is arranging and having required works carried out to the premises. Suppose that the landlord can show that a new lease would have started immediately following the lease ending[58] but due to the tenant's breach works were required which took the landlord six months to arrange and have executed. The landlord will seek the loss of rent for this six-month period. It has been suggested, although there is no case law on the point, that a landlord may not have to show that the premises would have been re-let, had the tenant complied with his repairing obligation; but that the landlord could base his claim on the loss of a chance that the premises could be re-let.[59] On that basis, where there is a real or substantial chance that the premises would have been re-let if the tenant had complied with his obligations, the landlord will be entitled to recover loss of rent, taking into account the chance of that actually taking place in the market prevailing at lease end.

As with the condition of the premises, causation, remoteness and mitigation of loss must also be considered. Each is discussed in turn below.

The state of the rental market at the time of lease expiry is important and expert advice on this should be sought. The tenant faced with a loss of rent claim in a damages action needs to consider whether the failure to return the premises to the landlord in the condition specified in the lease has caused loss of rent, etc to the landlord or whether, due to market conditions, the landlord would not have been able to re-let the premises immediately following lease end in any event. If the supply of rental properties outstrips demand the landlord might have had the premises on the market without securing a new lease regardless of the condition of the premises. Suppose the evidence is that the premises would have had to be on the market for a period of time, for instance 12 months, to secure a new lease and the works were done within two months, the outgoing tenant would not be liable for 12 months' loss of rent, and, indeed, might not be liable for any loss of rent. The landlord might be able to demonstrate that the premises could not be marketed until the works were carried out in which case the tenant would be liable for two months' loss of rent only.

The loss of rent is assessed taking into account the rent the landlord would obtain if the property was re-let, not the rent that was being paid by the tenant under the lease at the time it ended. Specific provision might be made in the lease for a sum to be paid to the landlord in respect of loss of rent which supersedes the position at common law.[60]

Where a prospective new tenant has been interested in the premises but decided, ultimately, not to take a lease it will be important to find out whether they would have taken a lease had the premises been in good condition and to gather any evidence to that effect for the loss of rent claim. The landlord might be able to show that had

---

[58] Commercial leases often allow the landlord to market the subjects for let towards the end of the lease. For instance the landlord might be permitted to market and show potential new tenants around the premises in the last three or six months of the lease.

[59] N Dowding et al, *Dilapidations: The Modern Law and Practice* (6th edn, 2017) para 32.05.

[60] On specific provision in the lease see **5.4.2**.

the tenant complied with his obligations in relation to repair and left the premises in the condition required by the lease, a new tenant (X) would have taken a lease at a certain rent. The landlord might seek to argue that as a result of the tenant's breach of the lease, resulting in works being required to put the premises into good condition, and consequent delay in re-letting, the market has changed such that he will not now be able to achieve the same level of rent on a new lease. The landlord might seek the difference between the rent that he had agreed with X and the lower rent he will now be able to obtain. For instance, if the rent with X would have been £250,000 per annum for a 10-year lease and the landlord would now only be able to re-let on the basis of a 10-year lease at £200,000 per annum, the landlord might seek the difference in rent over the 10-year period.[61] If it can be shown that the only reason X did not take a lease at £250,000 per annum is because of the condition of the premises then it can be said that the tenant's breach has caused the loss. However, this is not sufficient in itself to allow the landlord to recover. The next question is whether the landlord's loss is too remote.

This is a difficult question. There is no case law covering the specific point. It could be said that the loss flows naturally from the tenant's breach of the lease, and, as such, would have been in the parties' contemplation.[62] Put another way, it is not unlikely that the landlord would suffer this loss.[63] Both landlord and tenant are commercial parties and, as such, will be aware that there can be movements in the rental market. It may also be said that as a loss of rent claim for the period within which necessary works are carried out, discussed above, would not be too remote, then a claim for loss of rent where a lower rent is achieved is not a loss of a different type or kind, only of a different extent, which is therefore recoverable.[64] On the other hand, it may be said that such a loss was not within the tenant's contemplation, particularly given the terms on which the landlord could re-let the premises at lease end would result in an indeterminate and unquantifiable liability at lease commencement. The tenant may also argue that he did not accept responsibility for such a loss, based on the decision in *The Achilleas*.[65] For Lords Hoffmann and Hope[66] whether parties entering into a contract would have assumed liability for the loss was an important factor to consider. In that case they found there to be a general understanding in the relevant market that

---

[61] The sum of £500,000 (£50,000 × 10) would not be awarded as it would have to be discounted to take account of the fact that the landlord would receive the sum following a decision in his favour rather than over a 10-year period. Account would also have to be taken of the fact that in the lease at £200,000 per annum there will likely be rent reviews, normally upwards only, that will result in a review of the rent during the 10-year period of the lease.

[62] *Hadley v Baxendale* (1854) 9 Ex 341.

[63] *Czarnikow v Koufos (The Heron II)* [1969] 1 AC 350.

[64] However, in some cases certain economic losses have been held to be recoverable, and others not: see *Victoria Laundry Ltd v Newman Industries Ltd* [1949] 2 KB 528 CA; *Balfour Beatty Construction (Scotland) Ltd v Scottish Power plc* 1994 SC (HL) 20. See the discussion of this issue in *McGregor on Damages* (20th edn, 2017) paras 8.190–8.193.

[65] *The Achilleas* [2008] UKHL 48, [2009] 1 AC 61. As *McGregor* notes it is difficult to determine the ratio of the case: see *McGregor on Damages*, para 8.174. The decision has been criticised and, while defendants have made use of the case, the courts have tended to use the "traditional" remoteness test in cases such as *Hadley v Baxendale* (1854) 9 Ex 341. See the discussion of the case and the aftermath in *McGregor on Damages*, paras 8.168–8.181.

[66] With whom Lord Walker agreed.

the losses claimed were not recoverable (a reduced daily rate over the period of a follow-on charter lasting 191 days, as a result of a lower rate having to be agreed for the follow-on charter because the defendants did not return the ship on time, in breach of contract). It may be that, in the commercial leasing sector, there is a general understanding that a loss of rent calculated by reference to the difference between what the landlord could have obtained on a new lease had the tenant left the premises in repair, and what he could ultimately obtain due to the tenant's breach is irrecoverable.

The landlord must also take steps to mitigate his loss. As such he cannot do nothing but bemoan the tenant's failure to leave the premises in the condition required by the lease and then seek to recover loss of rent for a protracted period. While there may be a period following lease expiry in which a landlord would reasonably discuss matters with the tenant with a view to negotiating settlement to obtain agreement on sums that will be paid by the tenant, there will come a point when the landlord should instruct works to the property and/or market it for rent. If he fails to do so he will not be able to recover loss of rent beyond the loss he would have suffered had he instructed the works and/or marketed the property.[67]

In addition to loss of rent, service charge and insurance premiums the landlord may also seek to recover any business rates that he has had to pay to the local authority. Here, the landlord will have to demonstrate that if the property had been in the condition required by the lease it would have been re-let to a new tenant, who would have been liable for those rates.[68]

5.3.3.3 *Costs*

While professional costs associated with actually carrying out the works, such as a project manager's fee, will be dealt with as part of the cost of the works, the landlord is likely to incur other professional fees associated with the tenant's breach of the repairing obligation. The landlord may have had to instruct surveyors to inspect the property and prepare a schedule of dilapidations. He may also have instructed a solicitor to serve a schedule of dilapidations and to negotiate with the tenant or tenant's solicitor. Such costs are, it is argued, likely to fall within the first limb of the test in *Hadley v Baxendale* as an ordinary consequence of the tenant's breach.

Where the landlord has raised a damages action he will seek the expenses of the action from the tenant as part of his claim. In terms of the rules in relation to expenses in litigation[69] the landlord can only recover specific costs and is unlikely to recover all of his out of pocket expenses even where expenses are awarded in his favour.

It is very common for specific provision to be made in the lease in relation to recovery of landlord's costs, so that such professional fees and costs can be sought as a payment rather than as a head of claim in damages or by way of expenses in a court action.[70]

---

[67] See the comments on mitigation in **5.3.3.1**.
[68] For empty properties some rates relief is available: see the Non-Domestic Rating (Unoccupied Property) (Scotland) Regulations 2018, SSI 2018/77.
[69] What can be recovered by the party awarded expenses can be found in the tables of fees printed in *The Scottish Law Directory: The White Book: Fees Supplement* published annually.
[70] As to which see **5.4.2**.

5.3.4 Retention

The landlord may seek to utilise the right to retain so that he does not need to perform his obligations under the lease while the tenant is in breach of his obligations in relation to the condition of the premises. The right to retain is based on the principle of mutuality in contract.[71]

The landlord will be able to retain performance only where the obligation in relation to which he is withholding performance is the counterpart of the obligation breached by the tenant.[72] There is, however, an assumption that the obligations undertaken by the landlord are the counterparts of the obligations undertaken by the tenant under the lease, unless an examination of the lease shows that the obligations are independent.[73] In most FRI leases the landlord will not have many obligations. He will be under an obligation to give possession to the tenant but other than that a landlord of a multi-occupancy building may have obligations to insure the premises or to perform services in relation to common parts.[74] The landlord will generally not wish to withhold performance of these obligations when faced by a breach by a tenant of the repairing obligations. Failing to maintain building insurance or perform services in relation to the common parts would put the landlord in breach of his obligations to other tenants. In addition, the risk involved in not having adequate insurance would be too great for the landlord.

It is suggested that it will only be where the landlord has other obligations vis-à-vis the tenant in breach alone that retention may be a useful remedy for the landlord.[75] This may arise, for example, where the tenant has an option to purchase contained in the lease which the tenant seeks to exercise. It has been held that such an option and the tenant's repairing obligations may be counterparts, such that a failure by the tenant to comply with his obligations in relation to the condition of the premises might result in the tenant being unable to enforce the sale in terms of a duly exercised option to purchase.[76] It is suggested that, for the same reason, a landlord may be able to refuse to consider an application for consent to assign

---

[71] For a detailed discussion of the right to retain see L Richardson, "The scope and limits of the right to retain contractual performance" 2018 Jur Rev 209.
[72] McBryde, *Contract*, para 20-47; *Bank of East Asia Ltd v Scottish Enterprise* 1997 SLT 1213; *Macari v Celtic Football and Athletic Co Ltd* 1999 SC 628.
[73] W M Gloag, *The Law of Contract* (2nd edn, 1929) p 594; *Inveresk plc v Tullis Russell Papermakers Ltd* [2010] UKSC 19, 2010 SC (UKSC) 106 per Lord Hope at paras 42 and 43.
[74] Discussed in Chapter 6.
[75] Professor Thomson in his analysis of *Macari v Celtic Football and Athletic Co Ltd* 1999 SC 628 suggests that a party faced with a breach by the other cannot retain performance of some of his obligations but not others: see J Thomson, "An unsuitable case for suspension?" (1999) 3 Edin LR 394. Macari concerned a contract of employment, in which there are particular policy considerations at play, which do not arise in commercial contracts more generally. Indeed, Professor Thomson's comments were made in the context of an employee when faced with a breach by his employer of the implied term of mutual trust and confidence. See also the comments, with reference to *Macari*, in *Hoult v Turpie* 2004 SLT 308. It is not clear why a party faced with a breach of contract must retain all of his obligations. This is especially the case where, if a landlord withheld certain obligations, regarding for instance work to the common parts, he would put himself in breach of obligations to his other tenants.
[76] *McCall's Entertainments (Ayr) Ltd v South Ayrshire Council (No 1)* 1998 SLT 1403; cf *Rafferty v Shofield* [1897] 1 Ch 937 but see the Inner House decision in *Penman v Mackay* 1922 SC 385 especially Lord MacKenzie at 394 and Lord Skerrington at 394–95.

or sub-let or consent for alterations where the tenant is in breach of his repairing obligations under the lease.[77]

For retention to be available, the tenant's breach must be material, as well as being a counterpart obligation to that retained by the landlord. There are doubts about how serious a breach has to be for retention to operate.[78] What is known is that the tenant's breach need not be so material that it would justify the landlord rescinding the lease.[79] As such, his breach need not go to the root of the contract.[80] At the other end of the spectrum, it would appear that the tenant's breach would have to be more than trivial or insignificant. The brief discussion of this issue in *McCall's Entertainments (Ayr) Ltd v South Lanarkshire Council (No 2)*[81] suggests that the seriousness of the tenant's breach may have to be relatively high before the landlord can withhold performance.

Finally, it should be noted that the courts can exercise equitable control over the right to retain to ensure retention is not used in an abusive fashion.[82] There are uncertainties about when a court is likely to consider retention has been used inequitably.

Given the uncertainties surrounding the right to retain performance, and the limited circumstances in which the landlord will wish to use the right, it may be that retention is not often resorted to by landlords for breach of the tenant's repairing obligations.[83]

5.3.5 Rescission

A landlord faced with material breach by the tenant may seek to rescind the contract. For rescission to be available the tenant's breach must go to the root of the contract.[84] The lease may make express provision for which breaches will be considered material, but where express provision is made in the lease the matter is generally dealt with in an irritancy clause.[85]

---

[77] Although note the discussion below on the need for the tenant's breach to be material and the court's equitable control of retention from abuse. In this situation the landlord is not refusing or consenting to the application subject to repairs being carried out, but is simply refusing to consider the request. In any event, a landlord seeking to ensure that the tenant complies with his obligations under the lease is not the landlord seeking to obtain a collateral benefit as part of the process of consent to assignation or sub-letting, as to which see the *obiter* comments in *Lousada & Co Ltd v J E Lesser (Properties) Ltd* 1990 SC 178 per the Lord Justice Clerk at 188 and Lord Dunpark at 192; *Scottish Tourist Board v Deanpark Ltd* 1998 SLT 1121.

[78] See the doubts expressed by McBryde as to the extent of materiality required: McBryde, *Contract*, paras 20.58–20.60; *Inveresk plc v Tullis Russell Papermakers Ltd* [2010] UKSC 19, 2010 SC (UKSC) 106 per Lord Hope at para 43; and *EDI Central Ltd v National Car Parks Ltd* [2010] CSOH 141, 2011 SLT 75 per Lord Glennie at para 111.

[79] *Inveresk plc* per Lord Hope at para 43; *EDI Central* per Lord Glennie at para 111.

[80] *Wade v Waldon* 1909 SC 571 per Lord President Dunedin at 576.

[81] *McCall's Entertainments (Ayr) Ltd v South Lanarkshire Council (No 2)* 1998 SLT 1403 at 1429.

[82] *McNeill v Aberdeen City Council* [2013] CSIH 102, 2014 SC 335 per Lord Drummond Young at para 30.

[83] See the further discussion of the effect of breach of the tenant's repair obligations on rights granted to the tenant under the lease at **5.5**.

[84] *Wade v Waldon* 1909 SC 571 per Lord President Dunedin at 576. See the other phrases used to describe material breach identified by McBryde, *Contract*, para 20.91.

[85] As to which see **5.4.3**.

Where no express provision is made, it is necessary to consider whether a breach is sufficiently material to allow the landlord to rescind. The critical issue is the nature of the tenant's breach, judged objectively.[86] As such, the extent of the tenant's defective performance of his repairing obligations must be evaluated. The consequences of the breach may illustrate the materiality of the breach but that is not the critical issue.[87] Whether the breach is material depends on the facts and circumstances at the time of formation of the lease and since.[88] As such, where there is no express provision, there may be doubts as to whether a breach by the tenant of his repairing obligations is sufficiently material to allow the landlord to rescind, bringing future performance of the lease to an end. Where the landlord purports to rescind due to material breach by the tenant, but the tenant's breach is not sufficiently material, the landlord, by purporting to rescind, will find himself in material breach, entitling the tenant to rescind.[89] Given these uncertainties it is unsurprising that most commercial leases will contain specific provision on irritating the lease in defined circumstances, with landlords rarely having to resort to the common law right to rescind.

A right to rescind is likely to be relied upon only when the lease makes no provision for irritancy. That was the position in *Crieff Highland Gathering Ltd v Perth and Kinross Council*.[90] In this case, the landlord purported to terminate the lease of a public park on the basis that the tenant was in material breach of its obligations to maintain the premises and keep them in a neat and tidy condition as required by the lease.[91] Lord Pentland found that the tenant was in breach of its obligations,[92] in failing to maintain the walls in the park and a pavilion that the tenant had erected on the premises. He also found that there was rubbish and debris in the park, and vegetation and weeds that should have been removed from the premises. However, Lord Pentland did not think that the breaches, either singularly or cumulatively, were material.[93] A number of considerations lead him to this conclusion: the premises had never been closed to the public and there had never been any difficulty in the public making full use of the facilities in the premises, as a result of the wants of repair. That this had been the case since lease commencement, 28 years before, indicated that "the essence of the contract had not been undermined".[94] Furthermore, there was no evidence that the landlord contemplated carrying out the repairs itself and seeking the cost of doing so from the tenant[95] or seeking an order of specific implement requiring the tenant to carry out the required repairs.[96] At no time had the landlord taken steps to call a formal meeting to discuss the wants of repair, which was provided for in

---

[86] McBryde, *Contract*, para 20.93–20.94.
[87] McBryde, *Contract*, para 20.94.
[88] McBryde, *Contract*, para 20.96.
[89] *Wade v Waldon* 1909 SC 571.
[90] *Crieff Highland Gathering Ltd v Perth and Kinross Council* [2011] CSOH 38, 2011 SLT 992.
[91] *Crieff Highland Gathering* at paras 6–8.
[92] *Crieff Highland Gathering* at paras 37 and 38.
[93] *Crieff Highland Gathering* at para 44.
[94] *Crieff Highland Gathering* at para 44.
[95] From the case report it is not clear that the lease contained the provision generally found in commercial leases that the landlord has the right to carry out repairs and recover the cost from the tenant.
[96] *Crieff Highland Gathering* at para 45.

the lease. In addition, the landlord took no steps to follow up the notice of wants of repair issued in November 2007 until 2009, indicating that the wants of repair were not a serious or urgent problem.[97] Lord Pentland also took account of the fact that the lease was for a period of 60 years (with 30 years still to run) and that the tenant had, by the date of the proof,[98] carried out repairs with a view to addressing the wants of repair. The tenant had also stressed its commitment to running the premises as an important public facility and fulfilling its contractual obligations going forward. Lord Pentland considered the tenant's future intentions important because:

> [T]he courts have traditionally been reluctant to allow a rural lease without an irritancy clause to be brought to an end in circumstances where the tenant has made it clear that it intends to perform its side of the contract during the remaining period of the lease.[99]

Finally, the works that had been carried out by the tenant had cost just over £9,000. All of these factors indicated that the tenant's breaches were not material and, as such, the landlord was not entitled to rescind the lease.

This case also highlighted a further potential limitation on the landlord's right to rescind: that the right to rescind a lease is a right to terminate for refusal by the tenant to perform his obligations *in the future*. This can be contrasted with the landlord's right to irritate, which is a right to terminate the lease for past breach. Lord Pentland noted that in this respect the right to rescind a lease for material breach is "somewhat narrower than the right to rescind other mutual contracts"[100] where rescission is available on material breach having occurred. Having considered the authorities,[101] Lord Pentland held that a landlord is entitled to rescind a lease only where three conditions are satisfied: (i) the tenant has committed a material breach of the lease; (ii) the landlord has given the tenant a fair and reasonable opportunity to remedy the breach;[102] and (iii) the tenant has demonstrated that he is unwilling or unable to perform his obligations in the future.[103] As such, the court must not only consider the position as at the date of the landlord's purported rescission of the lease but must take into account the conduct and attitude of the tenant up until decree is sought.[104]

There is doubt, however, that rescission is only available in relation to anticipated breaches by the tenant of future obligations.[105] It seems strange that, in relation to leases only, the right to rescind is restricted to the tenant's repudiatory breaches in respect of future obligations, when for other mutual contracts a past material breach

---

[97] *Crieff Highland Gathering* at para 45.
[98] A court hearing at which evidence is heard.
[99] *Crieff Highland Gathering* at para 46; see also the discussion in paras 49–54.
[100] *Crieff Highland Gathering* at para 50.
[101] Discussed in *Crieff Highland Gathering* at paras 51–53.
[102] As to which see the discussion of the Law Reform (Miscellaneous Provisions) (Scotland) Act 1985 below.
[103] *Crieff Highland Gathering* at para 54. For further discussion see M Hogg, "To irritate or rescind: two paths for the landlord?" 1999 SLT (News) 1.
[104] *Crieff Highland Gathering* at para 54.
[105] A McAllister, *Scottish Law of Leases* (4th edn, 2013) para 4.36.

by one of the parties is sufficient to give the other the right to rescind.[106] While a lease may, and often does, create a real right in favour of the tenant, and as such different policy considerations may apply to lease termination than to other types of contracts, that has been considered and dealt with in respect of commercial leases by the protections found in the Law Reform (Miscellaneous Provisions) (Scotland) Act 1985.[107] As such there is no need for what appears to be an anomalous common law rule, based on thin authority decided prior to the 1985 Act coming into force. Lord Pentland's comments on this aspect of the case in *Crieff Highland Gathering*[108] should be considered *obiter* given he found there was no material breach of the lease by the tenant. A restricted right to rescind would also create practical problems and further uncertainty as to when the landlord would be able to use the right. This is unsatisfactory given rescission is a self-help remedy.[109] A landlord should be able to make an assessment of whether there has been a material breach of contract by the tenant[110] and whether he has given the tenant a reasonable period of time to remedy breaches which are remediable.[111] However, the landlord may be unable to determine with any certainty whether the tenant is unwilling or unable to perform his contractual obligations going forward in the absence of a clear statement to that effect from the tenant, which may not be forthcoming. Indeed, a tenant might initially state that he is unwilling to perform his obligations going forward, so that the landlord rescinds, but then change his mind such that the landlord would not be able to seek decree to remove the tenant from the premises.[112] With this uncertainty a landlord cannot be confident, when rescinding, that he is able to rescind and bring the lease to an end.

As noted above, the Law Reform (Miscellaneous Provisions) (Scotland) Act 1985 sets out certain provisions to protect tenants from termination of their lease. These provisions can be found in sections 4 to 6 of the Act. Section 5 (relating to non-monetary breaches of the lease) is the relevant section when considering the landlord's remedies for breach of the tenant's repairing obligations. The requirements of section 5 will be considered in detail when considering irritancy of the lease[113] but, for present purposes, it should be noted that section 5 applies not only to irritancy of the lease by the landlord. It also applies where the landlord seeks to terminate the lease, and thus must be considered where a landlord seeks to rescind.[114]

---

[106] Although note the comments of Lord Thomson in *Lindley Catering Investments Ltd v Hibernian Football Club Ltd* 1975 SLT (Notes) 56 at 57 that where the breach can be remedied so that the contract as a whole can thereafter be implemented, the innocent party is not entitled to treat the contract as rescinded without giving the other party an opportunity to remedy the breach. However, a "right to cure" has not subsequently developed in Scottish case law and this statement may be explained as evidencing that a breach that can easily be remedied is unlikely to be material: H L MacQueen and J Thomson, *Contract Law in Scotland* (4th edn, 2016) para 5.41.
[107] Discussed below.
[108] *Crieff Highland Gathering Ltd v Perth and Kinross Council* [2011] CSOH 38; 2011 SLT 992.
[109] MacQueen and Thomson, *Contract Law in Scotland*, para 5.27.
[110] Although, as noted above, without express provision in the lease as to which breaches are material there is likely to be some uncertainty.
[111] Although as noted in **5.4.3.1** there may be arguments about what a reasonable period is.
[112] See *The Kilmacolm Hydropathic Co Ltd v Hall* (1922) 38 Sh Ct Rep 233.
[113] See **5.4.3**.
[114] 1985 Act, s 5 does not refer to irritancy but to termination of the lease and specifically refers to any act or omission of the tenant being deemed by a provision of the lease to be a material breach of contract: s 5(1)(b).

5.4 REMEDIES SPECIFICALLY PROVIDED FOR IN THE LEASE

In addition to the remedies set out above, the parties may agree to certain remedies and make provision for them in the lease. The landlord is likely to wish to do so, given some of the difficulties he may encounter with the general contract law remedies available to him.

5.4.1 Landlord can carry out works to the premises and recover the costs from the tenant

Where, following an inspection of the property[115] the landlord discovers that the tenant is in breach of his repairing obligations, the landlord may wish to carry out works in order to safeguard the condition of the premises and prevent further deterioration. To be able to do this, the landlord must have a right to do so in terms of the lease, as the right is not implied,[116] and without it any works to the premises by the landlord will be an interference with the tenant's right to possession of the premises.[117] The tenant will, however, want to be protected from the landlord simply arriving at the premises to carry out works at any time given the significant disruption this is likely to cause. As such, it is common to find a term in a commercial lease that the landlord must serve a notice of wants of repair[118] on the tenant and give the tenant a reasonable opportunity to remedy same before the landlord will be able to enter the premises and do the works himself.[119] As well as having the right to enter and do the works, the landlord will wish to recover the cost of doing so from the tenant, and specific provision is generally made for this in the lease.[120]

Where the landlord wishes to enter the premises for the purpose of carrying out the work, but is denied access by the tenant, he may have to raise an action of specific implement that the tenant permits such access, or seek an order for interim possession of the leased subjects.[121] A landlord may, however, face difficulties in obtaining such an order on the balance of convenience[122] if the works are likely to cause significant disruption to the tenant and the operation of his business from the premises. The court will take into account the fact that the landlord will have

---

[115] As to which see **4.6**.
[116] K Gerber et al, "Landlord and Tenant" (Re-issue) in the *The Laws of Scotland: Stair Memorial Encyclopaedia* vol 10 (2001), para 500.
[117] *Possfund Custodial Tr Ltd v Kwik-Fit Properties Ltd* [2008] CSIH 65, 2009 SLT 133.
[118] See the discussion of such notices in **4.6**.
[119] See clause 4.3 of Schedule Part 6 of the style multi-occupancy lease in *Greens Practice Styles: Commercial Leases*, pp 113–211 although the terms of clause 4.3.3 suggest the landlord could enter upon the premises and carry out work if the tenant is in default of his repairing obligations without the need to serve a notice of wants of repair and allow the tenant time to carry out the works first. Such a provision should be resisted by the tenant.
[120] See clause 11.1 of Schedule Part 9 of the style multi-occupancy lease in *Greens Practice Styles: Commercial Leases*, pp 113–211.
[121] In terms of the Court of Session Act 1988, s 47(2) in the Court of Session or the Courts Reform (Scotland) Act 2014, s 88 in the sheriff court. For discussion of this remedy in the Court of Session see *William Collins & Sons Ltd v CGU Insurance plc* [2010] CSIH 37, 2010 SLT 607.
[122] See the discussion of balance of convenience in relation to interim specific implement in **5.3.1**. For discussion of the criteria considered in making a decision on the grant of interim decrees, see *Macphail's Sheriff Court Practice*, paras 21.89–21.92; and *Court of Session Practice*, paras H424–465; as to interim specific implement see the discussion in *Whyte and Mackay Ltd v Capstone International Incorporated* [2010] CSIH 87, 2011 SC 221.

other remedies available to him to deal with the tenant's breach of the lease such as claiming damages.[123]

5.4.2 Payment

The lease may make provision for the tenant to pay a sum of money to the landlord in lieu of the tenant being required to carry out work to bring the condition of the premises to the standard required by the lease.[124] Such a provision is generally at the landlord's option.[125] What the tenant will have to pay will depend on the clause agreed by the parties. Generally, the tenant will have to pay an amount in respect of the condition of the premises. This might be determined, for instance, by the landlord producing a costed schedule of dilapidations[126] or a sum certified by the landlord as being equivalent to the cost of carrying out the works.[127] The clause may, additionally, provide that a sum be paid to the landlord for loss of rent, for instance that the tenant will pay the landlord a sum of money equivalent to the rent due under the lease (immediately prior to expiry) for a certain period of time. This might be for the period it would take for works to be carried out.[128] Provision will also generally be made that any costs and professional fees incurred by the landlord as a result of the tenant's breach of the lease are payable by the tenant on demand.[129]

Such clauses are useful to the landlord as they avoid some of the difficulties noted above.[130] In particular, the landlord does not need to prove that he has suffered a loss as a result of the tenant's breach of the lease and does not need to mitigate his loss. Where the parties have agreed that the tenant will pay certain sums, the landlord can seek payment and, failing which, raise an action for payment rather than seeking damages.

Such payment clauses have been the subject of judicial analysis in the Inner House. In *Grove Investments Ltd v Cape Building Products Ltd*[131] the landlord sought payment of £10,299,912 from the tenant, that being the total amount set out in the schedule of dilapidations that had been served on the tenant. In terms of the lease the tenant was obliged:

---

[123] See the discussion of this issue, in the context of entry being sought to carry out works to common parts, in *William Collins & Sons Ltd v CGU Insurance plc* [2010] CSIH 37, 2010 SLT 607.
[124] An example of such a provision can be found in clauses 9 and 10 of Schedule Part 9 of the style multi-occupancy lease in *Greens Practice Styles: Commercial Leases*, pp 113–211; see also the provisions discussed in *Grove Investments Ltd v Cape Building Products Ltd* [2014] CSIH 43, 2014 Hous LR 35 and *@SIPP Pension Trs Ltd v Insight Travel Services Ltd* [2015] CSIH 91, 2016 SLT 131, both set out below.
[125] Clauses 9 and 10 of Schedule Part 9 of the style multi-occupancy lease in *Greens Practice Styles: Commercial Leases*, pp 113–211; see also the provisions discussed in *Grove Investments* and *@SIPP Pension Trs*.
[126] As to which see **4.6**.
[127] Clauses 9 and 10 of Schedule Part 9 of the style multi-occupancy lease in *Greens Practice Styles: Commercial Leases*, pp 113–211.
[128] See clause 8.5 of Schedule Part 12 of the style multi-occupancy lease in *Greens Practice Styles: Commercial Leases*, pp 113–211.
[129] See clauses 14.2 and 14.3 of Schedule Part 9 of the style multi-occupancy lease in *Greens Practice Styles: Commercial Leases*, pp 113–211.
[130] See the discussion at **5.3.3** *et seq*.
[131] *Grove Investments Ltd v Cape Building Products Ltd* [2014] CSIH 43, 2014 Hous LR 35.

to flit and remove from the premises at the expiry or sooner termination of this lease ... and to pay to the landlords the total value of the Schedule of Dilapidations prepared by the landlords in respect of the tenants' obligations under Articles Fifth and Sixth hereof, declaring that the landlords shall be free to expend all moneys recovered as dilapidations as they think fit ...[132]

Article Sixth obliged the tenant to return the premises to the landlord at the expiry of the lease in "good and habitable condition and repair". It also provided:

> that on expiry or earlier termination of this lease the landlords may require the tenants to make a financial settlement with the landlords in lieu of their obligations under this Article which the landlords consider to be outstanding at the date of expiry or earlier termination.[133]

The tenant argued that these provisions meant that he was only obliged to make payment to the landlord of the loss actually suffered by the landlord as a result of the tenant's breach of the lease. If the provisions were construed otherwise, the landlord might recover a sum that bore no relation to any loss suffered by the landlord.[134] The tenant also argued that the provisions were intended to reflect and reinforce the common law, in terms of which the landlord would be entitled to the loss actually sustained, which might be calculated using a number of different methods.[135] The landlord argued that the tenant had to pay a sum representing the total value brought out in the schedule of dilapidations. The Inner House found in the tenant's favour. The court was particularly influenced by the fact that the landlord's construction achieved a result that was "radically different from the rules of the common law" and that was a factor that indicated that the landlord's construction of the provisions in the lease was commercially unreasonable.[136] The court noted that if the parties intended a result different from the common law there needed to be "definite indications to that effect".[137] This case therefore indicated that if parties wished to make provision for payment of a sum of money to the landlord for the tenant's breach of the repairing obligation, beyond the damages claim available to the landlord at common law, the lease provisions had to be very clear that that is what the parties intended. Given the terms of this lease, in particular the fact that the lease expressly provided that the landlord could spend the money recovered as dilapidations as they thought fit, it seemed that this may be quite difficult to achieve.

However, shortly after *Grove* the Inner House had occasion to consider again a payment provision for breach of the tenant's repairing obligation. The court in *@SIPP Pension Trs Ltd v Insight Travel Services Ltd* sought to distance itself from the decision reached in *Grove*.[138] In this case the lease obliged the tenant:

---

[132] *Grove Investments* at para 2.
[133] *Grove Investments* at para 2.
[134] *Grove Investments* at para 4.
[135] *Grove Investments* at para 4. As to the different methods that can be used to calculate a landlord's loss see **5.3.3**.
[136] *Grove Investments* at para 12. See the discussion of this case in **4.2.3**.
[137] *Grove Investments* at para 20.
[138] *@SIPP Pension Trs Ltd v Insight Travel Services Ltd* [2015] CSIH 91, 2016 SLT 131. See the discussion of *@SIPP Pension Trs* at **4.2.3**.

> At the expiry or sooner termination of the ... Lease ... to surrender to the Landlord the leased subjects ... in such state and condition as shall in all respects be consistent with a full and due performance by the Tenant of the obligations herein contained ... Provided always that if the Landlord shall so desire at the expiry or sooner termination of the ... Lease they may call upon the Tenant, by notice in writing (in which event the Tenant shall be bound), to pay to the Landlord at the determination date ... a sum equal to the amount required to put the leased subjects into good and substantial repair and in good decorative condition in accordance with the obligations and conditions on the part of the Tenant herein contained in lieu of requiring the Tenant himself to carry out the work.[139]

The court considered that this case could readily be distinguished from *Grove*. In *Grove* the clause contained no notice provision and was concerned with parties reaching a financial settlement in relation to the "value" of the schedule of dilapidations without any reference to the cost of repairs.[140] The court set out a number of reservations to the approach to interpretation that had been taken by the court in *Grove*.[141] The court noted:

> the observations in *Grove* predated the guidance provided by the Supreme Court in *Arnold*[142] and must, accordingly, be regarded with an appropriate degree of caution. Finally, it is important to note that *Grove* did not lay down any general rule to the effect that the landlord in a commercial lease is, at termination, if repairs are outstanding only entitled to be compensated for capital loss actually suffered. Whilst the court concluded, in *Grove*, that that was the outcome that accorded with commercial commonsense, the context was its interpretation of the relevant clause in that lease ...[143]

The Inner House noted that, in interpreting the provision, the court had to determine what the parties meant by the language used by ascertaining what a reasonable person with all the background knowledge available to the parties would have understood the parties to have meant, looking for the natural and ordinary meaning.[144] For the Inner House in *@SIPP*, the common law should not be used as a benchmark. The court was satisfied that the only natural and ordinary meaning of the provision was that it was a payment clause and the sum due was the cost of repair.[145] The words used clearly indicated that if, at lease termination, the premises were not in the condition required by the lease, the landlord was entitled to payment of a sum equal to the cost of bringing them up to that standard.[146] The words used made this position clear. The fact that that was different to the position at common law and might result in the landlord receiving more than the actual loss he had suffered did not justify departing from the parties' agreement as set out in the lease.

While *Grove* has not been overturned it is unlikely to be followed, other than in relation to a clause in the exact same terms, given the decision in *@SIPP*, in which the Inner House drew on Supreme Court guidance[147] on the correct approach to

---

[139] *@SIPP Pension Trs* at para 2.
[140] *@SIPP Pension Trs* at para 42.
[141] See the further discussion of these issues in **4.2.1–4.2.3**.
[142] This case is discussed in **4.2.1**.
[143] *@SIPP Pension Trs* at para 44.
[144] *@SIPP Pension Trs* at para 36.
[145] *@SIPP Pension Trs* at para 37.
[146] *@SIPP Pension Trs* at para 38.
[147] *Arnold v Britton* [2015] UKSC 36, [2015] 2 WLR 1593, discussed in **4.2.1**.

contractual interpretation. As a result of *@SIPP*, it is suggested that provisions giving the landlord the right to seek payment from the tenant are enforceable, provided they are sufficiently clear.[148] Indeed, in *Tonsley 2 Trust Trs v Scottish Enterprise*[149] Lord Doherty followed *@SIPP* notwithstanding that the clause in question was in similar terms to the clause in *Mapeley Acquisitions Co (3) Ltd (in receivership) v City of Edinburgh Council*,[150] in which he had previously followed the decision in *Grove*.[151] In *Tonsley*, Lord Doherty noted that the decision in *@SIPP* had provided important guidance, which was applicable in this case, and which he was bound to follow.[152] The clause in *Tonsley* was closer to the provision in *@SIPP* than to that in *Grove*.[153]

5.4.3 Irritancy

There are two forms of irritancy: legal irritancy and conventional irritancy. The former is a right to irritate by operation of law, without the need for any express provision to that effect in the lease. There is one ground of legal irritancy: non-payment of rent for two years.[154] As such legal irritancy is not a remedy available to a landlord for breach by the tenant of his repairing obligations. Conventional irritancy arises where express provision is made in the lease. A commercial lease will normally make provision allowing the landlord to irritate the lease in certain circumstances. Generally a commercial lease will provide that the landlord will be entitled to irritate the lease on the following grounds: non-payment of rent or other sums due under the lease; breach by the tenant of any of his non-monetary obligations under the lease; the tenant becoming insolvent.[155] Conventional irritancy may therefore be a remedy open to the landlord where the tenant has not complied with his obligations in relation to the condition of the premises.[156] Where this option is open to a landlord, he may decide not to use it as it may be better for the landlord to have a tenant in the premises, albeit one who is not fully complying with his lease obligations, rather than bring the lease to an end.

The right to irritate may be subject to certain conditions specified in the lease, such as the landlord giving notice to the tenant of remediable breaches and giving him a period of time to remedy them before irritating the lease.[157] Even where the lease provides the landlord with an unconditional right to irritate, the landlord's

---

[148] It is unlikely that such clauses will be held to be penalties if the landlord seeks the cost of works given the landlord's legitimate interest in the repairing obligations being complied with: see *Makdessi v Cavendish Square Holdings BV* [2015] UKSC 67, [2016] AC 1172.
[149] *Tonsley 2 Trust Trs v Scottish Enterprise* [2016] CSOH 138, 2016 GWD 31-554.
[150] *Mapeley Acquisitions Co (3) Ltd (in receivership) v City of Edinburgh Council* [2015] CSOH 29, 2015 GWD 13-234.
[151] Indeed Lord Doherty noted that if he had had the benefit of the guidance provided in *@SIPP* and *Arnold v Britton* he would likely have found in favour of the landlord rather than for the tenant: see *Tonsley 2 Trust Trs v Scottish Enterprise* [2016] CSOH 138 at para 24, 2016 GWD 31-554.
[152] *Tonsley 2 Trust Trs* at para 21.
[153] *Tonsley 2 Trust Trs* at para 20.
[154] McAllister, *Scottish Law of Leases*, para 5.4.
[155] See clause 13 of Schedule Part 16 of the style multi-occupancy lease in *Greens Practice Styles: Commercial Leases*, pp 113–211.
[156] For discussion of the landlord's remedy of irritancy more generally see McAllister, *Scottish Law of Leases*, ch 5 and Rennie et al, *Leases*, ch 17.
[157] This is provided in clause 13.3 of Schedule Part 16 of the style multi-occupancy lease in *Greens Practice Styles: Commercial Leases*, pp 113–211.

right is restricted due to the Law Reform (Miscellaneous Provisions) (Scotland) Act 1985, section 5. This section provides that a landlord shall not be entitled to rely on a provision in the lease which purports to enable the landlord to terminate it[158] if in all the circumstances of the case a fair and reasonable landlord would not seek so to rely. Section 5(3) further provides that where a breach of the lease is capable of being remedied in reasonable time, regard will be had to whether a reasonable opportunity has been afforded to the tenant to remedy the breach in considering whether a fair and reasonable landlord would seek to rely on the breach. As such, prior to irritating the lease for breach of the tenant's repairing obligation, the landlord will have to notify the tenant of the breaches of the lease and give him a reasonable time to remedy them.

5.4.3.1 *Giving time to remedy the breach*

What is a reasonable time will depend on the works needed to bring the premises up to the standard required by the lease. Prior to giving any such notice a landlord would be well advised to discuss matters with a surveyor to find out how long the works are likely to take, bearing in mind the extent of the works and the time of year that the works will have to be carried out.[159] Where a landlord issued a notice to a tenant requiring an undertaking, within seven days from the date of the notice, that specified works would be carried out; that workmen would be on site within 21 days from the date of the notice to commence the works; and that the works would be completed within 60 days of the notice, he was held not to have given the tenant a reasonable opportunity to remedy the breach.[160] This was despite the fact that prior to the notice being served on the tenant requiring him to do the works, under threat of irritancy, the tenant had been advised that works needed to be carried out and had engaged in meetings with the landlord and others in relation to the works. The tenant's expert was of the opinion that it would take nine to twelve months to complete the works. Lord Macfadyen found that the timetable set by the landlord was impossible for anyone to comply with – accordingly, the tenant had not been given a reasonable opportunity to remedy the breach of the lease.[161]

5.4.3.2 *The fair and reasonable landlord test*

The test set out in section 5 of the 1985 Act requires consideration of "all the circumstances of the case" in determining whether a fair and reasonable landlord would rely on the tenant's breach to irritate the lease. It has been recognised that this is a wide test.[162] However, case law has indicated some limits on the circumstances

---

[158] As noted in **5.3.5** this provision applies to a landlord rescinding the lease as well as irritancy.
[159] Certain works may take a longer period during more difficult weather conditions.
[160] *Euro Properties Scotland Ltd v Khurshied Alam and Randall Mitchell* 2000 GWD 23-896; official transcript available at https://www.scotcourts.gov.uk/search-judgments/judgment?id=125487a6-8980-69d2-b500-ff0000d74aa7.
[161] *Euro Properties Scotland Lt*d at para 34.
[162] *Blythswood Investments (Scotland) Ltd v Clydesdale Electrical Stores Ltd (in receivership)* 1995 SLT 150 per Lord Cullen at 155, quoted with approval by Lord Macfadyen in *Aubrey Investments Ltd v DSC (Realisations) Ltd (in receivership)* 1999 SC 21 at 42. See also *Irritancy of Leases* in Land (Scots Law Com DP No 117, 2001) para 3.42. *Aspects of Leases: Termination* (Scots Law Com DP No 165, 2018) notes that the scope of s 5 can often lead to lengthy proofs, para 7.15.

that can be taken into account. The fair and reasonable landlord has the knowledge of the particular landlord in question. As such, circumstances that the landlord did not know about are not taken into account in determining whether he has acted as a fair and reasonable landlord would. However, where it is shown that a fair and reasonable landlord would have made inquiries that the actual landlord did not make, the fair and reasonable landlord has the additional knowledge that would have been obtained in making those further inquiries.[163] In addition, the time at which the landlord will be judged, to determine if he is acting as a fair and reasonable landlord would, is the time at which the landlord issues the notice irritating the lease.[164] No account is taken of circumstances arising after the landlord issues the notice and before decree of removing is granted. Irritancy is available at the landlord's option. Where the landlord irritates the lease that brings it to an end without the need for a decree to that effect.[165] Looking at events after termination of the lease, by the landlord irritating, involves directing attention away from the landlord's decision to irritate.[166]

Section 5 sets out a single criterion, which is to consider how a fair and reasonable landlord would behave in a given set of circumstances.[167] However, that does not preclude examining the separate elements of the criterion if different aspects of the circumstances bring them into focus in different ways.[168] The purpose of the test is to provide an objective criterion against which to consider the actions of the actual landlord.[169] It does not depend on what the court thinks is fair and reasonable.[170] The landlord may take a different view of the situation from the court but that does not necessarily mean that the landlord is not acting as a fair and reasonable landlord.[171] Furthermore, the fact that some landlords would refrain from irritating the lease does not establish that a fair and reasonable landlord would not irritate. Allowance must be made for the unduly lenient landlord, and the landlord who has his own reasons not to irritate. The fair and reasonable landlord test will only be failed if it can be shown that any landlord adhering to standards of fairness and reasonableness would, in all the circumstances, decide not to irritate.[172]

The fair and reasonable landlord test cannot be reduced to a balance of hardship. The factors to be weighed in the balance are not capable of being reduced to a

---

[163] *Aubrey Investments Ltd v DSC (Realisations) Ltd (in receivership)* 1999 SC 21 at 42.

[164] *Maris v Banchory Squash Racquets Club Ltd* [2007] CSIH 30; 2007 SC 501 at para 18; *Aubrey Investments Ltd* at 44, cf Lord Macfadyen's position on this issue in *Euro Properties Scotland Ltd v Khurshied Alam and Randall Mitchell* 2000 GWD 23-896 at para 45 but the Inner House in *Maris* found this to be unsound: see para 22.

[165] Although the landlord may seek declarator of irritancy in his action of removing against the tenant.

[166] *Maris v Banchory Squash Racquets Club Ltd* [2007] CSIH 30, 2007 SC 501 at para 18.

[167] *Maris v Banchory Squash Racquets Club* at para 24; *Aubrey Investments Ltd v DSC (Realisations) Ltd (in receivership)* 1999 SC 21 at 44.

[168] *Euro Properties Scotland Ltd v Khurshied Alam and Randall Mitchell* 2000 GWD 23-896 at para 24.

[169] *Aubrey Investments Ltd v DSC (Realisations) Ltd (in receivership)* 1999 SC 21 at 44.

[170] *Aubrey Investments Ltd* at 42; *Blythswood Investments (Scotland) Ltd v Clydesdale Electrical Stores Ltd (in receivership)* 1995 SLT 150 at 155.

[171] A similar approach is taken in relation to a landlord's consent to assignation, where his consent is not to be unreasonably withheld – see, e.g., *Burgerking Ltd v Rachel's Charitable Trust Ltd* 2006 SLT 224.

[172] *Aubrey Investments Ltd v DSC (Realisations) Ltd (in receivership)* 1999 SC 21 at 45.

common unit of measurement.[173] A fair and reasonable landlord would not ignore his own commercial interests.[174] However, he would not look exclusively to his own interests and would take account of the impact which irritancy would have on the tenant's interests.[175] The mere fact that a particular course of action brings collateral benefit to the landlord does not taint it with unfairness and unreasonableness.[176] It has been said that the most difficult part of applying the fair and reasonable landlord test is to judge what weight is to be attached to each of the multifarious considerations that such a landlord would take into account from all the circumstances of the case. All that can be done, after a critical examination of all the circumstances, is to take an overall view, bearing in mind that the fair and reasonable landlord is one who is prepared to irritate the lease unless it is unfair and unreasonable to do so.[177] It is for the tenant to show that the landlord is not acting as a fair and reasonable landlord would.[178]

As will be apparent from the discussion above, the judiciary have experienced difficulties when applying the fair and reasonable landlord test.[179] It has been noted that the width of the test has created difficulties for the courts.[180] Indeed, the Scottish Law Commission has found that the need to examine all of the circumstances of the case may lead to expensive and protracted proof hearings. The Commission has also found evidence to suggest that irritancy no longer operates as an effective remedy in many cases.[181] Given these problems the Commission, in 2003, recommended reform of the law of irritancy.[182] However, the Commission's recommendations have not been implemented. More recently, the Commission has consulted on whether the law of irritancy currently requires reform.[183]

5.4.3.3 *Irritating for breach of the repairing obligation*

In relation to what a fair and reasonable landlord would do where a tenant has breached his repairing obligations, Lord Macfadyen has noted that irritancy is a course "rarely adopted by fair and reasonable landlords".[184] A fair and reasonable landlord is more likely to carry out the works and seek the cost of doing so from the

---

[173] *Aubrey Investments* at 45.
[174] *Aubrey Investments* at 50.
[175] *Aubrey Investments* at 45.
[176] *Aubrey Investments* at 50.
[177] *Aubrey Investments* at 50.
[178] *Aubrey Investments* at 43.
[179] *Blythswood Investments (Scotland) Ltd v Clydesdale Electrical Stores Ltd (in receivership)* 1995 SLT 150 per Lord Cullen at 155–56; see also the difficulties experienced by Lord Macfadyen in applying the test in *Aubrey Investments Ltd v DSC (Realisations) Ltd (in receivership)* 1999 SC 21.
[180] Report on *Irritancy of Leases in Land* (Scots Law Com No 191, 2003) paras 1.11–1.14; *Irritancy of Leases in Land* (Scots Law Com DP No 117, 2001) paras 3.39–3.48, in particular paras 3.44–3.48. This has been reiterated in the recent Discussion Paper on *Aspects of Leases: Termination* (Scots Law Com DP No 165, 2018) para 7.15.
[181] Report on *Irritancy of Leases in Land*, para 1.14.
[182] The recommendations for reform are set out in Chapter 3 of the Report on *Irritancy of Leases in Land*.
[183] Discussion Paper on *Aspects of Leases: Termination*, para 7.27.
[184] *Euro Properties Scotland Ltd v Khurshied Alam and Randall Mitchell* 2000 GWD 23-896 at para 40.

tenant.[185] By irritating the lease, the landlord would deprive the tenant of carrying on his business from the premises. This would lead to a reduced chance that the tenant would be in a position to pay the cost of the works to the landlord.[186] Furthermore, by irritating the lease the landlord would deprive himself of the rental income from the premises. While the landlord may be able to re-let, if there was an available market, there would likely be a delay in doing so and, as such, a period within which the landlord would receive no rent from the premises. As a result, irritating the lease would be in the landlord's interests only if by doing so a more favourable lease could be entered into, with a rental stream better than that under the irritated lease by a sufficient margin to outweigh the disadvantages in interrupting the rental stream.[187] As noted above, a fair and reasonable landlord might not necessarily come to the same view as the court, and might come to the view that irritating would be in his financial interests when the court has a more pessimistic view. However, a fair and reasonable landlord would consider the financial implications of irritating the lease prior to doing so. In *Euro Properties Scotland*[188] the court found that the landlord had not taken any advice on his ability to re-let the premises and on what terms. A fair and reasonable landlord would not have done so.

5.4.3.4 *Oppression*

Having considered the statutory controls on the landlord's right to irritate, a few words should be said regarding the common law defence of oppression. This defence is available where the landlord is using the right to irritate oppressively, that is where he is abusing or misusing his right to irritate.[189] Oppression requires some impropriety of conduct on the part of the landlord, who is using irritancy to procure unfair consequences on the tenant.[190]

While the defence exists,[191] it is not often used by tenants seeking to challenge irritancy. This is because a defence of oppression is unlikely to succeed.[192] Indeed, there have been no cases since the 19th century where oppression has been used successfully.[193] Oppression has been interpreted narrowly, with the courts not wishing to interfere with the right to irritate that parties have expressly agreed to in the lease.[194] The narrow scope of the defence can be seen in *HMV Fields Properties Ltd v Skirt 'n' Slack Centre of London Ltd*[195] in which Lord Mayfield had to consider

---

[185] Assuming the landlord has a right to do so – as to which see **5.4.1**.
[186] *Euro Properties Scotland* at para 40.
[187] *Euro Properties Scotland* at para 40.
[188] *Euro Properties Scotland Ltd v Khurshied Alam and Randall Mitchell* 2000 GWD 23-896.
[189] *Lucas's Executor v Demarco* 1968 SLT 89 per Lord Guthrie at 96.
[190] *Lucas's Executor v Demarco* per Lord Guthrie at 96.
[191] The Scottish Law Commission recommended that it be abolished: see *Report on Irritancy of Leases in Land*, paras 3.11–3.12, although the Commission has recently consulted on whether the law of irritancy currently requires reform: see Discussion Paper on *Aspects of Leases: Termination*, para 7.27.
[192] McAllister, *Scottish Law of Leases*, para 5.16.
[193] McAllister, *Scottish Law of Leases*, para 5.16, although see McAllister's argument that greater use may be made of the defence in the future: paras 5.19–5.20.
[194] See Lord President Clyde's comments in *Lucas's Executor v Demarco* 1968 SLT 89 at 95; Lord Fraser in *Dorchester Studios (Glasgow) Ltd v Stone* 1975 SC (HL) 56 at 72.
[195] *HMV Fields Properties Ltd v Skirt 'n' Slack Centre of London Ltd* 1982 SLT 477.

whether a landlord had validly irritated a lease for non-payment of rent. The pursuer landlord notified the defender tenant that it had become landlord of the premises two days before the rent was due. The landlord had done so by sending a notice and invoice for the rent in a buff envelope to the leased premises. The tenant did not think that the envelope contained important information and, as was the tenant company's practice, sent the envelope on to the tenant company's head office to be actioned. It was not until some time after the rent had become due that the tenant paid the rent. The landlord sought to irritate the lease as the rent had not been paid on time. Lord Mayfield found that for oppression to be established it must be shown that there was clear abuse or impropriety of conduct by the landlord.[196] He held that the landlord's motive in irritating the lease was irrelevant.[197] The tenant averred that the landlord had irritated the lease because directors of the landlord company were also directors of a separate company, which was a trade competitor of the tenant. The trade competitor had premises directly across the street from the leased premises. The tenant argued that the landlord's motivation in irritating the lease was to remove it as a trade competitor of that other company. This was found to be irrelevant in determining whether there was oppression. Finally, Lord Mayfield stated that the failure by the tenant to pay the rent was an oversight on the part of the tenant. That oversight had not been adequately explained. In Lord Mayfield's opinion it was necessary that the tenant's oversight be excluded before the defence of oppression could be relevant.[198]

5.4.3.5 Use of irritancy as a remedy

As will be apparent from the discussion above, it is likely to be difficult for a landlord of a commercial lease to irritate for breach of the tenant's repairing obligations, and for that reason it is seldom used as a remedy for breach of that obligation. In summary, there are a number of difficulties for the landlord in seeking to utilise this remedy:

(a) It has been held that a fair and reasonable landlord is unlikely to irritate the lease where he has the ability to do the works and claim the costs of doing so from the tenant.[199] An FRI lease will usually provide for this. As such, a landlord would likely have to be able to point to particular facts and circumstances such that a fair and reasonable landlord would nonetheless irritate the lease.[200]

(b) There are several potential grounds for challenging an irritancy, which mean that it is not an attractive remedy for a landlord. Prior to irritating the landlord must give the tenant a reasonable opportunity to remedy his breaches of the lease. Whether a reasonable period has been given to the tenant may be disputed. Thereafter, the tenant may question whether a fair and reasonable landlord would irritate, which may result in a lengthy and

---

[196] *HMV Fields Properties Ltd* at 481.
[197] *HMV Fields Properties Ltd* at 481.
[198] *HMV Fields Properties Ltd* at 481.
[199] *Euro Properties Scotland Ltd v Khurshied Alam and Randall Mitchell* 2000 GWD 23-896 per Lord Macfadyen at para 40.
[200] In this way the burden of proof seems to be inverted.

costly court action with the court having to hear evidence on a range of circumstances surrounding the landlord's decision to irritate.

That said, a landlord faced with a tenant in breach of his repairing obligations may as a first step issue a notice requiring the wants of repair to be carried out within a reasonable period, under threat of irritancy. If the tenant does not remedy the breaches specified in that notice he takes the risk that the landlord will seek to irritate at the expiry of the period given to the tenant to do so.

5.5 EFFECT OF TENANT'S BREACH OF REPAIRING OBLIGATION ON RIGHTS THE TENANT HAS UNDER THE LEASE

As noted in **5.3.4** above, breach of repairing obligations by the tenant may allow the landlord to retain performance of obligations incumbent upon him. Breach by the tenant of his repairing obligations can also impact on the exercise of particular rights that the tenant may have under the lease; for example, an option to purchase the leased subjects[201] or a break option in terms of which the tenant can bring the lease to an end earlier than the full term. Tenants and those advising them should be alive to this issue where a tenant is considering exercising any such rights.

Breach by the tenant of his repairing obligations may result in him losing the benefit of an option to purchase the leased subjects.[202] It has been held that where a tenant is in material breach of his repairing obligations under a lease that will not prevent him from exercising the break option and thereby accelerating lease end.[203] The reason for this is that the principle of mutuality allows the party not in breach, the landlord, to withhold performance of his contractual obligations, when faced with a breach by the tenant. However, when the tenant exercises a break there is no counterpart obligation that the landlord must perform that he can then withhold.[204] The tenant's right to terminate is "unilateral".[205] However, the lease might expressly provide that the break option cannot be exercised where the tenant is in breach of any of his obligations under the lease.[206] If that is the case a condition for exercising the right to terminate the lease early will not be met where the tenant is in breach of his repairing obligations, such that the tenant will not be able to utilise the break option.

5.6 TENANT'S REMEDIES FOR BREACH OF THE LANDLORD'S OBLIGATIONS IN RELATION TO THE CONDITION OF THE PROPERTY

An FRI lease will generally not impose obligations on a landlord in relation to the condition of the leased premises. However, exceptionally, a commercial lease may provide that some aspect of repair of the premises will be undertaken by the

---

[201] For discussion see **5.3.4**.
[202] *McCall's Entertainments (Ayr) Ltd v South Ayrshire Council (No 1)* 1998 SLT 1403; see the discussion on this issue at **5.3.4**.
[203] *Allied Dunbar Assurance plc v Superglass Sections Ltd* 2003 SLT 1420.
[204] *Allied Dunbar Assurance plc* at 1423.
[205] *Allied Dunbar Assurance plc* per Lord Eassie at 1423.
[206] As was the case in *Arlington Business Parks GP Ltd v Scottish & Newcastle Ltd* [2014] CSOH 77, 2014 GWD 14-261.

landlord. As such, it is important that the terms of the lease are checked. Breach by the landlord of an obligation regarding repair is more likely to arise in relation to a landlord's obligations to maintain and keep common parts of the property in good condition and repair.[207]

A commercial lease is unlikely to make express provision for remedies available to the tenant on breach of the lease by the landlord. For present purposes, it is sufficient to note that the remedies available to a tenant for breach by the landlord of his repairing obligations are the same as the common law remedies available to a landlord discussed in **5.3** above. It should be noted that the heads of loss for damages would be assessed on a different basis, with the tenant receiving damages for any losses caused by the landlord's breach of the lease. A tenant faced with breach of the lease by the landlord may seek to retain his performance under the lease.[208] As noted above, the lease will impose more obligations on the tenant than on the landlord. The tenant may retain performance of any obligations that are counterparts of the landlord's repairing obligation.[209] One of the most significant obligations on a tenant under a lease will be paying the rent. In many FRI leases, parties contract out of the common law right of retention insofar as the tenant's obligation to pay rent is concerned, with the lease providing that the tenant must pay the rent without any deductions, retentions, rights of set-off or counter-claims.[210] This means that the tenant is unable to retain payment of the rent in response to the landlord's breach of the lease. Finally, while section 5 of the Law Reform (Miscellaneous Provisions) (Scotland) Act 1985 places controls on the landlord's right to terminate the lease, whether by rescission or irritancy, those controls do not apply to the tenant's ability to rescind the lease for material breach by the landlord.[211]

---

[207] As to which see Chapter 6.
[208] Retention can be used to seek to force the landlord to perform his obligations or to secure a damages claim the tenant may have against the landlord due to the landlord's breach: see L Richardson, "The scope and limits of the right to retain contractual performance" 2018 Jur Rev 209; Rennie et al, *Leases* paras 17.53–17.54.
[209] See the discussion of this and the other requirements for retention of performance at **5.3.4**.
[210] See clause 1.3 of Schedule Part 7 of the style multi-occupancy lease in *Greens Practice Styles: Commercial Leases*, pp 113–211.
[211] For discussion of material breach entitling rescission see **5.3.5**.

Chapter 6
Common Parts and Service Charge

6.1 INTRODUCTION

Having considered obligations placed upon the tenant in relation to the condition of the leased premises in Chapter 4, this chapter considers obligations in relation to those parts of the building, within which the leased premises are situated, that are not leased to a tenant. Often these parts of the building are common parts. This chapter discusses the obligations a commercial FRI lease may place on the landlord in relation to the building (in particular, the common parts) as well as the tenant's obligation to pay service charge. The landlord of a multi-occupancy building[1] is likely to retain various obligations in relation to the repair and maintenance of the building. He will typically recover the cost of performing those obligations through payment of a service charge by the tenants of the building.

This chapter begins by considering what a common part of a building is, before going on to discuss the obligations placed on the landlord in relation to common parts. Services which the landlord may provide in relation to the building are also considered. The tenant's obligation to pay service charge is then analysed. Payment of service charge and works to common parts are often areas of dispute between landlord and tenant. The main areas where such disputes arise are highlighted and some steps that may be taken to prevent disagreements are identified. The chapter concludes by setting out remedies available to both parties when faced with a breach by the other in relation to the common parts and service charge.

6.2 WHAT IS TYPICALLY A COMMON PART AND WHY?

What a common part is depends on the lease in question. It is, therefore, essential that the terms of the lease are consulted to determine how a common part is defined in it. Common parts are generally found in multi-occupancy buildings, as discussed in Chapter 2. The common parts of a building are usually those parts of the building that are not leased to any tenant. Typical examples of parts of a building that are common parts[2] include the structure of the building (external walls and roof) including the foundations; escape, service and fire corridors; lift shafts, escalators and stairs; and common areas such as reception areas and atria.[3] Common parts will often

---

[1] As to which see **2.3**.
[2] Consideration is given to services the landlord is to provide in relation to the building in **6.3**.
[3] See, e.g., clauses 2 and 3 of Schedule Part 2 of the style multi-occupancy lease in *Greens Practice Styles: Commercial Leases*, pp 113–211.

include areas of ground around and serving the building – for example, car parks; access roads; yards and delivery areas; boundary walls and fences; and landscaped areas.[4] Media for providing services are also often included within the definition of the common parts, and this would include items such as pipes, drains, conduits and cables.[5] Some leases may provide that service media are common parts where they do not exclusively serve any premises let to any of the tenants. Mechanical and electrical plant and equipment used in the building are also frequently included. This would include items such as lifts and their related machinery; heating and lighting systems; fire alarm and security systems.[6]

It can be important to determine whether the part of the building in need of attention is part of the premises let to a tenant (in which case the repair will be the tenant's responsibility, in terms of his repairing obligation) or whether the part in question is a common part (in which case it will be the landlord's responsibility). A landlord of a multi-occupancy building will generally want to ensure that the entirety of the building falls within either the definition of the premises let to each tenant or the definition of the common parts. If there is a part of the building that does not fall within either of those definitions, the landlord will be responsible for repair and maintenance of that part[7] without being able to recover the costs of doing so from the tenants of the building in the service charge.

It should be noted that there is no common law in relation to what is or is not a common part[8] that can be called upon to deal with any gaps in the express provisions of the lease.[9] It is, therefore, crucial that adequate provision is made regarding the common parts of a commercial property, as well as the service charge provisions. Where the drafting gives rise to doubt, the matter is determined using the ordinary rules for the interpretation of contracts.[10] As such, a lease is likely to define common parts broadly, such as "all parts and pertinents of the building excepting premises let to tenants",[11] before going on to set out in more detail that the common parts

---

[4] See, e.g., clauses 4–6 and 10 of Schedule Part 2 of the style multi-occupancy lease in *Greens Practice Styles: Commercial Leases*, pp 113–211.

[5] See, e.g., clause 7 of Schedule Part 2 and clause 1.1.43 of the style multi-occupancy lease in *Greens Practice Styles: Commercial Leases*, pp 113–211.

[6] See, e.g., clause 8 of Schedule Part 2 and Schedule Part 3 of the style multi-occupancy lease in *Greens Practice Styles: Commercial Leases*, pp 113–211.

[7] Although he will not have obligations regarding the repair or maintenance of that part in terms of the leases with his tenants, he will have certain obligations in relation to the condition of that part of the property, e.g. under the Occupiers' Liability (Scotland) Act 1961 or the Building (Scotland) Act 2003.

[8] *Marfield Properties v Secretary of State for the Environment* 1996 SC 362.

[9] Cf *Dolby Medical Home Respiratory Care Ltd v Mortara Dolby UK Ltd* [2016] CSOH 74, 2016 GWD 19-344 where Lord Woolman noted in relation to a licence to occupy, that where the term "common parts" was used but not defined it is generally understood to refer to areas from which both parties derive benefit and where there is a dispute about what constitutes a common part this can be the subject of evidence: see para 15.

[10] *Marfield Properties v Secretary of State for the Environment* 1996 SC 362. The court noted, at 365, that it would not interpret the provision in question *contra proferentem* against the landlord, as it is assumed that commercial leases were entered into between two parties on an equal footing with the lease terms being agreed by mutual adjustment. This case is discussed in **2.4.3**. For the rules of interpretation of contracts see **4.2**.

[11] See, e.g., the introductory wording of Schedule Part 2 of the style multi-occupancy lease in *Greens Practice Styles: Commercial Leases*, pp 113–211.

include, but are not limited to, various items,[12] such as those mentioned above. To avoid disputes, the lease should contain as much detail as possible regarding what the common parts include.

As discussed in Chapter 4, in an FRI lease a landlord seeks to contract out of all of his common law obligations regarding the condition of the leased premises. Why then does the landlord of a multi-occupancy building, who has agreed FRI leases with his tenants, retain obligations in relation to the common parts? It is suggested that there are two principal reasons for this. The first is that many of the common parts are crucial to the integrity of the landlord's building and, as such, his investment. For instance, if repairs are required to the external walls of the building and these are not carried out when required this may have grave consequences. The problem is likely to become worse as time passes, with the result that more significant repairs will eventually have to be carried out. The second reason for retaining obligations in relation to the common parts is a practical one. There may be a number of tenants in the building. In a shopping centre, for example, there might be 30 or more different tenants. It is unlikely that the tenants would be able to come together and agree on a course of works to the common parts.[13] Even where the tenants could agree, it would likely take some time to consult with each other and agree on the proposed works. By retaining responsibility for the common parts, the landlord does not need to consult with, and obtain the agreement of, all of the tenants regarding works to the common parts.[14] The works can, therefore, be carried out more quickly by the landlord than by seeking agreement among the tenants.

6.3 OBLIGATIONS IN RELATION TO COMMON PARTS AND SERVICES

Having identified parts of the property likely to be common parts in a commercial lease, consideration will now be given to what the landlord is required to do in relation to the common parts. Again, this is determined by the terms of the lease. The lease should set out that the landlord is obliged to carry out works and provide services in relation to the common parts, rather than there simply being provision for payment for such works or services by the tenant, should the landlord wish to carry them out.

The obligations imposed on the landlord regarding the common parts will impact on the tenants' service charge liability. Accordingly, the tenants have an interest in ensuring that the obligations are not too wide, thereby allowing the landlord to carry out extensive work which the tenants will have to pay for. The tenants will, however, want to ensure that the common parts will be adequately repaired and maintained,

---

[12] See the introductory wording of Schedule Part 2 of the style multi-occupancy lease in *Greens Practice Styles: Commercial Leases*, pp 113–211.

[13] Consider the difficulties experienced by owners of tenement properties, which the introduction of the Tenant Management Scheme by the Tenements (Scotland) Act 2004 has tried to alleviate.

[14] Unless the lease so provides. While the landlord may not be obliged, in terms of the lease, to consult with tenants transparency and communication are noted as core principles in dealing with service charge by the Royal Institute of Chartered Surveyors: see RICS Professional Statement on *Service Charges in Commercial Property* (2018), available at http://www.rics.org/uk/upholding-professional-standards/sector-standards/real-estate/service-charges-in-commercial-property-1st-edition, pp 11–12.

to allow them to carry out their business from the premises let in the building. For example, tenants on the top floor of a shopping centre have a clear interest in knowing that the lifts and escalators will be adequately repaired and maintained by the landlord, as without these items being in good working order their businesses will suffer from lower footfall.

In an FRI lease of a multi-occupancy building the landlord will generally:

- be obliged to repair and maintain, and if necessary, renew, rebuild and reinstate the common parts. This obligation is frequently stated to apply regardless of the age or state of dilapidation of the common parts or the cause of damage, destruction or deterioration.[15] This means that the landlord is obliged to do the work, and the tenants will have to pay for it, even where the work is an extraordinary repair, for which the landlord would be liable at common law,[16] and regardless of the reason for the repair;[17]
- be under an obligation to decorate the common parts;[18] keep them clean and tidy;[19] lit; and heated or cooled as appropriate;[20]
- be responsible for inspection, operation and servicing of plant and equipment and service media.[21] This means that the landlord must inspect and service, for instance, the lifts, generators and boilers in the building, where those items come within the definition of common parts; and
- carry out works to the common parts to ensure that they comply with statute.[22]

Where the landlord proposes to carry out works to the building, he or his solicitor should carefully check the terms of the lease as to whether the works proposed fall within his obligations in relation to the common parts.[23]

As well as the lease obliging the landlord to repair, maintain and replace the common parts, an FRI lease of a multi-occupancy building is also likely to require the landlord to provide certain services in relation to the common parts. These might include paying the rates[24] and other outgoings such as electricity and water.[25]

---

[15] See clause 1.1.1 of Schedule Part 11 of the style multi-occupancy lease in *Greens Practice Styles: Commercial Leases*, pp 113–211.
[16] For the landlord's common law repairing obligations see **3.2** and **3.3**.
[17] Although note the comment below that a tenant should seek to exclude paying for works as a result of problems with the design and/or construction of the building.
[18] See clause 1.1.2 of Schedule Part 11 of the style multi-occupancy lease in *Greens Practice Styles: Commercial Leases*, pp 113–211.
[19] Clause 1.1.3 of Schedule Part 11 of the style multi-occupancy lease in *Greens Practice Styles: Commercial Leases*, pp 113–211.
[20] Clauses 1.1.3–1.1.5 of Schedule Part 11 of the style multi-occupancy lease in *Greens Practice Styles: Commercial Leases*, pp 113–211.
[21] Clause 1.8.3 of Schedule Part 11 of the style multi-occupancy lease in *Greens Practice Styles: Commercial Leases*, pp 113–211.
[22] Clause 9 of Schedule Part 11 of the style multi-occupancy lease in *Greens Practice Styles: Commercial Leases*, pp 113–211.
[23] See **6.4.1** *et seq* for discussion of the extent of the landlord's obligation.
[24] Clause 1.3 of Schedule Part 11 of the style multi-occupancy lease in *Greens Practice Styles: Commercial Leases*, pp 113–211.
[25] Clause 1.4 of Schedule Part 11 of the style multi-occupancy lease in *Greens Practice Styles: Commercial Leases*, pp 113–211.

The lease may also require the landlord to provide other goods and services such as containers for refuse disposal, arranging refuse collection from the building,[26] or operating the car park.[27]

In a shopping centre, the services may include steps taken by the landlord to promote the centre. In *Boots UK Ltd v Trafford Centre Ltd*,[28] the court found that Christmas decorations, a Santa grotto, entertainment and an advertising screen (to the extent that it advertised external parties or individual retailers, rather than provided information about the centre) did not fall within "promotion", defined in the lease as "advertising and other forms of promotion of the Centre intended to bring additional custom to the Centre". While these features could be described as benefits, attractions or facilities, they were not forms of promotion.

The services to be provided by the landlord may extend to the landlord employing people to carry out services in relation to the building. The lease may provide that the landlord is to employ security staff for the building[29] or managing agents to manage the building.[30] The lease will also normally provide that the landlord is responsible for providing any premises within the building that such staff require to carry out their functions.[31] In *Douglas Shelf Seven Ltd v Co-operative Wholesale Society Ltd*,[32] the lease required the tenant to pay a proportion of repairs to and insurance of the common parts, the "professional charges of the Landlord's surveyors, as common factors of the whole subjects" in connection with those payments, and "in general in connection with the management and administration of the whole subjects". The landlord argued that this provision was wide enough to include the costs of providing security guards and other security services for the property, which costs the landlord's surveyors had invoiced to the tenants. The court disagreed, holding that the provision required the tenants to pay the surveyors' professional charges, which required that the charges related to their profession. As such, the tenants were liable only for the cost of the surveyors' professional activities in providing services in relation to the property, and not for any outlay that they had incurred on the landlord's behalf.

From the discussion above, it will be apparent that the obligations imposed on the landlord can extend beyond works to the common parts and can include services in relation to the building as a whole. Many leases also include what is known as a "sweeper clause". This is a clause that permits the landlord to

---

[26] Clause 1.7 of Schedule Part 11 of the style multi-occupancy lease in *Greens Practice Styles: Commercial Leases*, pp 113–211.
[27] Clause 10 of Schedule Part 11 of the style multi-occupancy lease in *Greens Practice Styles: Commercial Leases*, pp 113–211.
[28] *Boots UK Ltd v Trafford Centre Ltd* 2008 EWHC 3372 (Ch). In this case the tenant was arguing that the disputed items fell within the definition of promotion because in that event the landlord was liable for 50% of the costs; the parties agreed that the disputed items did otherwise properly fall within the service charge, which the tenants had to pay.
[29] Clause 5 of Schedule Part 11 of the style multi-occupancy lease in *Greens Practice Styles: Commercial Leases*, pp 113–211.
[30] Clause 1.14 of Schedule Part 11 of the style multi-occupancy lease in *Greens Practice Styles: Commercial Leases*, pp 113–211.
[31] See clause 1.5 of Schedule Part 11 and clause 1.1.24 of the style multi-occupancy lease in *Greens Practice Styles: Commercial Leases*, pp 113–211.
[32] *Douglas Shelf Seven Ltd v Co-operative Wholesale Society Ltd* [2009] CSOH 3, 2009 GWD 3-56.

provide other services in relation to the building, for which no other provision is made in the lease.[33] While such a clause can be beneficial, especially in a longer term lease where further services, not yet foreseen, might be useful, the tenants have an interest in limiting the scope of such a clause given they will be responsible for paying for any further unspecified services. As such, tenants will not want to give the landlord an unqualified right to provide (and charge for) additional services. Tenants can protect their position by qualifying the landlord's ability to provide such additional services – for instance, by specifying that services may be provided where they are "reasonably necessary" or "in the interests of good estate management".

Given the extent of the landlord's obligations in relation to the common parts and service, and the concomitant obligation on tenants to pay for them, many tenants may be tempted to revise the lease to delete work to be done or services to be provided. It is suggested that tenants do not necessarily benefit from the landlord being restricted in the work to the common parts or services to be provided in relation to the building. As noted above, tenants have an interest in these being performed, so that the building operates well and allows them to carry on their businesses from the leased subjects. Where tenants should be more circumspect is in agreeing which work and services they will pay for.

It should be noted that where a landlord borrows funds in order to do work or provide services, the cost of borrowing is not recoverable from the tenants unless the lease clearly provides for recovery of such costs.[34] The lease should provide that where works are required as a result of damage caused to the building by an insured risk, the costs of such work will be excluded from the service charge. Similar exclusion from the service charge should be made for costs incurred where the landlord carries out redevelopment work to the building during the currency of the lease. It should also be possible, in an appropriate case, to exclude works to the building required as a result of problems incurred in its initial design and construction.[35] This may be particularly important where the tenant leases premises in a newly constructed or refurbished development.[36] A particular issue may be the provision of equipment in the building. The tenants will not want to have to pay for items via the service charge that should have been provided as part of the fitting out of the building.[37] In older buildings, it may be appropriate to record the condition of the common parts at lease commencement,[38] and provide that the tenant will not be obliged to pay for works to the common parts which improve their condition beyond that shown in the schedule of condition.

---

[33] An example can be found in clause 17 of Schedule Part 11 of the style multi-occupancy lease in *Greens Practice Styles: Commercial Leases*, pp 113–211.

[34] *Boldmark Ltd v Cohen* (1987) 19 HLR 135.

[35] The terms of such an exclusion must be clear: see *AWG Business Centres Ltd v Regus Caledonia Ltd and Cheshire West and Chester Council* [2017] CSIH 22, 2017 GWD 9-131.

[36] It has been suggested that a tenant may be prepared to be liable for the costs of such work provided he has collateral warranties or the landlord's rights against the design and construction team assigned to him, together with appropriate insurance: see R Rennie et al, *Leases* (2015) para 26.40. However, the best position for the tenant is to have no liability for the cost of this work and to leave it to the landlord to carry out the work and pursue any rights he may have against the design and/or construction teams.

[37] D Cockburn and R Mitchell, *Commercial Leases* (2nd edn, 2011) para 6.17.

[38] See the discussion of a schedule of condition in para **4.5**.

Beyond this, the exclusions the parties agree on are likely to depend on their respective bargaining strengths and the prevailing market conditions. A tenant might seek to exclude paying for items of plant being replaced with improved systems or the introduction of new items, unless they can be economically justified.[39] To be economically justified, the capital outlay would have to result in ongoing annual savings to the service charge to offset the capital sum expended. Such a provision would allow the landlord to replace items or introduce new ones but would qualify his ability to do so in the interests of the tenants.

Matters between the landlord and other tenants, such as costs associated with entering into new leases, enforcing a particular tenant's obligations under his lease and applications for consent should be explicitly excluded. This is unlikely to be controversial, given the landlord's cost for these matters will generally be recoverable from the tenant in question under his lease. It may be useful to specifically exclude from the service charge work done or costs incurred by the landlord in promoting the development to potential new tenants.

Tenants may also wish to restrict the costs of managing agents' fees, and any management fee levied by the landlord that forms part of the service charge. Managing agents or the landlord's in-house management team are likely to spend some of their time carrying out functions for the landlord in relation to the property that do not benefit the tenants or relate solely to the provision of services. Tenants will wish to pay only for the time that the managing agents or management team are carrying out work related to the provision of services to the building, with the landlord paying the managing agents for any work carried out solely for his benefit. Tenants may wish to limit the amount that can be charged by way of a management fee, either to a financial limit for each year, or by qualifying the obligation to pay such fees to when they relate to work reasonably and necessarily carried out in performing the services which the landlord is obliged to provide under the lease.

As well as considering items that tenants will want to exclude from the service charge expenditure, tenants should also seek to make provision for those common parts that generate income.[40] Where, for instance, the car park is a common part this will be maintained at the tenants' cost via payment of the service charge. Where those parking in the car park are charged for doing so, the car park is generating income. If no provision is made in the lease in relation to this income the landlord will make a profit at the tenants' cost.[41] As such, tenants should seek to provide in the lease that income generated from common parts should be credited to the service charge account,[42] thereby reducing the service charge that the tenants will have to pay.

---

[39] Cockburn and Mitchell, *Commercial Leases*, para 6.18. Such a provision would reinforce the position at common law in relation to the replacement of plant and equipment: see *Fluor Daniel Properties Ltd v Shortlands Investments Ltd* [2001] 2 EGLR 103.
[40] Cockburn and Mitchell, *Commercial Leases*, para 6.24.
[41] The RICS Professional Statement includes mandatory requirements, one of which is that the landlords and their agents must seek to recover no more than 100% of the proper and actual costs of the provision of services: see p 10. Indeed, the Professional Statement provides that where the service charge has either provided the initial capital or ongoing services for the income stream the income is to be treated as a service charge credit: see para 4.11.3.
[42] As to which see **6.5.3**.

6.4 FACTORS TO TAKE INTO ACCOUNT REGARDING WORKS TO COMMON PARTS OR SERVICES

Beyond considering whether the works proposed or carried out by the landlord are to common parts, and chargeable to the tenants through the service charge, there are a number of other factors to be considered.

6.4.1 Whether the costs incurred need to be fair and reasonable

In *Finchbourne Ltd v Rodriguez*,[43] the court implied a term into the lease that the costs claimed from the tenants should be fair and reasonable. In that case, the court found that the parties could not have intended the landlord to have unfettered discretion to adopt the highest conceivable standard in relation to repairs and services and recharge the costs thereof to the tenants. While the case has been followed[44] and also referred to in a number of cases,[45] it has been distinguished in others. In *Victor Harris (Gentswear) Ltd v The Wool Warehouse (Perth) Ltd*,[46] the tenant was obliged to pay the landlord all insurance premiums, with the landlord being entitled to insure the property for such sum as he deemed to represent the full reinstatement value of the property. The tenant refused to pay the premium and argued that there was an implied term that the amount of the premium would be reasonable. The sheriff held that there was no such implied term. He found that the decision in *Finchbourne* was limited to its own facts, and those facts were "totally different" from the facts in the present case. In *Finchbourne*, the matter at issue was whether the landlord could carry out improvements to the property at the tenant's cost. In that situation the sheriff could:

> well understand the need for reasonableness in controlling such costs, as otherwise there would be no limit on a landlord's extravagance in increasing the value of his property with exorbitant improvements for which he did not require to pay and of which he would be the ultimate beneficiary.[47]

As such, whether a fair and reasonable qualification will be implied to costs recoverable from the tenant by way of service charge depends on what the service charge payment relates to. Where it relates to payment of an insurance premium there will be no qualification and the tenant will have to pay the landlord the premiums demanded.[48]

While tenants will have some protection by the implied term discussed above, tenants should seek to protect themselves by express provision in the lease. This is particularly important given that a term will be implied only where necessary for business efficacy or where it is so obvious that it goes without saying.[49] The tenant's

---

[43] *Finchbourne Ltd v Rodriguez* [1976] 3 All ER 581.
[44] *Beech v Kennerley*, 20 October 2010, unreported, although this case did not relate to a lease but to an obligation to contribute to cleansing and maintenance found in the titles to the property.
[45] *Morgan v Stainer* (1993) 25 HLR 467 and *Firstcross Ltd v Teasdale* (1983) 8 HLR 112.
[46] *Victor Harris (Gentswear) Ltd v The Wool Warehouse (Perth) Ltd* 1995 SCLR 577.
[47] *Victor Harris (Gentswear)* at 578.
[48] For cases to the same effect, although without distinguishing *Finchbourne*, see *Haveridge Ltd v Boston Dryers Ltd* (1994) 49 EG 111 and *Berrycroft Management Co Ltd v Sinclair Gardens Investments (Kensington) Ltd* (1997) 29 HLR 444.
[49] *Marks and Spencer plc v BNP Paribas Securities Services Trust Co (Jersey) Ltd* [2015] UKSC 72, [2016] AC 742.

solicitor should, therefore, revise the lease to include express provision that the costs incurred in carrying out works to the common parts or providing services to the building can only form part of the service charge cost where they have been reasonably incurred by the landlord.[50] Furthermore, the tenant's solicitors must ensure that this protection is not rendered redundant by a service charge provision which states that the landlord or his agent will certify the service charge due from the tenant, with the certificate being final, binding or conclusive. Where there is such a provision, it has been held that it prevents the tenant from looking beyond the terms of the certificate to argue that sums included in the service charge were not reasonably incurred.[51]

6.4.2 Determining whether costs are fair and reasonable

Having determined that there is an implied term that certain costs claimed from the tenant by way of service charge should be fair and reasonable, and that it is good practice to include an express term to that effect in the lease, the question is how to decide whether costs are fair and reasonable. In *Scottish Mutual Assurance plc v Jardine Public Relations Ltd*[52] the court had to determine whether work charged to the tenant had been "reasonably and properly incurred". At the outset, the court considered both repair options available to the landlord (short-term cheaper repairs and longer-term, more expensive, repairs), as well as the factors that led the landlord to carry out the more expensive work. The court found that the more expensive repair costs in relation to roof repairs were not reasonably and properly incurred, because the works went significantly beyond what was required for the landlord to perform his contractual obligations to the tenant under the lease. The works carried out were a long-term solution, while the lease in question was only for three years, and the works were instructed within the last six months of the lease. As such, the length of the lease and the extent of the unexpired portion are relevant factors to take into account when determining whether the costs are fair and reasonable. This is an important factor, given that landlords are more likely to be considering works required to the property towards the end of a lease. Leaving consideration of works to common parts until late in the life of the lease could result in successful challenges by tenants. In *Scottish Mutual*, the court was also influenced by the fact that, prior to the more costly works, short-term repairs had been carried out on parts of the roof, and there was no evidence that such repairs were ineffective. Furthermore, the court found that the longer-term roof works were, in fact, instructed because a prospective tenant of the property was prepared to enter into a lease only if the more extensive roof works were carried out, rather than to comply with the landlord's obligations to his existing tenant.

In *Plough Investments Ltd v Manchester City Council*[53] the court noted that, while the landlord's decision on works carried out to common parts had to be reasonable, the tenant could not insist that cheaper works be carried out.[54] The test is whether an owner of the property, bearing the costs himself, might reasonably decide to have

---

[50] In *Lowe v Quayle Munro Ltd* 1997 SC 346 Lord Penrose suggested that "reasonably incurred" and "properly incurred" meant the same thing – see the discussion at 352.
[51] *WW Promotions (Scotland) Ltd v De Marco* 1988 SLT (Sh Ct) 43, discussed in **6.5.3.1**.
[52] *Scottish Mutual Assurance plc v Jardine Public Relations Ltd* [1999] EG 43 (CS).
[53] *Plough Investments Ltd v Manchester City Council* [1984] 1 EGLR 244.
[54] See also *Fluor Daniel Properties Ltd v Shortlands Investments Ltd* [2001] 2 EGLR 103.

carried out the works. It is for the landlord to decide how to go about providing the services he is obliged to provide in terms of the lease, provided he acts reasonably.[55]

A landlord will not be entitled to incur costs, which the tenant is required to pay via the service charge, where the service performed by an item of plant or equipment is being rendered to the standard required by the lease; where the plant or equipment is in proper working order; and the proposed works are not reasonably required to maintain that service.[56] There is thus a clear link between the works to the common parts and whether the works are needed to provide the service the landlord is required to provide in terms of the lease.[57]

It has been noted that whether works amount to repair or renewal is a question of fact and degree in each case.[58] Taking the example of a roof, it might be that parts of the roof are renewed, but this is simply repair of the roof as a whole.[59] The fact that the works can be categorised as repairs rather than replacement does not, however, mean that the costs of the repair works have been fairly and reasonably incurred.[60] That needs to be considered, taking account of the factors discussed above.

It has been held that whether a common part should be repaired or replaced is a question of fact and degree, having regard to the nature and extent of the defect in the common part, and the costs involved in repair and replacement.[61] As such, tenants may be liable for the cost of replacement items, via the service charge, where that is a reasonable course for the landlord to adopt taking into account the disrepair; the cost to carry out a repair or replacement; how effective the repair or replacement will be vis-à-vis the respective costs of each; and the unexpired duration of the lease.

It is not reasonable for a landlord to replace an item of plant and equipment simply because it is at or nearing the end of its economic life.[62] To be able to replace such items, the landlord would generally have to be able to show that the plant or equipment was suffering from a defect such that replacement plant or equipment was needed. Evidence from service records of the frequency and duration of breakdowns, together with details of repairs that could be carried out, the cost of the repairs and their likely improvement to the service provided by the item of plant, and the cost and improvement to the service where the plant is replaced would have to be considered. Where an item of plant is replaced, there is likely to be an element of betterment, given the replacement will be a new item that has been manufactured to modern standards. This is incidental betterment, which the tenant will not be able to object to, provided replacement plant was required rather than repair.[63]

It is suggested that where a landlord has failed to carry out works to the common parts over a period of time, such that the works required become more significant and,

---

[55] *Fluor Daniel Properties*.
[56] *Fluor Daniel Properties*.
[57] This was also a factor in *Scottish Mutual Assurance plc v Jardine Public Relations Ltd* [1999] EG 43 (CS).
[58] *Scottish Mutual Assurance plc* relying on *Ravenseft Properties Ltd v Davstone Holdings Ltd* [1980] QB 12 and *McDougall v Easington District Council* [1984] 1 EGLR 93.
[59] As was found in *Scottish Mutual Assurance plc v Jardine Public Relations Ltd* [1999] EG 43 (CS).
[60] See the discussion of *Scottish Mutual Assurance plc* above.
[61] *Fluor Daniel Properties Ltd v Shortlands Investments Ltd* [2001] 2 EGLR 103.
[62] *Fluor Daniel Properties*.
[63] See the discussion of incidental betterment in relation to the tenant's repairing obligation in **4.4.3**.

as a result, more costly, the tenant will be able to challenge this higher expenditure.[64] A tenant could argue that he is not liable for the increased costs of maintaining or replacing a common part, which is incurred as a result of the landlord failing to comply with his obligations under the lease in earlier years. However, an allowance may have to be made for the fact that the tenant was not charged for certain repairs in the years in which the landlord had not been carrying out sufficient repairs to those common parts now in need of significant works.

6.4.3 Timing of works to common parts

As noted above, the timing of the works has a bearing on whether the expenditure incurred by the landlord regarding the common parts is fair and reasonable. Another issue to bear in mind is that the tenant is generally liable only for expenditure incurred on common parts or services until lease expiry. The landlord, therefore, should not leave it too late in the lease for works to common parts to be considered, especially where it may take some time to tender or instruct works, and the works to be completed thereafter. If the works are not completed by lease end, the tenant will not be liable for any part of the works carried out following expiry of the lease.

Solicitors acting for landlords should also ensure that provision is made in the lease for the tenant to pay service charge following lease end for works carried out during the lease, and that payment of service charge is not limited to payment during the period of the lease.[65]

6.4.4 RICS Professional Statement on Service Charges

The Royal Institute of Chartered Surveyors previously produced a Code of Practice in relation to service charges in commercial property.[66] The Code was superseded on 1 April 2019 by the RICS Professional Statement on Service Charges in Commercial Property.[67] The Professional Statement contains mandatory requirements that must be adhered to by those regulated by RICS, as well as best practice guidance. The Statement builds on and updates what was set out in the Code. The mandatory requirements include that all expenditure sought to be recovered must be sought in accordance with the terms of the lease; that the landlord or his agent must not seek to recover more than 100% of the proper and actual

---

[64] An analogy may be drawn here with the position at common law where a tenant is not relieved of his obligation to carry out ordinary repairs where the defect has become so significant, due to the tenant's failure to repair, that extraordinary repair is now needed: see *Co-operative Insurance Society Ltd v Fife Council* [2011] CSOH 76 per Lord Glennie at para 13, 2011 GWD 19-458. Ordinary and extraordinary repairs are discussed in **3.4**.

[65] Payment of service charge by the tenant is discussed in **6.5**. See clause 6.5 of Schedule Part 10 of the style multi-occupancy lease in *Greens Practice Styles: Commercial Leases*, pp 113–211. However, clause 5 of this style lease obliges the tenant to pay rent (defined as including service charge) for the duration of the lease. This provision appears in conflict with clause 6.5 of Schedule Part 10.

[66] RICS Code of Practice, *Service Charges in Commercial Property* (3rd edn, 2014).

[67] The Professional Statement is effective for all service charge periods commencing from 1 April 2019: *Service Charges in Commercial Property* (2018), available at http://www.rics.org/upholding-professional-standards/sector-standards/real-estate/service-charges-in-commercial-property-1st-edition/.

COMMON PARTS AND SERVICE CHARGE

costs in the provision of services; and that landlords and their agents are required to provide service charge budgets and accounts annually to tenants.[68]

The Statement is designed to promote best practice in relation to service charges of commercial premises. It sets out core principles, as well as recommendations and guidance on how the Statement can be followed. The core principles include: that services should be procured on a value-for-money basis, with the use of competitive quotes for work; that the landlord should not profit from a service charge but should be reimbursed for costs incurred; and that there should be communication and consultation between landlords, or their agents, and tenants so that tenants are clear on the works carried out and services provided and the associated costs to them.[69]

The Statement goes on to note that effective communication between landlords, or their agents, and tenants is key. Landlords' agents are encouraged to have regular meetings with tenants, and to seek feedback on performance and service delivery.[70] The Statement notes that it is best practice to consult with tenants prior to incurring costs that will be included in the service charge, even where there is no requirement to do so in terms of the lease. This is to ensure that the standards of service to be provided by the landlord (the cost of which will be paid for by tenants via the service charge) do not unnecessarily go beyond the reasonable needs and requirements of the tenants.[71] Such action may help identify areas of concern or potential dispute between landlord and tenants in advance of the landlord incurring such costs.

The Statement itself is clear on the fact that it cannot override the lease provisions in relation to service charge.[72] It may, however, provide useful information to landlords and their agents in dealing with service charge, as long as the Statement is read alongside the lease and recognised to be subordinate to its terms. In a dispute in relation to service charge, it may be that the Statement is a relevant factor to consider, where it is shown that it was within the factual matrix or relevant background circumstances at lease commencement.[73] In some leases, express reference may be made to the Code or Statement, with the landlord being obliged to take into account the provisions of the Code or Statement, as appropriate, in dealing with the service charge.[74] Where that is the case then the provisions of the Code/Statement become part of the lease, and must be adhered to by the landlord.

6.5 THE TENANT'S OBLIGATION TO PAY SERVICE CHARGE

As noted above, while the landlord will be obliged to carry out works to keep the common parts in good repair, and to provide certain services, the landlord will seek to recover the costs involved in doing so from the tenants of the property by way

---

[68] RICS Professional Statement, p 10.
[69] RICS Professional Statement, pp 11–12.
[70] RICS Professional Statement, para 4.3.1.
[71] RICS Professional Statement, para 4.3.2.
[72] RICS Professional Statement, para 1.1.
[73] For discussion of the use of background circumstances in interpretation see **4.2.2**.
[74] See the style leases in multi-occupancy buildings drafted by the Property Standardisation Group, available at http://www.psglegal.co.uk/leases.php. At the time of writing update style leases are being produced by the Property Standardisation Group.

of the service charge. The lease in a multi-occupancy property will provide for the tenant to pay a certain proportion or percentage of the service expenditure. This is the service charge that the tenant will have to pay. From the landlord's perspective, the percentages due from the various tenants should amount to 100%, to ensure that the landlord can recover all of the costs of dealing with the common parts and providing the services. However, tenants should ensure that the landlord is obliged to pay the service charge in respect of any unlet premises in the building. This ensures that the service charge account receives all of the money that it should in order to pay for works to common parts and services, but that tenants are not being asked to pay more than the share of the service charge attributable to their premises.

6.5.1 Basis of apportioning service charge among tenants

There are a number of ways in which the landlord can apportion service charge among tenants. The lease should specify which method of apportionment has been agreed between the parties. Each of the various methods of apportioning the service charge has advantages and disadvantages.[75] For instance, a fixed service charge provides parties with certainty, but has no flexibility. Where flexibility is sought, particularly in the event that the building changes over the course of the lease, there is likely to be scope for dispute between the parties.

The service charge may be apportioned on the following bases:

- *A fixed percentage*: the lease will simply set a fixed percentage of service charge payable by the tenant. There may be some dispute between the parties at the outset as to what that fixed percentage should be. In addition, a fixed percentage will not reflect any changes that may occur in the building during the life of the lease.
- *Floor area occupied by the tenant*: this may be either the gross internal area of the leased premises[76] or net floor area.[77] This method apportions service charge based on the proportion of the total floor area comprised within the leased premises in relation to the building as a whole. This method of apportionment allows flexibility, so that if the building within which the leased premises are situated increases during the life of the lease, the proportion of service change payable by the tenant will be altered to reflect that change. However, this method does not take account of the fact that the cost of providing a service may not relate to the amount of space occupied by the tenant.
- *Weighted floor area*: this method of apportionment seeks to reflect the different costs in servicing differently sized units. Such an apportionment discounts the percentage payable by the tenant over a certain size.[78] This takes account of the fact that it does not cost, for instance, 10 times more to service a unit at 5,000 square metres compared with servicing a unit of 500 square metres.[79]

---

[75] For discussion of this issue see M Noor and M Pitt, "A discussion of UK commercial property service charges" (2009) 8 Journal of Retail & Leisure Property 119.
[76] This measure is often seen for warehouses or premises in industrial estates.
[77] Net floor area is the usable area of the premises. This measure is often used for retail or office premises.
[78] RICS Professional Statement para 4.2.8.
[79] This form of apportionment is common in shopping centres.

- *Rateable value*: with this method of apportionment, the service charge payable by the tenant is determined by considering what the rateable value of the leased premises bears to the overall rateable value of the building of which the leased premises form part. There may be practical problems in using this method of apportionment, such as where the rateable value of the building or the leased premises is not known when the lease is entered into. Furthermore, the rateable values assigned to a property can be appealed and, in the event of a successful appeal by either the landlord or the tenant, the proportion of service charge payable by the tenant would need to be changed in the landlord or managing agent's records. Finally, the rateable value does not relate to the costs of providing services to the leased premises.[80]
- *A fair proportion*: there is clear scope for disagreement between the landlord and tenant as to what the tenant's "fair" proportion is.[81] The lease is likely to provide that it is for the landlord to determine what the fair proportion is.[82]
- *A fixed amount*: this is rarely seen in commercial leases. However, given difficulties and disputes associated with service charge, some landlords have opted to provide leases where a higher rent is charged, to take account of works to common parts and services provided by the landlord, without there being payment of a separate service charge. While the rent may be reviewed during the term of the lease, the tenant will be paying a fixed amount for the services provided by the landlord as part of the rent. The benefits are that the rent is set out as a fixed sum in terms of the lease, so the parties are clear on the sum due. The disadvantages are that a fixed amount paid as part of the rent is rigid and inflexible to changes in the services and the cost of providing them, and changes to the building of which the leased premises forms part.

It is also possible that the parties will agree to an apportionment that is a combination of some of the methods set out above; for instance, a fixed percentage with the landlord having the right to alter the apportionment in the future.[83] Such an apportionment would allow the landlord to amend the proportion of service charge payable by the tenant to reflect changes in the building, such as an extension with more lettable units and more tenants.

Where the landlord has agreed a lease with an anchor tenant of the building, including the apportionment of service charge, there is unlikely to be much scope for negotiation or significant revision of the service charge provisions with other tenants. It is highly unlikely that the landlord will agree to a different basis of apportionment to that agreed with the anchor tenant. The landlord wants uniformity in the leases across the whole building, to keep administration in relation to service charge at a minimum. In addition, the landlord is seeking to ensure that, across all

---

[80] The RICS Code of Practice noted that this method of apportionment was no longer recommended: para 1.5.6. This is repeated in the Professional Statement, para 4.2.6.
[81] See the discussion on this issue in **6.5.2**.
[82] See the definition of service charge in clause 1 of the Model Commercial Lease of Part of a Building (Office) produced by the Property Standardisation Group (VI.3, September 2018), available at http://www.psglegal.co.uk/leases.php. At the time of writing the Property Standardisation Group is updating the lease (to VI.4) but it has not yet been published.
[83] See clause 1.1.41 of the style multi-occupancy lease in *Greens Practice Styles: Commercial Leases*, pp 113–211.

of the leases, all sums incurred by him in relation to the common parts and services are fully recoverable from the tenants. Essentially, the landlord wants to ensure that, when he adds up all of the proportions payable by tenants, 100% of the costs can be recovered from the tenants.

Where the building is a mixed-use development, for instance shops on the ground floor and offices above, the landlord may consider dividing the service charge expenditure between the different uses of the building, to take account of different services provided to the different parts. The landlord may then wish to apportion the service charge on a different basis among the tenants of these separate parts. For example, the landlord might determine that for the retail units the service charge should be based on the net floor area relative to the floor area of the retail space available, and for the offices a weighted floor area.

6.5.2 Paying an equitable or fair proportion of service charge costs

In *Bradford & Bingley Building Society v Thorntons plc*[84] the lease provided that the tenant would pay an equitable share of common repair costs, determined on the basis of either floor area or rateable value, with the landlord having the choice between these two bases. The court found that the use of the term "equitable share" implied some restraint on the landlord in selecting the method of apportionment. Lord Hamilton found that, by specifying that the tenant would pay "an equitable share", the parties had intended to import into the landlord's decision a measure of objective fairness. As such, the landlord had to act equitably in making his choice between the two bases of apportionment provided by the lease. Lord Hamilton noted that, in certain circumstances, it may be that either choice could be regarded as equitable and, if that is the case, the landlord's choice would be determinative. However, where the choice made by the landlord was not one that a landlord acting equitably could have made, it was open to challenge.

There will be a similar restraint on the landlord where he has to determine the "fair proportion" of the service charge costs payable by a tenant, unless the lease specifies that the fair proportion is to be determined in the landlord's sole discretion. Tenants should avoid agreeing to such unfettered discretion by the landlord in determining service charge apportionment. Tenants should ensure that the requirement that the tenant pay a fair proportion is not cut across by a provision that the service charge due is to be certified by the landlord or his agent, with this certificate being binding or conclusive. It seems that such a clause would prevent the tenant from going beyond the terms of the certificate to argue that the proportion charged to the tenant was unfair.[85]

Where the lease provides that the landlord is to determine the "fair proportion" payable by the tenant, and notify the tenant of this, it is important that the landlord notifies the tenant of his proportion. It has been held that providing the tenant with estimates of service charge or year-end reconciliation certificates[86] is not notifying

---

[84] *Bradford & Bingley Building Society v Thorntons plc* 1998 GWD 40-2071; official transcript available at https://www.scotcourts.gov.uk/search-judgments/judgment?id=4c4287a6-8980-69d2-b500-ff00 00d74aa7.

[85] See the *obiter* comments on this issue in *WW Promotions (Scotland) Ltd v De Marco* 1988 SLT (Sh Ct) 43, especially those at 46. This case is discussed in **6.5.3.1**.

[86] As to which see **6.5.3**.

the tenant of the fair proportion of service charge that he has to pay.[87] Where the tenant has not been notified of the proportion of service charge attributed to him, the service charge apportionment can be challenged notwithstanding the fact that the lease provides that an end of service charge year certificate is conclusive evidence of the service charge payable by the tenant.[88]

6.5.3 Payment of service charge

The terms of the lease must be consulted to determine what needs to be paid by the tenant by way of service charge, and when payments are to be made. Where the words used in the service charge provision have a clear meaning, the parties will be held to that meaning, even if the bargain is disastrous for one of the parties.[89] Commercial common sense cannot be invoked to protect a party from a bad bargain.[90] In *Arnold v Britton*, the Supreme Court, reluctantly, held tenants of holiday chalets liable to pay a service charge that started at £90 per annum but would increase to over £550,000 per annum by the end of the 99-year term of the lease.[91] This was the effect of the service charge provisions agreed to in the leases.[92]

It is common for commercial leases to make provision for payment of service charge as follows. The lease establishes a service charge year. The landlord or his agent is obliged to provide an estimate of service charge for the service charge year, either in advance of, or shortly after, the start of the service charge year.[93] The tenant is obliged to pay the estimated service charge quarterly throughout the service charge year. Often, payment of this on-account service charge is paid on the same days that rent is due. Funds paid by tenants to the landlord in respect of service charge should be held in a separate account: the service charge account. Interest accrued on this account should be credited to the service charge account.[94] Following the end of the service charge year, the landlord or his agent is to calculate the amount actually spent on works and services in the service charge year. In doing so, the landlord or his agent will discover if the landlord spent more or less on works and services in the service charge year than the landlord received from tenants by way of the on-account service charge, based on the service charge estimate for the year. Shortly after the end of the service charge year, the landlord or his agent will send a certificate to the tenants certifying the cost of works and services in the service charge year.[95] If the landlord has spent less on works and services than he received from tenants, the surplus is carried forward and used as a credit for on-account service charge payments

---

[87] *Mars Pension Tr Ltd v County Properties and Developments Ltd* 1999 SC 267, in particular Lord Penrose at 276.
[88] *Mars Pension Tr Ltd v County Properties and Developments Ltd* 1999 SC 267.
[89] Unless a case based on rectification can be made, as was the case in *Britannia Invest A/S v Scottish Ministers* 2018 SLT (Sh Ct) 133, 2018 GWD 9-112.
[90] *Arnold v Britton* [2015] UKSC 3, [2015] 2 WLR 1593. See the discussion of this case in **4.2.1**.
[91] *Arnold v Britton*; see Lord Neuberger's comments in paras 30–32.
[92] Although the landlord was willing to agree amendments to the leases to mitigate the effects of the service charge provisions: see *Arnold v Britton* per Lord Neuberger at para 64.
[93] The RICS Professional Statement states that budgets for on-account service charge should be issued at least one month before the start of each service charge year: see 4.5.6.
[94] These are mandatory requirements in the Professional Statement, principles 6 and 7, p 2.
[95] The RICS Professional Statement states that this should occur within four months of the end of the service charge year: see para 4.5.6.

due from tenants in the next service charge year. If the landlord has spent more on works and services than he received from tenants' payments of on-account service charge, the landlord will seek payment of the shortfall from tenants. The shortfall will generally have to be paid on demand, or within a short period of the demand, such as 14 or 21 days.[96]

In an attempt to reduce the possibility of discussion or dispute in relation to sums spent by the landlord in carrying out works or providing services, or a tenant's liability to pay an amount by way of service charge, commercial leases often provide for certification by the landlord or his agent of the service expenditure and sums to be paid by the tenants. Often, the lease will provide that the certificate is binding[97] or conclusive evidence of the sums paid in doing the works and providing the services and/or the sums due by the tenants. Some leases will qualify this by stating that the certificate is binding or conclusive, save in the case of manifest error. Lease provisions such as these have not been entirely successful in preventing challenges to service charge costs or calculations, and a number of disputes have been heard by the courts.

6.5.3.1 *Certification of service charge expenditure*

Where the lease makes no provision regarding the finality or conclusiveness of the service charge certificate it is open to challenge. Where the lease provides that the landlord's certificate is final, the parties are not normally entitled to look beyond the terms of the certificate. Indeed, in *WW Promotions (Scotland) Ltd v De Marco*,[98] Sheriff Principal Caplan held that, where the lease provided that the landlord's surveyor's certificate was to be final, the tenant could not look beyond the certificate to determine whether the surveyor had made a mistake. Nor could the tenant seek to show that the costs incurred by the landlord were unreasonable.[99] However, in *Franborough Properties Ltd v Scottish Enterprise*[100] the court considered a provision which obliged the tenant to pay the cost and expense (or due proportion thereof) attributable to repair and maintenance of the main structure of a building, and in providing services to common parts. That cost and expense or due proportion was to be certified by the landlord's surveyor, whose certificate was final and conclusive except in the case of manifest arithmetical error. Lord Penrose held that, while the surveyor's certificate was final and conclusive as to the quantification of costs, it was not conclusive as to whether an item was properly a common part or a service and, as such, whether the cost of providing it could be recovered by the service charge. To avoid any doubt as to the ability to challenge a service charge certificate, a tenant should be unwilling to agree to a service charge provision in a lease that provides that the end of year certificate is final and binding without qualification.

A lease might qualify the finality of the certificate issued by the landlord or his agent by providing that the certificate is final and binding, save in the case

---

[96] See the provisions on paying service charge in Schedule Part 10 of the style multi-occupancy lease in *Greens Practice Styles: Commercial Leases*, pp 113–211.
[97] See clause 5 of Schedule Part 10 of the style multi-occupancy lease in *Greens Practice Styles: Commercial Leases*, pp 113–211.
[98] *WW Promotions (Scotland) Ltd v De Marco* 1988 SLT (Sh Ct) 43.
[99] See the discussion of this issue in **6.4.1–6.4.2**.
[100] *Franborough Properties Ltd v Scottish Enterprise*, 14 June 1996, Lord Penrose, unreported.

of manifest error.[101] An error is manifest where it is so obvious and clear as to be beyond reasonable contradiction.[102] In *Scottish Mutual Assurance plc v Jardine Public Relations Ltd*,[103] the tenant was obliged to pay service charge of a fair proportion, fairly and reasonably determined by the landlord's surveyor, of the amounts expended on the property. The lease also provided that a certificate in writing by the landlord showing the amount of the service charge was to be conclusive evidence of the amount the tenant was to pay, save in the case of manifest error. The tenant successfully challenged the inclusion of substantial costs in relation to roof repairs in the service expenditure. The court found that including such costs in the service charge expenditure was a manifest error, because the apportionment to the tenant did not take account of the short duration of the tenant's lease, the short length of the unexpired term, the fact that substantial amounts had recently been spent on short-term repairs to the roof (which had not been shown to be failing), and that the works were not carried out to allow the landlord to fulfil his obligations to the tenant under the lease but to appease a prospective incoming tenant of the leased premises.[104] It is questionable whether the landlord was in manifest error, given the need to make a proper enquiry into the facts in order to determine these issues. As was noted in a Scottish case regarding an expert decision on partnership accounts, "Once elaborate (or any) argument and counter-argument is required, it is clear that one is not in 'manifest error' territory".[105]

It has been said that the process of certification is purely procedural, and that while the existence of the certificate is conclusive evidence of the sum payable, the absence of the certificate does not prevent the landlord from recovering the service charge.[106] However, in *Leonora Investment Company Ltd v Mott MacDonald Ltd*, the Court of Appeal noted that the service charge provisions in a lease were important, characterising them as the "contractual route down which the landlord must travel to be entitled to payment".[107] As such, a landlord was not entitled to payment of the service charge where he had not complied with the provisions on seeking payment provided for in the lease. The landlord had failed to include certain items of expenditure in the service charge year end statement and had invoiced the tenant for payment of those items separately. The court found that he could not seek payment in this way. The landlord would, however, be able to seek payment by issuing another, correct, end of year statement, including these costs. Where the lease provides that the certificate produced by the landlord or his agent will be final and binding, the landlord must ensure that the sums set out in the

---

[101] See clause 5 of Schedule Part 10 of the style multi-occupancy lease in *Greens Practice Styles: Commercial Leases*, pp 113–211.
[102] *MacDonald v Livingstone* [2012] CSOH 31, 2012 GWD 11-218, see in particular paras 9 and 10.
[103] *Scottish Mutual Assurance plc v Jardine Public Relations Ltd* [1999] EG 43 (CS).
[104] These were the same factors the court took into account in coming to its decision that the costs had not been reasonably and properly incurred: see the discussion of the case at **6.4.2**.
[105] *MacDonald v Livingstone* [2012] CSOH 31 per Lord Malcolm at para 10, 2012 GWD 11-218.
[106] *Scottish Mutual Assurance plc v Jardine Public Relations Ltd* [1999] EG 43 (CS).
[107] *Leonora Investment Co Ltd v Mott MacDonald Ltd* [2008] EWCA Civ 857, [2008] 2 P&CR DG15 per Tuckey LJ at para 22. The Upper Tribunal (Lands Chamber) took the same view in *Akorita v Marina Heights (St Leonards) Ltd* [2011] UKUT 225 (LC) with the tribunal finding that in terms of the lease a surveyor's certificate certifying the amount due as service charge was a condition precedent to the tenant's liability to pay.

certificate are correct – otherwise he may not be able to recover the correct service charge amount.[108]

In *Universities Superannuation Scheme Ltd v Marks & Spencer plc*[109] the service charge certificate erroneously did not include everything the landlord could charge the tenant by way of service charge. The tenant paid the amount set out in the certificate and argued that, having done so, he had fulfilled its obligation to pay service charge. The Court of Appeal disagreed. The court noted that the service charge provisions had a clear purpose; allowing the landlord, who had reasonably incurred liability for costs in maintaining the property for the benefit of his tenants, to recover the full cost of doing so from the tenants. The provisions of the lease were to be given an effect which fulfilled, rather than defeated that purpose, so far as the lease provisions allowed.[110] The lease provided that the tenant was to pay the service charge "calculated in accordance with the fifth schedule" to the lease. It did not provide that the tenant was to pay the service charge "as certified in accordance with the fifth schedule". As such, paying the sum certified did not relieve the tenant of its obligation to pay the service charge actually due, absent provision in the lease to the contrary effect.[111] In terms of the lease, the service charge year end certificate was not final, binding or conclusive.

The cases suggest that the courts are trying to balance the interests of the landlord and tenant. The courts do not wish to impose technical or procedural obstacles to recovery of service charge but acknowledge that the landlord has agreed to follow a particular route to recovering the service charge, which the tenant should be able to rely upon.

6.5.3.2 *Who certifies service charge costs?*

As well as considering how the service charge is to be certified, consideration must also be given to who certifies the service charge. When drafting the service charge provisions, thought should be given to the independence or impartiality of the person tasked with certifying the annual service charge to be paid by the tenants. If the lease provides that the service charge is to be certified by the landlord's agent, it must be carried out by someone other than the landlord.[112] However, the courts have not insisted on complete independence, and have had no difficulty with the person certifying the service charge being the landlord's agent, often his managing agent, surveyor or accountant.[113] Where the lease provides that service charge costs will be determined by the landlord's surveyor, it is the surveyor, and not someone else, such as the landlord's solicitor[114] or the landlord's accountant[115] who can do so.

---

[108] This was not the position in *Leonora Investment Co*. In that case the lease simply provided for an end of year service charge statement to be produced by the landlord, with the tenant being liable for any costs in excess of the on-account service charge.

[109] *Universities Superannuation Scheme Ltd v Marks & Spencer plc* [1999] L & TR 237.

[110] *Universities Superannuation Scheme* at 243.

[111] *Universities Superannuation Scheme* at 243.

[112] *Finchbourne Ltd v Rodrigues* [1976] 3 All ER 581.

[113] See clause 2.1 of Schedule Part 10 and clauses 2 and 3 of Schedule Part 2 of the style multi-occupancy lease in *Greens Practice Styles: Commercial Leases*, pp 113–211 where the "Accountant" is defined as the accountant, surveyor or managing agent appointed by the landlord.

[114] *Jacey Property Ltd v De Sousa* [2003] EWCA Civ 510.

[115] *Akorita v Marina Heights (St Leonards) Ltd* [2011] UKUT 225 (LC).

While there is benefit in the person certifying the service charge being someone who is familiar with the building and costs incurred in relation to it during the service charge year, the landlord's agent is unlikely to be truly impartial. The RICS Professional Statement emphasises the need for those certifying service charge expenditure to do so in an impartial way, noting that those certifying must act in a professional, non-partisan manner, and must not think that their only task is to recover as much as they can for the landlord.[116] The Statement further notes that the certifier has a duty of care to the landlord and the tenants to act with professional care, diligence, integrity and objectivity.[117] However, the fact that such statements have to be made perhaps says something about the mindset of agents employed by landlords. Such agents have a relationship with the landlord, one that is likely to extend beyond the building in question. The agents are engaged by and paid by the landlord. It is suggested that in these circumstances landlords' agents may have some difficulty in being completely objective in certifying service charge. It is suggested that, in drafting service charge provisions, the tenant considers independent verification of the service charge account,[118] with the landlord having to provide access to the information used to produce the end of year service charge certificate; or that certification is carried out by an independent party.[119] While both of these routes may result in some further costs in terms of professional fees, or perhaps some delay in finalising the service charge each year, given the sums involved in service charges of commercial properties this could be a sensible option for tenants to ensure this important task is completed objectively and accurately.

The knowledge and skills needed by the person certifying must also be taken into account when specifying who is to certify the end of year service charge.[120] Some leases allow the landlord to certify the amount. As well as issues regarding impartiality, the question must be whether the landlord has the necessary skills and professional competence to be able to do this. In a similar vein, are managing agents or surveyors adequately equipped to deal with service charge accounts that can be complex and deal with large sums of money? It is suggested that an accountant might, in certain circumstances, be specified as the party responsible for certifying the annual service charge as a professional appropriately qualified for the task.

The RICS Professional Statement recommends that service charge accounts contain a comprehensive list of accounting policies and principles on which the statement is prepared[121] and that tenants be given a reasonable period[122] in which to raise queries or request further information about the service charge year end

---

[116] See para 4.5.3.2 of the Professional Statement.
[117] See para 4.5.3.2 of the Professional Statement.
[118] The Professional Statement provides that for leases entered into after 1980 this auditing should be carried out in accordance with ISA 800 (UK); and for leases entered into before 1980 the parties may not have anticipated the work required by the modern auditing framework, and, as such, the landlord or his agent should consider whether an audit provides best value: see para 4.5.3.4. Provision is also made in the Professional Statement for an independent review rather than an audit: see para 4.5.3.5.
[119] A period within which to challenge the service charge certificate should also be provided in the lease or the certificate should not be final, binding or conclusive.
[120] See para 4.5.3.2 of the Professional Statement.
[121] See para 4.5.1 of the Professional Statement.
[122] Paragraph 4.5.7 of the Professional Statement suggests four months from issue of the year end reconciliation.

certificate.[123] It must be remembered that the provisions of the Professional Statement cannot override the provisions of the lease, so that where the end of year certificate is stated to be final, or final except in the case of manifest error, the landlord will not be obliged to answer queries or provide further details.[124] Inclusion of such a provision in the Professional Statement appears to highlight a change in the mindset of landlords towards a more transparent approach to the recovery of service charge. However, many leases provide that any shortfall in the service charge, against what has been paid by the tenant by way of on-account service charge, must be paid by the tenant within a short period of time,[125] which does not give the tenant much opportunity to ask questions or obtain further information. The Professional Statement also sets out some minimum levels of information that should be included in the end of year certificate, to give tenants sufficient details of what they are being charged for, and how this compares to the budget issued at the beginning of the service charge year,[126] again promoting the need for transparency when dealing with service charge costs.

6.5.3.3 *A changing approach to service charge?*

In the past, some landlords and their agents have acted with disregard for the tenants' position when seeking recovery of service charge. "Landlord-friendly" lease terms allowed landlords to behave in this way. Often, reconciliations were not carried out until many months, or even years, after the end of the service charge year in question, resulting in financial uncertainty for tenants as to their liability for that year.[127] There were problems not only with the end of year certificate but also problems with the service charge budget provided at the start of the service charge year. Delay in providing this to the tenant would often result in a demand for "underpaid" on-account service charge, based on an increased estimated service charge at some point during the service charge year.[128] As well as timing issues, there were issues with the accuracy of the annual estimate of service charge provided to the tenant.[129] Where the budget does not reasonably reflect the sums likely to be expended on the building in that year, tenants could be faced with having to pay a significant shortfall,

---

[123] See para 4.5.7 of the Professional Statement.
[124] See the discussion at **6.5.3.1**.
[125] See the discussion at **6.5.3**.
[126] Paragraph 4.5.2 of the Professional Statement recommends including an analysis of any material variances between budget and actual expenditure, with a detailed commentary to explain trends and variances where these are significant.
[127] There may be some doubt about whether any shortfall due following a late reconciliation would be due by the tenant where a landlord was obliged to prepare the year end reconciliation certificate within a reasonable time following the end of the service charge year. However, some leases seek to deal specifically with landlord tardiness by providing that any delay of such certification would not entitle the tenant to withhold or delay payment of the service charge: see clause 5 of Schedule Part 10 of the style multi-occupancy lease in *Greens Practice Styles: Commercial Leases*, pp 113–211.
[128] Many leases provide that where a service charge estimate is not provided at the start of the new service charge year the tenant will pay the same amount on-account service charge as was paid in the previous year and that on the new budget being made available, the tenant is required to pay any shortfall as a result of any increase in the on-account payments at the quarter day following the new budget being made available. See, for instance, clause 6.4 of Schedule Part 10 of the style multi-occupancy lease in *Greens Practice Styles: Commercial Leases*, pp 113–211.
[129] M Noor and M Pitt, "A discussion of UK commercial property service charges" (2009) 8 Journal of Retail & Leisure Property 119 at 136.

often within a very short period of time.[130] Against this, tenants need to be able to budget for their service charge expenditure. While rent due under the lease is clear, the service charge is sometimes viewed as a hidden cost of the lease by the tenant,[131] with some considering it a "money-making agenda for [landlords]."[132]

Lack of transparency on the part of landlords and their agents is also a problem for tenants, with landlords or their agents reluctant or slow to provide information or respond to questions.[133] The need for transparency and communication between landlords and tenants have been highlighted in the RICS Professional Statement.[134]

Given these difficulties, it is hardly surprising to find tenant frustration at landlords' handling of the service charge. While tenant satisfaction increased slightly in the three years to 2012, in 2012 commercial tenants in the UK scored service charge arrangements at 4.7 out of 10,[135] indicating that there remains significant discontent in this area.

More recent court decisions have indicated that landlords must adhere to the terms of the lease in order to be paid the service charge, and such decisions appear to be having some effect on thinking among landlords' agents. There is also the Professional Statement and, prior to that, the Code of Practice. While these documents cannot, of course, override or permit derogations from the terms of the lease, their promulgation by the surveying profession is likely to have an effect on the perceptions of landlords and their agents in dealing with service charge, and their solicitors, when drafting service charge provisions. Indeed, as noted above, some leases expressly refer to the Code itself in the service charge provisions.[136]

For some, the problems in dealing with a service charge – from what works and services can be recovered via the service charge to the certification process – are simply too great. For some landlords and tenants the solution has been the use of rent-only leases, in terms of which the landlord in consideration of payment of the rent (but not a separate service charge) continues to carry out works to common parts and provide the services needed in a multi-occupancy building.[137] The rent paid is higher to take account of the works and services provided. The benefits of such an arrangement are increased clarity and certainty for both parties: tenants know what they have to pay each year and can budget accordingly, and landlords also know the sums they will receive from their tenants. However, this certainty means there is no room for flexibility. The landlord may end up not recovering enough to cover the

---

[130] See **6.5.3**.
[131] Noor and Pitt, "A discussion of UK commercial property service charges" at 129.
[132] Noor and Pitt, "A discussion of UK commercial property service charges" at 127.
[133] Noor and Pitt, "A discussion of UK commercial property service charges" at 127.
[134] These are core principles 6 and 7, with best practice guidance set out in para 4.3.
[135] Property Industry Alliance, *Occupier Satisfaction Survey* (2012) available at http://bco.org.uk/Research/Publications/Occupier-Satisfaction-Survey.aspx. This is the most recent survey that is publicly available.
[136] See, e.g., the service charge provisions in the Model Commercial Lease of Part of a Building (Office) produced by the Property Standardisation Group (VI.3, September 2018). At the time of writing the Property Standardisation Group is updating the lease (to VI.4) but this has not yet been published.
[137] McAllister notes that this method of collection is widely used in England: see McAllister, *Scottish Law of Leases*, para 13.13.

RESERVE OR SINKING FUNDS

costs needed to properly maintain the common parts or provide adequate services. More likely, maintenance of common parts and services would suffer. Conversely the tenant may end up paying more (by way of the higher rent) than it costs for the landlord to service the common parts and provide the services. This, of course, is a risk that both parties will need to take into account in deciding to use a rent-only lease, and in determining the appropriate level of rent in such leases.

6.6 RESERVE OR SINKING FUNDS

The discussion so far has concentrated on costs incurred in a particular service charge year. There are, however, costs that are incurred in carrying out works to the common parts that may not arise each year. They may arise frequently, although not annually, for instance external redecoration; or may occur infrequently, such as replacing a major item of plant, for example, the air-conditioning system serving the building. The purpose of reserve and sinking funds is to build up a pot of money to deal with larger items of expenditure on the common parts, so that the service charge payable does not fluctuate significantly in the years in which such expenditure occurs.

A reserve fund is built up to equalise spending on regularly occurring but infrequent items.[138] Such a fund is defined in the RICS Professional Statement as:

> A fund formed to meet anticipated future costs of maintenance and upkeep in order to avoid fluctuations in the amount of service charge payable each year (for example, for external cleaning or redecorations).[139]

This fund is built up by the tenants paying a sum by way of service charge that includes an amount to be put into the reserve fund, rather than simply to pay for works to the common parts or on the provision of services in the service charge year in question.[140] Payment is made to this fund so that in a service charge year in which, for instance, redecoration of common parts takes place the service charge due for that year does not increase by a significant amount. Essentially, the cost of these regular, but non-yearly, works or services are evened out by paying an additional amount of service charge each year to build up the reserve fund. It is important to ensure, as a tenant, that in any year in which this additional expenditure is incurred it is paid for from the reserve fund, rather than having an increased service charge cost for that year, with sums continuing to accrue in the reserve fund.

A sinking fund is built up in the same way as a reserve fund, by paying an amount by way of service charge that is used to accumulate a pot of money available to pay for more significant items of expenditure. Similarly, when work has been carried out that should be paid for from the sinking fund, it should be paid for from that fund, rather than by way of a sharp increase in the service charge payments for that year. What is different is that a sinking fund is used to pay for infrequently incurring expenditure, for example, the replacement of an item of plant and equipment or significant works to the common parts, for example replacing the roof covering. A sinking fund is defined in the RICS Professional Statement as:

---

[138] For example redecoration of common parts which may take place at three- or five-yearly intervals.
[139] RICS Professional Statement, para 4.8.4.
[140] See, e.g., clause 17 of Schedule Part 11 of the style multi-occupancy lease in *Greens Practice Styles: Commercial Leases*, pp 113–211.

A fund formed by periodically setting aside money for the replacement of a wasting asset (for example, heating and air-conditioning plant, lifts and equipment, etc).[141]

For landlords, the advantage of such funds is that money is available to pay for the works when they are required, rather then having to seek recovery from tenants after the landlord has paid for the works.[142] A sinking fund would require all tenants who benefit from the common part to contribute to its repair or replacement, rather than a significant burden falling on the party who happens to be the tenant when major repairs are needed to the common parts or an item of plant needs to be replaced. Given the importance to tenants of being able to budget for service charge[143] such funds may be useful, as they protect against significant fluctuations in any service charge year.

However, tenants are paying in advance for works that will, or are likely to be, carried out in the future. Major tenants, who would have no difficulty in paying for works through an increased service charge in any particular service charge year, may be reluctant to hand money over to the landlord in advance of the works being carried out. A very important issue for the tenant is that the money in a reserve or sinking fund is not the landlord's, and he will be keen to ensure it is protected, especially from the landlord's creditors, until used to pay for the works.[144] For landlords there are also disadvantages, including administering such funds, as well as tax complications.[145] As a result, reserve or sinking funds are utilised relatively rarely, and even where the lease makes provisions for a reserve or sinking fund, it may not be used. It may be the case that shorter lease durations are having a negative impact on the use of reserve and sinking funds, with tenants seemingly unwilling to put aside money for works that will not be required during the term of their lease.

6.6.1 Lease terms providing for reserve and sinking funds

As noted above, a tenant will want to ensure that he is adequately protected where a reserve or sinking fund is established. This should be done by the tenant's solicitor ensuring adequate protection in terms of the lease. The most important requirement is that sums for the reserve or sinking fund are held separately from the landlord's assets. The funds should be in trust for the benefit of the tenants,[146] in a discrete bank account bearing a competitive rate of interest. In addition, responsibility for making payments to such funds in respect of unlet units should rest with the landlord.[147]

The tenant can also be protected by the landlord being required to calculate the sum to be paid into the reserve or sinking fund based on anticipated expenditure on identified items on which expenditure will be or is likely to be required, rather than

---

[141] RICS Professional Statement, para 4.8.4.
[142] Although given service charge is paid on-account the landlord will have some funds from which to pay for works carried out during the year.
[143] Discussed in **6.5.3.3**.
[144] See the discussion of this issue in **6.6.1**.
[145] For a brief overview of the main issues see para 4.8.1 of the Professional Statement.
[146] This point is made by the RICS in their Profesional Statement – see para 4.8.4.6. For a lease provision stipulating such a requirement see clauses 16.2 and 16.3 of Schedule Part 11 of the style multi-occupancy lease in *Greens Practice Styles: Commercial Leases*, pp 113–211.
[147] As is the position with service charge in respect of unlet units generally – see **6.5**.

sums simply being saved in the reserve or sinking funds just in case some additional expenditure is incurred in the future. In this way, no more than is anticipated to be needed is placed in the reserve or sinking fund.[148] The tenant may, additionally, only be prepared to pay into such a fund in respect of expenditure anticipated to arise during the life of the lease. If that is the case, this additional qualification should be added to the way in which sums to be provided for future costs are calculated. Provision may also be made for any dispute in respect of this calculation to be referred to the decision of an expert or arbitrator.[149] Where the tenant is unwilling to pay towards expenditure beyond the life of his lease, provision should be made for return of any money paid into the reserve or sinking fund which has not been utilised to pay for works during the lease.

The courts have had to consider whether unused funds should be returned to the tenant at lease end. In *Secretary of State for the Environment v Possfund (North West) Ltd*[150] the tenant had paid £600,000 into a fund earmarked for replacing air-conditioning plant. At lease end, the tenant sought repayment of this money as the air-conditioning plant had not been replaced, and the money in the fund had therefore not been spent. The court found that the fund belonged to the landlord. The decision turned on the provisions in the lease but, in coming to his decision, Rimer J was clearly influenced by commercial sense, noting that during the lease the tenant had enjoyed the benefit of the air-conditioning, which was a depreciating asset, and that the landlord would at some point in the future have to replace it.[151]

However, in *Brown's Operating System Services Ltd v Southwark Roman Catholic Diocesan Corporation* the Court of Appeal held that *Possfund* did not lay down general principles, but simply interpreted the provisions of the lease in question.[152] In *Brown's Operating System*, the lease was different in a number of material respects. The lease provided that the service charge could include:

> such sum as the Landlord shall in its reasonable discretion think fit as being a reasonable provision for expenditure likely to be incurred in the future in connection with [the landlord's obligations under the lease in relation to the common parts and services].

So, while the lease did allow the landlord to build up a reserve of funds for future works, he could only make provision for future expenditure that would be incurred during the period of the lease, that being the period during which the tenant was under an obligation to pay service charge.[153] There was no obligation on the tenant to contribute to the costs of works following the end of the lease. The court was clearly influenced by the fact that the lease did not make provision for the creation of a reserve fund. While funds could be held by the landlord "in reserve" for future expenditure, that did not mean that the money was held in a reserve fund. The sums

---

[148] This is also advocated by the RICS in the Professional Statement – see para 4.8.4.6.
[149] See Cockburn and Mitchell, *Commercial Leases*, para 6.10.
[150] *Secretary of State for the Environment v Possfund (North West) Ltd* [1997] 2 EGLR 56.
[151] *Secretary of State for the Environment*.
[152] *Brown's Operating System Services Ltd v Southwark Roman Catholic Diocesan Corporation* [2007] EWCA Civ 164, [2007] L &TR 25 at para 30 per Smith LJ, with whom Longmore and May LJJ agreed.
[153] *Brown's Operating System* at para 27 per Smith LJ.

for future expenditure were "lumped together", with any excess left following an end of year service charge reconciliation. The amount held in reserve was not designed to cover any specific repair or renewal, but was used along with any excess following a service charge reconciliation in a year of light expenditure, to help meet the costs of a heavy year of service charge expenditure.[154] The lease did not specify what was to happen to money held in reserve by the landlord at lease end. As such, the court inferred that any unspent money at the expiry of the lease belonged to the tenant and had to be returned to the tenant.

The discussion in the cases, especially *Brown's Operating System*, shows that, as with many aspects of the law of commercial leases, the terms of the lease are of paramount consideration.

Where a reserve or sinking fund is to be established, this should be clearly provided for, including what the fund can be used for, that the fund is held separate from the landlord's assets, and what is to happen with any money in the fund, that has been contributed by the tenant, at the end of the lease.

6.7 TENANT'S REMEDIES FOR THE LANDLORD'S BREACH OF THE LEASE

Having considered so far what the service charge is, what it is paid for and how it is paid, the remainder of the chapter focuses on when either of the parties to the lease fails in relation to their obligations regarding the service charge or common parts and services.

Where the landlord fails to fulfil his obligations in relation to the common parts or services, the tenant will have common law remedies which he can use against the landlord. It is unlikely that a commercial lease will provide any remedies available to the tenant for breach of the lease by the landlord.

A tenant will be able to seek specific implement to compel the landlord to carry out works or perform services,[155] although it should be noted that some leases may be drafted in such a way that the landlord need only use his best endeavours to carry out works to the common parts or provide services,[156] which is likely to make such an order more difficult to obtain.[157]

Where the tenant can show that he has suffered a loss due to the landlord failing to carry out works to the common parts or provide services, he will be able to obtain damages. As with all actions for damages, the tenant, as pursuer, has to prove that the landlord's breach caused his loss, and that the loss was not too remote. The tenant

---

[154] *Brown's Operating System* at para 29 per Smith LJ, although the evening out of service charge is one of the functions of a reserve fund.
[155] See the discussion of this remedy in **5.3.1**. Interim specific implement may also be sought.
[156] See, e.g., clause 4.1 of Schedule Part 14 of the style multi-occupancy lease in *Greens Practice Styles: Commercial Leases*, pp 113–211. Such clauses should be resisted by tenants' solicitors. The landlord is adequately protected if he has an obligation to carry out the works and provide the services with a clause exempting him from liability for loss, damage or inconvenience where the works cannot be carried out or services performed due to a cause outwith the landlord's control – for such a clause see clause 4.2 of Part 14 of the style multi-occupancy lease in *Greens Practice Styles: Commercial Leases*.
[157] The need to be very clear in the interlocutor for specific implement may be problematic – as to which see L Macgregor, "Specific performance in Scots law" in J Smits, D Haas and G Hesen, *Specific Performance in Contract Law: National and Other Perspectives* (2008) pp 67–92 at 84–86.

will also be unable to recover losses beyond those he would have incurred had he taken reasonable steps to mitigate his loss.[158] It may be difficult to prove that it was the landlord's failure to comply with his obligations in relation to common parts or services which resulted in the tenant's loss, given the number of factors that may impact on how well a tenant operates and his profits.[159]

Potentially more useful to the tenant is the remedy of retention,[160] in terms of which the tenant can withhold performance of his counterpart obligations under the lease[161] until the landlord performs his obligations in relation to the common parts/services. However, in practical terms, this remedy may be unavailable to the tenant as commercial leases almost invariably include a provision in terms of which the tenant contracts out of this common law right. However, it should be noted that if the tenant has simply contracted out of the right to retain the rent[162] he would be able to retain other obligations, monetary or otherwise, while the landlord is in breach of his obligations in relation to the common parts or services.

Finally, the tenant could rescind[163] the lease for failure by the landlord to comply with his obligations in relation to the common parts/services, provided the landlord's breach is material. The lease is unlikely to set out what breaches by the landlord will be material and, as such, there may be doubt about whether the landlord's breach is sufficiently serious to entitle the tenant to rescind. The tenant is less likely to seek to utilise this remedy, particularly given that the tenant will be found to be in material breach of contract himself where he purports to rescind the lease where rescission is not justified by the landlord's breach.[164]

However, it may be more likely that a dispute will arise between landlord and tenant regarding works that the landlord intends to carry out, rather than those he is not carrying out. The tenant may dispute that the works intended by the landlord are necessary for the landlord to comply with his obligations in relation to common parts or services, and/or dispute the extent of the works. Significant works carried out to common parts may not only be expensive in terms of the service charge but may also be very disruptive to the tenant's business operated from the leased premises. This will be especially so where the landlord requires entry onto the premises let to the tenant in order to carry out works to the common parts.[165]

---

[158] These matters are discussed in detail in **5.3.3** *et seq.*

[159] The problems in proving that loss is due only to a breach of the lease may be seen in a different context in *Douglas Shelf Seven Ltd v Co-operative Wholesale Society Ltd* [2007] CSOH 53, 2007 GWD 9-167.

[160] See the discussion of this remedy in **5.3.4**.

[161] Note the assumption that the obligations undertaken by the landlord are the counterparts of the obligations undertaken by the tenant under the lease unless an examination of the lease shows that the obligations are independent, discussed in **5.3.4**.

[162] As occurs in clause 1.3 of Schedule Part 7 of the style multi-occupancy lease in *Greens Practice Styles: Commercial Leases*, pp 113–211. However, some leases specify that the service charge is payable as further or second rent, which would be caught by a clause in terms of which the tenant contracts out of his right to retain the rent.

[163] See the discussion of this remedy in **5.3.5**.

[164] See the discussion of this issue in **5.3.5** and the case of *Wade v Waldon* 1909 SC 571.

[165] Commercial leases generally contain a term that the landlord can take access to the premises for a number of purposes, including carrying out works to the common parts – see clause 3.1.1 of Schedule Part 6 of the style multi-occupancy lease in *Greens Practice Styles: Commercial Leases*, pp 113–211.

COMMON PARTS AND SERVICE CHARGE

Where the tenant has a basis on which to dispute that the works are necessary, he may seek to interdict the landlord from carrying them out,[166] on the basis that this would interfere with the tenant's possession of the leased premises.[167] Indeed, where access to the tenant's premises is needed for the works to be done, the tenant may simply refuse that access.[168] Where a tenant seeks an interim interdict, or seeks to oppose an order for interim possession of the premises by the landlord, he will have to show a *prima facie* case that the works are not necessary, are excessive, or otherwise go beyond what the landlord is required to do in terms of the lease. The tenant will also have to show that the balance of convenience that the works not be carried out is in his favour. The fact that the landlord will not be able to carry out the works before the end of the lease, and accordingly will not be able to recover the cost of them via the service charge,[169] does not seem fatal to the tenant's case. The landlord would have a remedy in damages against the tenant for failing to allow him to carry out the works.[170]

6.8 LANDLORD'S REMEDIES FOR THE TENANT'S BREACH OF THE LEASE

The landlord has a number of remedies where the tenant fails to pay the service charge. Some of these remedies are available at common law, while others must be provided for in the lease to be available to him.

6.8.1 Common law remedies[171]

Where the tenant has failed to pay the service charge, the landlord could raise an action for payment against the tenant. Such actions are rare, however, as commercial leases are generally registered for execution.[172] Where the lease is not registered for execution, a landlord may issue a statutory demand[173] seeking payment of the

---

[166] See the discussion of this remedy in **5.3.2**.
[167] *Possfund Custodial Tr Ltd v Kwik-Fit Properties Ltd* [2008] CSIH 65, 2009 SLT 133 at paras 12 and 13. McAllister notes that once in the property the tenant has the right to be maintained in possession and the landlord must not do anything that would deprive or partially deprive the tenant of possession. This is known as the obligation not to derogate from the grant: see McAllister, *Scottish Law of Leases*, para 3.11 and also paras 3.14–3.17.
[168] This occurred in *William Collins & Sons Ltd v CGU Insurance plc* [2006] CSIH 37, 2006 SC 674 where the landlord sought an order for interim possession of the leased premises.
[169] As to which see **6.4.3**.
[170] *William Collins & Sons Ltd v CGU Insurance plc* [2006] CSIH 37, 2006 SC 674.
[171] Where the lease provides that the service charge is payable as further or second rent it may be possible to utilise the landlord's right of hypothec where the tenant fails to pay service charge – see McAllister, *Scottish Law of Leases*, para 13.13. Given the abolition of sequestration for rent (by the Bankruptcy and Diligence, etc (Scotland) Act 2007, s 208) the landlord's right of hypothec is substantially weakened and is unlikely to be of significant use to many landlords seeking payment of service charge; for details of the use that can now be made of the landlord's right of hypothec see A McAllister, "The landlord's hypothec: down but is it out?" 2010 Jur Rev 65.
[172] See **6.8.2.1** on this issue.
[173] See the Bankruptcy (Scotland) Act 2016, s 16(1)(i) and the Insolvency Act 1986, s 123(1)(a). The form of statutory demand for individuals and partnerships is found in the Bankruptcy (Scotland) Regulations 2014 (SSI 2014/225) Sch 1 Form 2. Rule 5.3 of the Insolvency (Scotland) (Receivership and Winding Up) Rules 2018 (SSI 2018/347) sets out the information to be included in a statutory demand served on a company.

sums due[174] rather than raising an action for payment. A statutory demand should be used only where there is no genuine and substantial dispute as to the debt.[175] Serving a statutory demand does not result in the landlord receiving the sums owed by the tenant. If three weeks pass and the statutory demand is not paid or denied (in the case of an individual or partnership) the landlord can seek the tenant's sequestration (if an individual or partnership)[176] or winding-up (if a company).[177] The landlord will generally not wish to go through a bankruptcy or winding-up process, but may seek to use the threat of being able to do so to prompt the tenant into paying sums due.

The landlord could also retain performance of his contractual obligations in face of a tenant failing to pay the service charge.[178] However, for the reasons discussed in Chapter 5, the landlord will not wish to retain performance of some of his obligations, such as those in relation to the maintenance of the common parts or insuring the building, even where he is entitled to do so. He may, however, decide to withhold performance of other obligations, such as considering an application to assign the lease or fulfilling obligations following the purported exercise of an option to purchase by the tenant, where the tenant is in breach by failing to pay the service charge.[179]

The landlord would also be able to rescind the lease where the tenant's breach in failing to pay the service charge is material.[180] A landlord will rarely use the remedy of rescission, given that provision for irritancy is invariably made in commercial FRI leases.[181]

6.8.2 Remedies provided for by the lease

6.8.2.1 *Summary diligence and charges for payment*

Most commercial leases are capable of being registered for execution. This means that the landlord can register the lease in the Books of Council and Session[182] and obtain an extract lease containing a warrant for diligence. Where the tenant owes money

---

[174] For a landlord to be able to issue a statutory demand he must be owed at least £1,500 where the tenant is an individual or partnership: Bankruptcy (Scotland) Act 2016, s 16(1)(i); and he must be owed at least £750 where the tenant is a company: Insolvency Act 1986, s 123(1).

[175] For corporate insolvency see *In re A Company* [1984] 1 WLR 1090; the Bankruptcy (Scotland) Act 2016, s 16(3)(b) provides that for individual and partnership debts the debtor can deny that there is a debt or that the debt is immediately payable by intimating this fact by recorded delivery to the creditor.

[176] Bankruptcy (Scotland) Act 2016, s 2(1)(b); although note the need for the landlord to be a qualifying creditor (owed £3,000 or more) to be able to petition for the tenant's sequestration. The petition could be brought by qualifying creditors (who are in aggregate owed £3,000 or more): 2016 Act, s 7(1).

[177] Insolvency Act 1986, s 122.

[178] See the discussion of retention in **5.3.4**.

[179] For further discussion see **5.3.4**.

[180] See the discussion of this remedy in **5.3.5**.

[181] Discussed in **6.8.2.2**.

[182] This is what is generally done although it is competent to register the lease in the Sheriff Court Books also: see G L Gretton, "Diligence and the Enforcement of Judgments" in *The Laws of Scotland: Stair Memorial Encyclopaedia* vol 8 (1991) para 122.

to the landlord, the landlord can proceed straight to carrying out diligence, such as arresting sums in a bank account or inhibiting the tenant,[183] without first having to raise proceedings. It has been remarked that "summary diligence is something of a misnomer, for the diligence involved is not summary", there being no difference between summary diligence and other forms of diligence.[184] What is different is that there is no need to raise proceedings and obtain a decree before exercising summary diligence.

It should be noted that not all forms of diligence will give the landlord access to the tenant's funds[185] or assets[186] that could be used to pay what the tenant owes to the landlord. For instance, an inhibition prevents the tenant from disposing or charging his heritable property in Scotland. The landlord does not obtain access to the tenant's heritable property in order pay off what is owed. The landlord uses the inhibition and its effect to try to prompt payment from the tenant of the sums due to the landlord – so that the inhibition will be discharged and the tenant will then be free to deal with his heritable property as he wishes.

Where the landlord has an extract registered lease, he can also serve a charge for payment on the tenant. If the tenant fails to pay the charge within 14 days, the expired charge can be used as evidence that the tenant is apparently insolvent[187] or unable to pay his debts.[188] This would allow the landlord to seek the tenant's sequestration or winding-up, the threat of which may prompt the tenant into paying sums due to the landlord. The benefit of using a charge, rather than a statutory demand, is that the tenant who is an individual or partnership cannot challenge or deny the existence of the debt by simply intimating this to the landlord.[189] If the tenant refutes the sums set out in the charge for payment, he would have to raise an action of reduction, seeking interim suspension and reduction of the charge.

Having a clause permitting the lease to be registered for execution is a powerful tool for the landlord. It means that the landlord can seek to take action to recover sums very quickly and fairly inexpensively. As such, summary diligence and/or charges for payment are often used by landlords where tenants have failed to pay sums due under the lease. It is clear that summary diligence is not only available where the sums due are set out in the lease, but can be used where the lease provides how an amount will be ascertained,[190] which will generally be the case for service charge in commercial leases. However, in order to be able to carry out summary diligence or

---

[183] For a discussion of the various forms of diligence see Gretton, "Diligence and the Enforcement of Judgments", para 133 *et seq*. It is advisable to use the online version, in which more recent developments in the law of diligence have been incorporated.
[184] Gretton, "Diligence and the Enforcement of Judgments", para 122.
[185] The landlord would obtain access to funds caught by an arrestment 14 weeks after service of the schedule of arrestment in terms of the Debtors (Scotland) Act 1987, s 73J, unless an objection is made in terms of s 73L of that Act. The landlord would also obtain funds caught by a money attachment where he successfully seeks a payment order in terms of the Bankruptcy and Diligence etc (Scotland) Act 2007, s 183.
[186] The landlord would be able to sell the tenant's assets and use the proceeds to pay the sum due to him, where an attachment has been carried out, followed by auction of the attached articles in terms of the Debt Arrangement and Attachment (Scotland) Act 2002, s 19.
[187] See Bankruptcy (Scotland) Act 2016, s 16(1)(f).
[188] Insolvency Act 1986, s 123.
[189] See the discussion of this in **6.8.1**.
[190] G Stewart, *A Treatise on the Law of Diligence* (W Green, Edinburgh, 1898) p 413.

serve a charge for payment, it is essential that the landlord or his agent has complied with the lease provisions on calculating service charge exactly.[191]

6.8.2.2 *Irritancy for monetary breach*

Irritancy was discussed in Chapter 5 as a remedy available to the landlord.[192] However, in that chapter the concern was a non-monetary breach by the tenant in relation to the repair and condition of the premises let. In this chapter, the tenant's breach concerns a monetary obligation in failing to pay service charge due in terms of the lease. An FRI lease will normally provide that the landlord can irritate the lease where the tenant fails to pay sums due under the lease.[193] An irritancy on this basis is a conventional irritancy, rather than a legal irritancy.[194]

Where a landlord seeks to irritate for a monetary breach, he must consider the Law Reform (Miscellaneous Provisions) (Scotland) Act 1985, section 4,[195] as well as the terms of the lease. It is easier[196] for a landlord to irritate a lease for a monetary breach rather than a non-monetary breach. This is due to the fact that, in order to irritate the lease for failure to pay, the landlord must simply give the tenant an opportunity to pay the sums due.[197] Section 4 of the 1985 Act provides that the landlord must serve a notice on the tenant requiring him to make payment of outstanding sums within a deadline specified in the notice. The tenant must be given a period of at least 14 days following service of the notice in which to make payment, or such longer period as the lease may provide.[198] The notice must be served by recorded delivery,[199] which has been held to be the Royal Mail recorded delivery service and no other form of recording delivery.[200]

The 1985 Act does not provide a form for such notice to the tenant,[201] but provides that the notice must state that the tenant should make payment of outstanding sums, and any interest thereon, within the period specified in the notice; and that the lease may be terminated if the tenant fails to do so.[202] There has been recent controversy

---

[191] The method of calculating and paying service charge and problems that have arisen are discussed in **6.5.3.1–6.5.3.3**.
[192] See **5.4.3** *et seq.*
[193] See clause 13.1 of Schedule Part 16 of the style multi-occupancy lease in *Greens Practice Styles: Commercial Leases*, pp 113–211.
[194] See the discussion of these terms in **5.4.3**. Where the lease provides for payment of the service charge by way of further rent, sometimes referred to as the second rent, the landlord could use legal irritancy. Given the service charge would have to remain unpaid for two years before legal irritancy would be possible and specific provision is almost invariably made in FRI leases such cases would arise very rarely.
[195] Rather than s 5 (discussed in **5.4.3–5.4.3.3**) with the difficulties that entails.
[196] Although not wholly without difficulty, as discussed below.
[197] He need not satisfy the fair and reasonable landlord test, discussed in **5.4.3.2**.
[198] Law Reform (Miscellaneous Provisions) (Scotland) Act 1985, s 4(3). It is not uncommon for commercial leases to give the tenant 21 days to make payment.
[199] Law Reform (Miscellaneous Provisions) (Scotland) Act 1985, s 4(4).
[200] *Kodak Processing Companies Ltd v Shoredale Ltd* [2009] CSIH 71, 2010 SC 113.
[201] Although a statutory form for such notices has been recommended by the Scottish Law Commission: see Report on *Irritancy in Leases of Land* (Scot Law Com No 191, 2003) para 3.69, although the Commission are seeking views on whether the law of irritancy requires any reform: see Discussion Paper on *Aspects of Leases: Termination* (Scot Law Com DP No 165, 2018) para 7.27
[202] Law Reform (Miscellaneous Provisions) (Scotland) Act 1985, s 4(2)(a).

about the level of detail required in such notices. In *Scott v Muir*[203] Sheriff Principal Stephen[204] held that, to be valid under the 1985 Act, an irritancy warning notice had to specify the periods in which the arrears had arisen. However, Sheriff Principal Murray[205] in the later case of *Inverclyde Council v John F McCloskey t/a Prince of Wales Bar*[206] held that, while providing this level of detail may be good practice, it is not a requirement of the 1985 Act. As such, an irritancy warning notice that simply stated the sum due and the deadline by which it had to be paid complied with section 4 of the 1985 Act. While these decisions seem to conflict, it is to be noted that in *Scott v Muir* the landlord sought payment of arrears and interest thereon. The point may be made that, without notice of the periods over which the sums became due, it will not be easy[207] for the tenant to calculate what interest is to be paid along with the arrears to prevent irritancy. That was not the position in *Inverclyde Council*, where the landlord sought payment of arrears only without interest. As such, it is suggested that these decisions can be distinguished from each other. Nonetheless, it would seem advisable that solicitors issuing irritancy warning letters on behalf of landlords provide details of the periods over which arrears have accrued.

While the 1985 Act does not require any further notice to be served on the tenant, it is invariably the case that another notice is issued, given that the irritancy warning letter will state that the landlord *may* terminate the lease if the tenant fails to pay the sums due within the time limit set. Solicitors acting for landlords generally send a further notice following the deadline passing without payment, confirming that the landlord has exercised his right to irritate the lease, as well as noting that the tenant is required to remove from the premises, the lease having come to an end by irritancy.

As discussed above,[208] it is important that the landlord or his agent complies strictly with the lease in relation to the calculation and invoicing of service charge from the tenant. When a tenant does not want the lease to come to an end, the tenant's solicitor is likely to scrutinise an irritancy warning letter very carefully to determine whether any arguments can be made that the notice is invalid due to the landlord having failed to comply with the terms of the lease regarding the service charge or irritancy, or the requirements of the 1985 Act.[209] While oppression is available to the tenant as a defence, he is unlikely to use it, or to be successful if he does,[210] to defend an action of removing,[211] following irritancy of the lease. It is much

---

[203] *Scott v Muir* 2012 SLT (Sh Ct) 179.
[204] Sheriff Principal Stephen was the Sheriff Principal of Lothian and Borders.
[205] Sheriff Principal Murray was Sheriff Principal of North Strathclyde.
[206] *Inverclyde Council v John F McCloskey t/a Prince of Wales Bar* 2015 SLT (Sh Ct) 57, 2015 GWD 6-126.
[207] Although it should be possible given the tenant should know, or be able to work out from the lease, when sums fall due under it.
[208] The same point was made in **6.8.2.1** in relation to summary diligence. See the discussion at **6.5.3.1–6.5.3.3**. regarding the method of paying service charge and problems that have arisen.
[209] Such challenges were made in *Scott v Muir* 2012 SLT (Sh Ct) 179; and *Inverclyde Council v John F McCloskey t/a Prince of Wales Bar* 2015 2015 SLT (Sh Ct) 57; GWD 6-126. It should be noted that the reasonable recipient test discussed in *Mannai Investment Co Ltd v Eagle Star Life Assurance* [1997] AC 749 is not applicable where the question is whether the irritancy warning notice complies with the Law Reform (Miscellaneous Provisions) (Scotland) Act 1985, as this is a matter of statutory interpretation: see *Kodak Processing Companies Ltd v Shoredale Ltd* [2009] CSIH 71, 2010 SC 113 per Lord Osborne, delivering the opinion of the court, at para 25.
[210] See the discussion of oppression and its very limited use in **5.4.3.4**.
[211] As to which see McAllister, *Scottish Law of Leases*, para 10.36.

more likely that he will try to make a case based on the invalidity of the irritancy notice, including that the sums set out in the notice are incorrect or not due. For that reason, and to ensure that a landlord is able to use irritancy effectively where the tenant fails to remedy his monetary breach of the lease, it is important that the terms of the lease regarding service charge are strictly followed.

6.8.3 Effect of the tenant's breach on rights the tenant has under the lease

As well as the landlord being able to exercise remedies, whether at common law or specifically provided for by the lease, the lease may grant certain rights to the tenant that he may be unable to exercise if he is in breach of the lease.[212] The tenant, and those advising him, should be alive to the fact that if he fails to pay the service charge it may impact on such rights, for instance, the ability to exercise a break option to bring the lease to an end, or the ability to exercise an option to purchase.[213]

---

[212] This may be based on retention, discussed at **6.8.1**, or the lease may specify that the tenant must have complied with all of his obligations to be able to exercise the rights conferred.
[213] These issues are discussed in **5.5**.

Chapter 7

Dispute Resolution

7.1 INTRODUCTION

The earlier chapters of this book cover the substantive law concerning the obligations of the parties to a commercial lease in relation to repairs, dilapidations and service charge. The nature of the remedies available to the parties in the event of breach of those obligations has also been explored. This chapter aims to introduce the practice and procedure of dispute resolution in dilapidations claims in particular, although it is not possible in a book of this nature to explore the topics in great detail. Summary diligence, covered in Chapters 5 and 6, receives no additional commentary in this chapter. The rarity of irritancy or lease termination actions resulting from breach of repairing/service charge obligations is such that they, too, are not covered in this part of the book.

Each case presents its own lease terms and alleged breach. More often than not, the landlord will require professional advice from its solicitors/counsel as to the most appropriate forum in which to seek to have the dispute resolved, and the time/costs involved. Discussed below are some of the key elements to be taken into account in those discussions. Taking one particular procedural step does not necessarily prevent parties from trying to resolve the dispute by other means – for example, parties are free to negotiate or mediate a claim, even though arbitration or litigation proceedings have been commenced.

7.2 NATURE OF THE DISPUTE AND REMEDY SOUGHT

The various remedies open to the landlord in the event of breach of a leasehold obligation are discussed in Chapters 5 and 6, although "enforcement" of the repairing obligation will normally be undertaken through one of the following types of action:

(a) Specific implement – where the landlord wants the tenant to carry out the works required in terms of the repairing obligation.
(b) Payment – where the lease provides for a payment of money to the landlord, such as service charge or a sum payable in lieu of dilapidations.
(c) Damages – where specific implement (as a remedy) is unwanted or unavailable, and the lease does not otherwise provide for a payment in lieu of dilapidations.

Specific implement in the context of terminal dilapidations at lease expiry is covered in **7.4** below. For the reasons explained, specific implement is sought and obtained in a relatively small number of cases, notwithstanding it is generally considered to be the "primary" remedy available under Scots law in respect of breach of contract.[1] A landlord might seek an order for specific implement and/or damages in the same action, or might seek damages only.

An action for payment is ostensibly less burdensome for the landlord, as is considered in detail in Chapter 5. A payment action is normally raised based on an unpaid invoice or certificate issued by reference to the terms of the lease, whether that is in respect of service charge or a payment in lieu of dilapidations.[2] The landlord is not required to quantify or prove loss/damages, and there is no requirement to consider whether steps have been taken to mitigate loss. However, that is not to say that the tenant need simply accept, without qualification or challenge, that the landlord's claim for payment is valid and accurate. Much will depend on the wording of the payment clause in question, and the extent to which any "certification" or apportionment of costs or liability is final and binding on the tenant.[3]

7.3 WHEN AND HOW ARE DILAPIDATIONS IDENTIFIED?

At some point prior to lease expiry, the landlord will be considering what is to happen with the property following the contractual expiry date of the lease. Options might include selling the property, re-letting to the current tenant, finding a new tenant, refurbishment or even total demolition/redevelopment of the property. Some of those options obviously require more forward planning than others.[4] This is the likely point at which the landlord will seek advice in relation to the current condition of the property, and the repairing obligations of the outgoing tenant. If the property is to be re-let to a new tenant then the landlord will want to minimise any rental void caused by the property not being in the state and condition required by the ingoing tenant.

Whether or not there is sufficient time to enforce the repairing obligation by way of an order for specific implement is considered below. If there is not then seeking damages for breach of contract or a payment in lieu of dilapidations will be the landlord's remaining "enforcement" options.

From the tenant's perspective, there is obviously going to be little desire to expend potentially significant amounts of money on premises in which the tenant has no future interest. Furthermore, it is likely that carrying out repairs/dilapidation works will impact on the tenant's ability to trade from the premises – for example, if they are retail premises and the tenant requires to strip out its own extensive fitting-out works. From a tactical perspective also, the tenant will no doubt want to investigate whether the landlord's future plans for the premises are such that the

---

[1] See H L MacQueen and L J Macgregor, "Specific implement, interdict and contractual performance" (1999) 3 Edin LR 239–46. That specific implement is the primary remedy available to the innocent party in the contract is disputed in W W McBryde, *The Law of Contract in Scotland* (3rd edn, 2007) at para 23-08, although it is not necessary for present purposes to explore the debate further.
[2] See Chapter 6 regarding the possible use of summary diligence.
[3] See Chapter 6 concerning certification. The issue of certification generally is discussed further in K Lewison, *The Interpretation of Contracts* (6th edn, 2016) paras 14.01–14.09.
[4] As the law stands, landlords and tenants should also be considering whether to serve a "notice to quit" to avoid the operation of *tacit relocation,* but that is not discussed further in this book. The issues of notices to quit and *tacit relocation* generally are discussed in the Scottish Law Commission's Discussion Paper *Aspects of Leases: Termination* (DP No 165, 2018) at chapter 3.

landlord's loss/claim for damages is reduced or removed altogether. Put shortly, it is unlikely to be in the tenant's interest to engage in meaningful discussions with the landlord about payment of damages in advance of lease expiry.[5]

Conversely, it is in the landlord's interests to raise proceedings at an early stage: (a) the landlord will hopefully obtain payment of sums due sooner rather than later, (b) evidence of the breach ought to be available (and not obscured by subsequent remedial works), and also (c) the tenant has less time and opportunity to investigate the landlord's future plans for the property and consider whether the costs claimed by reference to a schedule of dilapidations properly reflect the landlord's loss/damages.

The landlord will normally instruct a building surveyor to inspect the premises and prepare a schedule of dilapidations, identifying the repairing and decorating obligations of the tenant at lease expiry. The RICS has produced a guidance note for its members entitled *Dilapidations in Scotland*, which sets out practice guidelines for property inspections, and the preparation and service of a schedule of dilapidations.[6]

Unless the lease is indisputably an all-encompassing FRI lease, with an absolute transfer of all ordinary and extraordinary repairs onto the tenant, it is worthwhile obtaining legal advice on the extent of the repairing obligation prior to production of any schedule of dilapidations. To do otherwise risks time and money being spent on investigations and production of a schedule of dilapidations that includes works for which the tenant is not liable. Notwithstanding this fact, and the provisions of the RICS note, it is often the case that potential "difficulties" for the landlord in the interpretation and application of the repairing clause in the lease are ignored or glossed over, in an attempt to set forth the best negotiating position thought to be available. Almost invariably, this simply leads to delay and additional expense as parties' surveyors and lawyers thereafter become entrenched in their own analyses of the wording of the clause, and its application to the premises/dilapidations in question. The party preparing any schedule of dilapidations should also bear in mind that his/her work (and credibility) may well end up being scrutinised in court.

It is also expected that the landlord's surveyors will produce a "Scott Schedule". This is a table of the individual claims under the schedule of dilapidations, cross-referenced to the relevant clause or clauses in the lease, with costings against each proposed item.[7] The Scott Schedule is exchanged between surveyors for the parties with a view to identifying what matters are agreed between the parties, and what matters are in dispute.

7.4 WHEN TO CONSIDER DISPUTE RESOLUTION – SPECIFIC IMPLEMENT AND DAMAGES

The repairing obligation in most commercial leases will be operative throughout the duration of the lease – i.e. the tenant is under an obligation to comply with

---

[5] Two matters that might encourage the tenant to do the works, or bring the tenant to the negotiating table are (1) a potential loss of rent claim if the works are not carried out, and (2) potentially advantageous VAT treatment if the tenant carries out the works itself.

[6] RICS, *Dilapidations in Scotland* (2nd edn, 2015) chapters 8 and 9.

[7] RICS, *Dilapidations in Scotland* at para 10.3 (with style Scott Schedule shown in Appendix D to the guidelines).

the repairing obligation at all times during the lease, and the landlord is entitled to enforce those obligations and require the tenant to effect any necessary works to the premises. As was pointed out in **4.4.4**, however, it is at lease expiry that most dilapidations issues and disputes come to the fore.

In that context, it is important to remember that the remedy of specific implement is available to the landlord only in respect of obligations that can be fulfilled during the duration of the lease, save where the lease provides otherwise.[8] As Lord Kinnear says in *Sinclair v Caithness Flagstone Co Ltd*:[9]

> I know of no authority in support of the pursuer's claim to require his tenants after the termination of the contract of lease to re-enter the subjects which, by their contract, they are bound to quit, in order to perform after their possession has come to an end, obligations which were applicable only to the period of their possession, and which they are alleged to have already broken. They cannot be liable to a decree for specific performance, except by virtue of their contract.

Lord Kingarth expands on this slightly in *PIK Facilities v Shell UK Ltd*[10] in which he says:

> Nor would it be right, in my view, to conclude that the decision [in *Sinclair*] was based simply or mainly on the fact that the tenants' right to occupation had ceased. Although that is mentioned, it is mentioned in the context that the corresponding right of the landlord to require the tenants to occupy the subjects and execute the works had come to an end. It would, I think, have been abundantly clear that the pursuer, in seeking specific implement, was prepared to allow access.
>
> ...
>
> What the pursuers are asking the defenders to do (namely to return to the subjects and put the pipelines, etc into a particular state in which they should have been left) is to do something which they did not contract to do.

Accordingly, if the landlord wants the tenant to undertake works prior to lease expiry (to implement the repairing obligation) then the following must be considered:

(a) identification of any breaches of the repairing obligation;
(b) the time required to secure agreement or independent determination of the breach/required remedial works; and
(c) the time required, following that agreement/determination, for the tenant to effect the required remedial works.

A dilapidations dispute might involve complex questions of fact and law, bearing in mind that the proper construction or interpretation of the repairing obligation is a question of law in itself. Unless the tenant is willing to accept that it is liable for all the repairs set out in the schedule of dilapidations (in which event there is not really a dispute) it is going to take some time for any dispute resolution procedure

---

[8] *PIK Facilities v Shell UK Ltd* 2003 SLT 155 (OH, Temporary Judge T G Coutts QC), and also 2005 SCLR 958 (OH, Lord Kingarth). It appears that the pleadings were the subject of two separate Outer House debates on the point.
[9] *Sinclair v Caithness Flagstone Co Ltd* (1898) 25 R 703, as followed in *PIK Facilities v Shell UK Ltd* 2005 SCLR 958.
[10] *PIK Facilities v Shell UK Ltd* at paras 36 and then 44.

to run its course. Timescales will vary according to the volume and complexity of the matters in dispute, but a timeframe of six to twelve months to achieve a first-instance decision is to be expected, even using expedited "Commercial Action" procedures available in the Court of Session and certain sheriff courts.[11] Whilst interim specific implement is technically available as a remedy,[12] it is difficult to envisage circumstances in which a court would ordain a tenant to implement on an interim basis (i.e. prior to full determination of the issue) a repairing obligation that it has challenged as a matter of fact and/or law.

The outcome of all of the above is that a landlord is unlikely to secure an order for specific implement of the tenant's repairing obligation prior to lease expiry, if the tenant legitimately challenges the nature and extent of the obligation and defends the action accordingly. Unless the lease provides for a contractual payment in lieu of dilapidations,[13] the landlord's remaining option is to seek damages in respect of the tenant's breach of contract. As mentioned above, the tenant is unlikely to be in any rush to enter into discussions/negotiations in that regard. Instead, it is more likely that the tenant will want to allow the lease to expire, see what if anything the landlord does with the premises, and consider whether the tenant has grounds for challenging the landlord's quantification of damages.

7.5 DISPUTE RESOLUTION OPTIONS

The main options open to parties seeking to resolve a dispute as to their rights and obligations under a commercial lease are as follows:

- Negotiation
- Mediation
- Arbitration
- Expert determination
- Litigation

7.5.1 Negotiation

It is of course open to the parties to discuss, negotiate and agree the nature and extent of a leasehold obligation, the extent to which a party is in breach of that obligation, and the damages payable as a result. Whilst lawyers and surveyors (with associated costs) are likely to be involved in that process, a negotiated settlement has the benefits of speed, and absence of additional costs/expenses associated with other dispute resolution procedures. Once the settlement is agreed, the settlement agreement itself is enforceable (by both parties) without reference to the lease.

Whoever is negotiating on behalf of the parties should be aware that an agreement can be reached, binding on the landlord and tenant, without the need for formal documentation entered into between solicitors. The key question is whether the parties (directly or through their respective agents) have reached a consensus on

---

[11] It should also be borne in mind that a first-instance decision on a matter of law, such as interpretation of the repairing obligation, might be appealed, extending further the dispute resolution time frame.
[12] See Chapter 5.
[13] See Chapter 5.

settlement of the claim. As Lord Malcolm puts it in *Fordell Estates Ltd v Deloitte LLP*:[14]

> The proper approach in law to questions of this kind is well settled, and is discussed in numerous cases, for example *Baillie Estates Ltd v DuPont (UK) Ltd [2009] CSOH 95, per* Lord Hodge at paragraphs 25/6. In summary, both parties must have manifested an intention to be immediately bound to all the legally essential elements of the bargain. In assessing this, the court adopts an objective approach, based upon what an informed reasonable person would have understood by the words and conduct of the parties or their agents.

The court in that case found that the terms of email correspondence between agents for the parties did not support the pursuer's assertion that parties had reached consensus on settlement of the claim.

Negotiations might be complicated by the presence of a sub-tenant with responsibility for some or even all of the dilapidations works under its separate sub-lease. In that event, the head-landlord will seek to agree a position with the tenant/mid-landlord, who then will attempt to reflect that agreement with the sub-tenant by reference to its obligations under the sub-lease – i.e. seek to pass on the financial settlement obligation in whole or in part, according to relevant liabilities.[15]

If there is a full transfer of the tenant's obligations onto a sub-tenant, then discussions might be short-circuited by a more straightforward discussion between the landlord and sub-tenant, although that would not affect the leasehold structure of contractual obligations should enforcement be necessary.

7.5.2 Mediation

Mediation is a voluntary process whereby parties meet to try to resolve a dispute. Mediation might be undertaken without recourse to more formal procedures such as arbitration or litigation, or can be arranged during an arbitration/litigation with a view to resolving matters in advance of determination by a court or arbitrator. It might be thought of as a facilitated negotiation between the parties, using an independent and neutral mediator to assist parties assess the strengths and weaknesses of their respective cases, and to highlight the benefits of reaching agreement outwith the other available procedures.[16]

Mediation is intended to be an entirely confidential process that can be undertaken at any point, even if litigation is underway for example. There is no obligation on parties who attend a mediation to reach agreement or compromise their position, although the process itself very often results in just such an outcome for the benefit of all concerned.

Mediation has a number of benefits in the context of a dilapidations claim, including the opportunity for clients, lawyers and surveyors to discuss the various issues at the same time – especially helpful if the dispute involves mixed questions of fact and law, such as whether certain dilapidations works might be classified

---

[14] *Fordell Estates Ltd v Deloitte LLP* [2014] CSOH 55 at para 13.
[15] See, e.g., *Dolby Medical Home Respiratory Care Ltd v Mortara Dolby UK Ltd* [2016] CSOH 74, 2016 GWD 19-344.
[16] See M Mantle, *Mediation: A Practical Guide for Lawyers* (2nd edn, 2017).

as extraordinary repairs, and whether the repairing obligation imposes liability for extraordinary repairs on the tenant.

Another key feature of mediation is the ability to consider wider commercial interests that might exist between the parties, such as agreeing new lease terms for the building in question, or landlord/tenant relationships elsewhere (actual or desired). In other words, mediation might result in dispute settlement proposals that go beyond the somewhat blunt instrument of damages for breach of contract.

7.5.3 Arbitration

Parties might seek resolution of a dilapidations dispute using arbitration rather than litigation. Arbitration allows parties to obtain a determination of the issue(s) in dispute from an independent third party, the arbitrator, in the form of a legally binding award, but without going through the more public route of a court action. Arbitration in Scotland is now governed mainly by the Arbitration (Scotland) Act 2010, with the Scottish Arbitration Rules themselves found in Schedule 1 to the 2010 Act. Section 1 of the 2010 Act sets out the following "founding principles" for arbitrations conducted under the 2010 Act:[17]

1 Founding principles

The founding principles of this Act are—
(a) that the object of arbitration is to resolve disputes fairly, impartially and without unnecessary delay or expense,
(b) that parties should be free to agree how to resolve disputes subject only to such safeguards as are necessary in the public interest,
(c) that the court should not intervene in an arbitration except as provided by this Act.

Anyone construing this Act must have regard to the founding principles when doing so.

Arbitration is often promoted as a speedier and more cost-effective dispute resolution procedure than litigation, but that is far from guaranteed, particularly if the procedure adopted in the arbitration simply replicates that found in litigation.[18]

The basis of any arbitration concerning the parties' obligations under a commercial lease is agreement between the parties that they wish the dispute in question to be determined by an arbitrator, in preference to undertaking litigation. An agreement to arbitrate might be found within the lease itself, or be agreed separately between the parties. Thus, if one party attempts to litigate a matter in court, but the other pleads the existence of a valid arbitration agreement, the court in question will sist the proceedings to allow the arbitration to take place. The

---

[17] For a fuller introduction to arbitration, see F Davidson et al, *Commercial Law in Scotland* (5th edn, 2018), ch 10 (Commercial Dispute Resolution). There are also a number of specialist textbooks, such as F Davidson, *Arbitration* (2nd edn, 2012) and *Dundas and Bartos on the Arbitration (Scotland) Act 2010* (2nd edn, 2014).

[18] Commercial action procedure in the Court of Session is discussed below. The case management role of the Commercial Judges, combined with the in-built flexibility of commercial action procedure, will often ensure that disputes are resolved as expeditiously as possible. The speed of determination is often a major factor in keeping costs to a minimum.

classic statement of the common law position is found in *Sanderson v Armour & Co*[19] – "[If] the parties have contracted to arbitrate to arbitration they must go." This approach is followed in section 10(1) of the 2010 Act.

The nature of arbitration is such that there are only limited rights to appeal against any award made by the arbitrator. The three grounds of appeal are:

(1) no jurisdiction[20]
(2) serious irregularity[21]
(3) legal error[22]

The ability of a party to an arbitration to found an appeal on legal error is in some ways controversial, and the 2010 Act permits parties to exclude appeals flowing from an alleged legal error. If parties are permitted to found an appeal based on legal error under rule 69, rule 70 (which is mandatory) contains a number of conditions for the operation of any such appeal. For example, a legal error appeal can be made only with the agreement of the parties, or with leave to appeal obtained from the Outer House of the Court of Session (normally dealt with by a Commercial Judge). Leave to appeal itself is only to be given if the applicant can satisfy the court that (a) deciding the point will substantially affect a party's rights, (b) the tribunal was asked to decide the point, and (c) on the basis of the facts found in the award (i.e. findings in fact), the tribunal's decision was obviously wrong or (where the point is of general importance) open to serious doubt.[23]

7.5.4 Expert determination

Expert determination is triggered by agreement between the parties that they wish their dispute to be resolved by an independent third party expert, who may be named or appointed in accordance with the parties' agreement. In very general terms, a remit to an expert is intended to provide advantages of cost, speed and finality by (a) putting the disputed issue into the hands of an expert in the field, and (b) removing the costs and delays associated with other dispute resolution procedures, such as litigation or arbitration.[24]

Agreement to remit a matter to an expert might be found within the body of the lease itself or be reached independently of it. The effect of such an agreement is to exclude, contractually, the jurisdiction of the courts to determine the matter in dispute, but only insofar as remitted to the expert. Establishing the extent (or limits) of any remit to an expert is a matter of interpretation of the contract between the parties.[25]

---

[19] *Sanderson v Armour & Co* 1922 SC (HL) 117 at 126.
[20] Scottish Arbitration Rule 67 (mandatory).
[21] Scottish Arbitration Rule 68 (mandatory).
[22] Scottish Arbitration Rule 69 (default, with option for parties to exclude any appeal on this ground).
[23] Scottish Arbitration Rule 70 (mandatory).
[24] For a fuller discussion of expert determination, see C Farrell and J Freedman, *Kendall on Expert Determination* (5th edn, 2015).
[25] *Ashtead Plant Hire Co Ltd v Granton Central Developments Ltd* [2018] CSOH 107, referring in this context (in particular) to *Campbell v Edwards* [1976] 1 WLR 403 per Lord Denning MR at 407F–G. Of course, this might lead to a court action to determine the extent of the expert's remit, as happened in the case of *Ashtead*, and the various cases referred to therein. The manner in which the court is to interpret or construe the contract itself is covered in Chapter 4.

One key point to consider is whether the expert's remit (instruction) includes determination of all matters of fact and/or law. For example, if an expert building surveyor is appointed to determine the extent of a dilapidations claim, have the parties agreed that the surveyor is also to determine the proper construction of the repairing obligation within the lease, that being a question of law?

Whilst the question is in each case to be answered by reference to the wording of the expert's remit, the Scottish courts have indicated that questions of law will be included within the expert's remit only when that is expressly provided for in the parties' agreement, or made crystal clear by implication. This is seen in the case of *Ashtead Plant Hire Co Ltd v Granton Central Developments Ltd*.[26] The case concerns the interpretation of a rent review clause in a commercial lease. The rent review clause specified that any dispute as to the revised "Open Market Rent" (as defined) was to be determined by an independent expert, whose decision was to be final and binding on the parties. The "Open Market Rent" was to be calculated using certain assumptions and disregards regarding the hypothetical leased subjects. The tenant (pursuer) sought a declarator as to the proper construction of the rent review clause in advance of the appointment of an expert, in order that any expert thereafter appointed would determine the Open Market Rent using the tenant's preferred basis of valuation (interpreting the assumptions and disregards).

The landlord (defender) argued that the expert determination clause within the lease was such that questions of interpretation of the rent review clause were within the expert's remit. On that basis, the landlord argued that the court did not have jurisdiction to hear the action. The Lord Ordinary (Doherty) found otherwise, stating:

> [21] [The] critical issue is whether on a proper construction of the lease the contracting parties expressly or impliedly agreed that the legal interpretation of "the leased subjects" and of the assumptions and disregards were remitted exclusively to the expert. I am not persuaded that they agreed that those issues of construction were removed from the court's jurisdiction. Even on the basis that the expert could obtain legal advice, it would be very surprising if the parties had agreed that a surveyor should have exclusive jurisdiction to decide the correct legal construction of such important provisions. A surveyor would not have the necessary skill and competence to make the required adjudication. He could only obtain and rely upon legal advice. In those circumstances I think that the lease would have to have made it very clear indeed (whether expressly or by implication) that exclusive jurisdiction was being conferred ...
>
> [22] I am not satisfied that the lease provides that the suggested exclusive jurisdiction is to be conferred on the expert here. On the contrary, in my opinion the more natural and common sense reading of the lease is that the expert is to carry out his functions on the basis of the correct interpretation of the lease's provisions, including the sound construction of "the leased subjects" and of the assumptions and disregards. If he fails to do that he will have departed from his instructions in a material respect and will have failed to comply with the terms of his reference. He will not merely have given the wrong answer to the right question.

Whilst the decision is in respect of a rent review clause, arguably a more complex clause than a repairing obligation, the reasoning provided suggests that questions of

---

[26] *Ashtead Plant Hire Co Ltd v Granton Central Developments Ltd* [2018] CSOH 107.

interpretation of a disputed repairing obligation would also fall outwith an expert surveyor's remit, unless the lease (or separate remit agreement) expressly provides otherwise.[27]

As the general intention of an expert determination clause is to allow the parties to achieve a cost-effective, speedy and final determination, parties will have only very limited rights to challenge the outcome of the determination – the parties are bound by any determination given honestly and in good faith, and in accordance with the instructions given to the expert.[28]

7.5.5 Litigation

Litigation procedure is a complex topic in its own right, and this book aims to give merely an overview of the main points to consider in the context of a dilapidations claim.[29]

7.5.5.1 *Jurisdiction*

Litigation in Scotland occurs in the Court of Session and in local sheriff courts. The local sheriff court has exclusive jurisdiction for actions of up to £100,000, although it can deal with cases with claims in excess of that figure. The Court of Session, whilst having Scotland-wide jurisdiction, cannot entertain any claim that does not exceed £100,000. Subject to that financial qualification on jurisdiction, the party instigating the litigation (the pursuer) may choose which court to litigate in. The choice will depend on a variety of factors, such as the complexity and extent of matters in dispute, involvement of counsel, and the pursuer's perception of which court is more likely to produce a definitive determination of its claim.

7.5.5.2 *Commercial action procedure*

The Court of Session has the benefit of expedited "commercial action" procedure, which is often utilised in dilapidations claims.[30] One of the key benefits for parties is that a judge experienced in commercial matters will be appointed to the case. That judge undertakes a case-management role, and is given a range of options and powers

---

[27] The decision in *Ashtead* was quickly followed by the decision of Lady Wolffe in *Cine-UK Ltd v Union Square Developments Ltd* [2019] CSOH 3. In that case, the expert's remit (also concerning a rent review) was expressly stated to be final and binding on questions of fact and law. Lady Wolffe, perhaps unsurprisingly, found that the pursuer (tenant) was precluded from challenging the expert's interpretation of the rent review clause in question.
[28] *Campbell v Edwards* [1976] 1 WLR 403 per Lord Denning MR at 407F–G; *Jones v Sherwood Computer Services plc* [1992] 1 WLR 277; and *Franborough Properties Ltd v Scottish Enterprise*, 14 June 1996, OH (Lord Penrose) unreported at p 15 (noted at 1996 GWD 27-1619).
[29] There are various reference works available for those who require to delve further into the topic, such as *Macphail's Sheriff Court Practice* (3rd edn, 2006); and *Greens Annotated Rules of the Court of Session 2019–2020*. A gentler introduction can be found in Davidson et al, *Commercial Law in Scotland*, chapter 10 (Commercial Dispute Resolution).
[30] See the Rules of the Court of Session 1994, Chapter 47 (Commercial Actions). Certain sheriff courts have adopted an equivalent commercial action procedure, although litigants are unlikely to benefit from the same degree of judicial specialism and experience as is found with the appointed Commercial Judges in the Court of Session.

to ensure that the action is progressed as speedily and efficiently as is possible in the circumstances. For example, the court may:

- direct that skilled persons (such as surveyors and lawyers) meet with a view to reaching agreement and identifying areas of disagreement, and order production of a joint note for the court identifying areas of agreement/disagreement, and the basis of any disagreement;[31] or
- appoint an expert to examine, on behalf of the court, any reports of skilled persons or other evidence submitted, and to report to the court.[32]

7.5.5.3 *Use of a reporter*

It is open to parties to invite the court to remit certain questions of fact to a "reporter" – usually a recognised expert in his field. This might be employed to limit the expenses of fact-finding and resolving differences between the parties. In the context of a dilapidations claim, for example, the questions might include:

(a) whether individual wants of repair identified in a schedule existed at a particular date;

(b) what works are required to remedy those wants of repair identified in response to question (a), and

(c) in light of the answers to question (b), (i) whether the costs of effecting works claimed by the pursuer are reasonable and, if not, (ii) what would be a reasonable cost.[33]

The general effect of such a remit is to exclude proof in court of the matters covered in the report. The reporter's remit is contractual, and any failure to implement the directions of his remit (including a failure to exhaust the remit) would form the ground of a legal challenge.[34]

7.5.5.4 *Third party procedure*

Third party procedure allows a defender in an action to seek to bring into that action any other party "liable to the defender in respect of a claim arising from or in connection with the liability, if any, of the defender to the pursuer".[35] It will be apparent that this might prove useful in the situation whereby an action has been raised against a defender tenant in respect of dilapidations, where that defender has or had in place a sub-tenant with liability in respect of some or all of the works in question.

---

[31] Rules of the Court of Session 1994, rule 47.12(2)(h) – particularly useful for mixed questions of fact and law.
[32] Rules of the Court of Session 1994, rule 47.12(2)(i). The commercial action rules previously also afforded the Court the opportunity to remit matters to a person of skill for determination, but that is no longer one of the available options under the rules.
[33] See, e.g., *BNP Paribas Securities Services Trust Co (Jersey) Ltd v Mothercare (UK) Ltd* [2015] CSOH 47, 2015 GWD 14-250.
[34] *BAM Buchanan Ltd v Arcadia Group Ltd* [2013] CSOH 107A, 2013 GWD 25-506, as applied in *BNP Paribas Securities Services Trust Co (Jersey) Ltd v Mothercare (UK) Ltd* [2015] CSOH 47, GWD 14-250.
[35] Rules of the Court of Session 1994, rule 26.1(1)(b)(ii) in respect of ordinary actions, and rule 47.7 in respect of commercial actions; Ordinary Cause Rules 1993, Chapter 20 (sheriff court).

7.5.5.5 *Use of tenders and pursuers' offers*

A tender is a form of judicial offer by a defender to settle a court action (and pay the expenses of the action to the date of the tender). It may be made at any time during the court proceedings, and equally might be withdrawn at any time after it is made (before acceptance). It is not brought to the attention of the judge or sheriff hearing the case.

In general terms, if a tender is made, but not accepted, *and* the court's eventual award to the pursuer is no greater than the tendered amount, then it is the pursuer who bears the expenses of the litigation subsequent to the date of the tender. The principle behind this is that, whilst the pursuer has been successful to an extent in the action, the litigation subsequent to the date of the tender was unnecessary, and the pursuer should bear those costs accordingly. A tender can be a useful tool for the defender, in that a suitable tender will ensure that a pursuer will think carefully of the costs and risks involved in proceeding with an action beyond the date of the tender.

A pursuer's offer is an offer to settle a claim against a defender. Unlike tenders, pursuer's offers are the subject of particular rules in the Court of Session and sheriff courts.[36]

If the following conditions are met, the court must (except on cause shown) award the pursuer an additional sum equal to 50% of its judicial expenses attributable to the period from which the offer could reasonably have been accepted to the date on which judgment was given.[37] The conditions are:

(a) a pursuer's offer is made and has not been withdrawn;
(b) the offer has not been accepted;
(c) the court has pronounced judgment;
(d) the judgment is at least as favourable in money terms to the pursuer as the terms offered; and
(e) the court is satisfied that the pursuer's offer was a genuine attempt to settle the proceedings.

Pursuers' offers were introduced relatively recently into the Court of Session and sheriff courts.[38] They are intended as a form of sanction on a defender who, having refused to accept an offer, loses the case outright, or at least does not achieve a lower award than that offered. It remains to be seen how effective they might be in the context of dilapidations claims, although those pursuing a claim, whether in the Court of Session or local sheriff court, should undoubtedly consider them carefully.

---

[36] Rules of Court of Session 1994, Chapter 34A; Ordinary Cause Rules 1993, Chapter 27A (sheriff court). As with defenders' tenders, there is no disclosure of the pursuer's offer until the issue of expenses is raised with the court.
[37] There are equivalent provisions regarding "late" acceptance of a pursuer's offer, where that offer is accepted prior to judgment.
[38] 3 April 2017.

Index

accession
    case law, 13, 14
    fixtures and, 12–13
    intention and, 13–14
    meaning, 12
action for payment, 112–13, 118–19
ad factum praestandum
    see specific implement
alterations
    interdict, 60
    removal of, 51, 54
    rent review and, 11n
    repairing obligation and, 54
arbitration, dispute resolution by, 124–25

break clause, 4, 83, 117

car park
    common part, as, 9, 86, 89
    service charge and, 91
charge for payment, 114–15
commercial action procedure, 127–28
commercial lease
    breach, remedies for, *see* remedies for breach of lease
    commercially sensible interpretation, 32–34
    common law and, *see* common law
    contextual approach to interpretation, 31–32
    interpretation, 7, 28–34
    landlord's right of inspection, 49
    literal interpretation, 29–30
    premises fit for purpose, 19
    registered for execution, 112, 113–14
    tenant's breach, effect, 117
    terms, 6

common law (*cont*)
    urban lease, 2
    see also FRI lease
commercial property
    meaning, 1–2
    investment in, 2–3
common law
    commercial leases and, 16–17
    common parts, 19
    contracting out of, 16–17, 28, 35
    default position, 35
    excepted repairs, 24–27
    fitness for purpose, implied warranty, 17–19
    landlord's repairing obligation, 2, 19–20, 21–24
    ordinary and extraordinary repairs, 21–24
    remedies for breach of lease, 56–72, 84, 110–14
    tenant's duty of care, 24
common parts
    car park, 9, 86, 89
    common law, at, 19
    defining, 9–10, 85–87
    fitness for purpose, 19
    income-generating, 91
    landlord's neglect of, 94–95
    landlord's obligations, 87–91
    lease terms, 88–89
    meaning, 7, 85–86
    obligations of parties, 85, 87–91
    repair or replacement, 94
    repairing obligation, 7, 85
    services, provision of, 88–89
    timing of works, 95

131

INDEX

damages for breach of lease
  assessment of loss, 61–67
  causation of loss, 63
  common law remedy, 61–67
  costs, recovery of, 67
  generally, 61, 110–11, 118, 122
  heads of, 62
  insurance premiums, recovery of, 64, 67
  landlord's breach, for, 84, 110–11
  loss of rent, 64–67
  mitigation of loss, 64, 67
  rates, recovery of, 67
  remoteness of loss, 63–64, 66–67
  tenant's breach, for, 61–67, 122
damnum fatale, 20, 51
decoration, tenant's obligation, 53
developer's shell, 5n
disability discrimination legislation, 53
dispute resolution
  action for payment, 113, 118–19
  arbitration, 124–25
  commercial action procedure, 127–28
  damages, 61, 84, 111, 118, 122; *see also* damages for breach of lease
  defender's tenders, 129
  expert determination, 125–27
  generally, 118
  jurisdiction, 127
  litigation, 127–29
  mediation, 123–24
  negotiation, by, 122–23
  options, 122–29
  payment in lieu of action, 118–19
  pursuer's offers, 129
  specific implement, 118–19
  third party procedure, 128
  timescales, 122

English law
  damages, assessment, 62–63
  putting and keeping in repair, 37
  repair and renewal, 44
  specific performance, 60
expert determination, 125–27
extraordinary repairs
  case law, 21–24
  identifying, 44
  repairing obligation, 8n, 21–24, 37–38

fair and reasonable landlord test, 78–80
fitness for purpose
  common parts, 19
  implied warranty of, 17–18
  tenant's acceptance of, 19, 35
fixtures
  accession, 12–13
  generally, 11
  meaning, 11–13
  severance of, 15
  trade fixtures, 11, 14–15
full repairing and insuring (FRI) lease
  common parts and, 87
  duration, 3, 4
  extraordinary repairs, 37–38
  good tenantable repair, 39–40
  interpretation, *see* commercial lease
  meaning, 3
  premises condition, 39–42
  premises defined, 36–37
  rationale for, 3
  repairing clause, 35–38
  repairing obligation, *see* repairing obligation
  services, provision of, 88–89
  tenant's acceptance of premises, 35
  tenant's repairing obligation, 35–38
  terms, 28

inspection of premises, landlord's right of, 49
insurance
  damages claims and, 64, 67
  repairing obligation and insured risk, 51–52
  service charge, 89, 92
interdict, remedy of, 60–61, 112
irritancy
  breach of repairing obligation, 80–81
  conventional irritancy, 77, 115
  defence to, 81–82, 116–17
  difficulties of, 82–83
  fair and reasonable landlord test, 78–80
  grounds for, 77
  law reform proposals, 80
  legal irritancy, 77
  limitations, 77–78
  monetary breach by tenant, 115–17

INDEX

irritancy *(cont)*
  oppression, defence of, 81–82, 116
  service of notice, 115–16
  timing, 78

mediation, 123–24
mixed-use development
  service charge, 99
multiple-occupancy building
  common parts, *see* common parts
  insurance, 51–52
  lease for, 9–10
  premises defined, 7, 9–10
  repairing obligations, 5, 7, 85
  services, provision of, 88–89

oppression
  defence to irritancy, 81–82, 116

plant and equipment
  repairing obligation, 36–37, 42–43
  replacement, 94
premises
  condition at lease commencement, 46–48
  defining, 7–10, 36–37
  fitness for purpose, 17–18, 19
  good tenantable repair, 39–42
  inspection, landlord's right of, 49
  sub-tenancy, 10
  tenant's acceptance of, 19, 35, 46–48
professional fees
  service charge and, 89, 91
rei interitus, 51
remedies for breach of lease
  action for payment, 113
  charge for payment, 114–15
  common law remedies, 56–72, 84, 110–14
  contractual remedies, 73–83
  damages, 61–67, 111
  interdict, 60–61, 112
  irritancy, 77–83, 115–17
  landlord carrying out works, 73–74
  landlord's remedies for tenant's breach, 112–14
  payment in lieu of notice, 74–77
  rescission, 69–72, 111–12, 113–14
  retention, 68–69, 111, 113

remedies for breach of lease *(cont)*
  specific implement, 56–60, 73
  statutory demand for payment, 113
  summary diligence, 115
  tenant's remedies for landlord's breach, 83–84, 110–12
  tenant's rights and, 83, 117
  wants of repair notice, 73
rent-only leases, 106–07
rent review, 11n
repairing obligation
  absence of, 24–27
  alterations and, 54
  case law, 39–42
  collateral warranties, 52
  common law, at, 21–24
  common parts, 87, 88
  condition of premises, 39–42, 46–48
  construction documents, 52
  duration, 120–21
  exclusions from, 51–52
  extent of obligation, 37
  extraordinary repairs, 21–24, 37–38, 44
  FRI lease, 35–38
  general principles, 38–39
  good tenantable repair, 37, 39–42
  improvement, 44
  insured risk, 51–52
  interpretation, 38–39
  landlord's, 21–24, 83–84
  lease end, at, 4–5, 45–46, 119–20
  multi-occupancy building, 5
  outgoing tenant, 119
  plant and equipment, 36–37, 42–43
  premises defined, 36–37
  remedies for breach, *see* remedies for breach
  replacement, test for, 43, 94
  schedule of dilapidations, 49–51. *See also* schedule of dilapidations
  service media, 8, 36
  single-occupancy building, 5, 6–7
  sub-tenant, of, 54–55, 123
  tenant, of, 35–36, 83
  triggering, 39
  work, extent required, 43–45
replacement, test for, 43, 94

133

INDEX

rescission of lease
  availability of remedy, 69, 71, 111–12, 113
  case law, 70–71
  irritancy and, 70, 71
  statutory protections, 72
reserve fund
  advantages and disadvantages, 108
  lease terms, 108–10
  meaning, 107
  protecting, 109
  unused funds, 109–10
retention by landlord, 68–69, 111, 113
RICS, *Dilapidations in Scotland*, 49n, 120
RICS Professional Statement on Service Charges
  accounting policies and principles, 104–05
  certification of expenditure, 104
  consultation, 87n
  generally, 49n, 95–96
  recovery of landlord's costs, 91n
rural lease, 1–2

schedule of condition
  photographs, 46
  purpose, 46, 48
schedule of dilapidations
  costed, 50
  format, 49
  interim, 49
  service of, 49, 50–51, 56
  terminal, 49, 120
"Scott Schedule", 120
security staff, service charge and, 89
service charge
  action for payment, 112–13
  administration and management charges, 89, 91
  apportionment, 97–99
  borrowing charges, 90
  car park, 91
  certification of expenditure, 101–05
  challenging, 101–03
  changing attitudes to, 105–07
  charge for payment, 114–15
  empty properties, 64n
  exclusions from, 90–91
  failure to pay, *see* remedies for breach of lease

service charge (*cont*)
  fair apportionment, 98, 99–100
  fair and reasonable test, 92–95
  fixed amount, 98
  fixed percentage apportionment, 97
  floor area apportionment, 97
  insurance premiums, 89, 90, 92
  irritancy for monetary breach, 115–17
  managing agents' fees, 91
  manifest error, 101–02
  mixed-use developments, 99
  payment after lease end, 95
  payment provisions, 100–01
  professional fees, 89, 91
  rateable value apportionment, 98
  rent-only leases, 106–07
  RICS Code of Practice, 95
  RICS Professional Statement, 95 *et seq*; *see also* RICS Professional Statement on Service Charge
  security staff, 89
  service charge year, 100
  service media, 86
  statutory demand, 112–13
  summary diligence, 114
  tenant's obligation to pay, 96–107
  tenant satisfaction with, 106
  uncertainty, 105
  unlet units, 97
  who may certify, 103–05
  see also reserve fund; sinking fund
service media
  repairing obligation, 8, 86
  service charge and, 86
single-occupancy building
  defining premises, 6–8
  repairing obligation, 5
sinking fund
  advantages and disadvantages, 108
  lease terms, 108–10
  meaning, 107–08
  protecting, 109
  unused funds, 109–10
specific implement
  availability of remedy, 73, 110–11, 121
  balance of convenience, 60, 73
  court discretion, 57
  interim, 59, 122

134

specific implement (*cont*)
  penal sanctions, 58
  timing, 58–59
statutory compliance, tenant's obligation, 53
statutory demand, 112–13
sub-tenancy
  defining the premises, 10
  repairing obligation and, 54–55
summary diligence, 115
"sweeper clause", 89–90

tacit relocation, 119n
terminal repairs, 4–5
third party procedure, dispute resolution, 128

urban lease, 1–2

wants of repair notice
  contractual remedy, 73
  service of, 49
  see also schedule of dilapidations